Governor Durkee

The Transcontinental Railroad Bonds

John V. Chamberlin

Cover image is provided by the Utah State Archives, as part of their photograph collection

DEDICATION

This Book is dedicated to the Memory of Governor Durkee and his achievements in life.

Special appreciation is given to Ms. Mary (Penny) Enroth of Pinehurst North Carolina who commissioned me to conduct research on the life of Governor Charles Durkee and the Paramount Lien Bonds.

Also dedicated to the Kemper Center Foundation of Kenosha which has supported this research and publication

Also by John Chamberlin

Yalta Top Secret: *The official records of the Yalta Conference, 1945*

Tehran Top Secret: *Conference records Tehran, Iran 1943*

The Moscow Conference 1943: *Records of Agreements, United States and the Soviet Union*

Churchill Stalin Moscow Conference 1944: *Records of Churchill's negotiations with Stalin, the Balkans and Poland*

The End of War Europe *Diplomatic records of the US Embassy in Moscow, Allies end the War of Europe*

Frantic Joe: *Air bases in Russia, 8th and 15th US Air Force 1944, the missions.*

Disclaimer

This publication was arranged by the Editors and Author citing official source material. Any digital images made, and those resulting images and content produced is Copyright protected as presented herein.

This is an original creative work based on sources found in the public record. The names, characters, places and incidents are those found within the public record and based on original and declassified documents authorized for public viewing by recognized public repositories.

The publisher does not have any control over and does not assume any responsibility, or any results, or third party uses of this content. Nor does the publisher assume any responsibility for activities that might have been published as source material.

Completion of the Transcontinental Railroad
East Meets West May 10 1869

Courtesy of the Utah State Railroad Museum at Ogden Union Station

Table of Contents

ACKNOWLEDGMENTS

I would like to thank Ms. Penny Enroth for her resourceful research and support of this project. Also, the Kemper Center Foundation for its financial support and the Palmer Foundation for their support.

The Durkee Research has spanned over 155 years of records in the states if Maryland, New York, Wisconsin, Nebraska, Iowa, Utah and California. We have used digital imaging of documents to retrieve copies where there was no other means to record. The result is a vast data base. These include original letters, newspaper articles, Congressional Records; Treasury Records and other data .

PREFACE

Governor Durkee and the Transcontinental Railroad

Governor Charles Durkee of the Territory of Utah was researched in a quest to search for Transcontinental Railroad Bonds which he owned at the time of his death in 1870. At that time, he had custody of numerous Primary Lien Bonds of the Transcontinental Railroads from the 1860's.

As one of the first to envision a railroad network that would span the continent and grow the nation, Durkee is recognized as a man of complex determination and courage: His world was a fledgling nation with tenuous roots in a dangerous landscape. Yet there is no question that he would shape American commerce. This became clear in the search for the financing bonds that would build the railroads. Still, the trail was elusive; the records sparse and the history foggy.

That Durkee was instrumental in building the railroads is indisputable. How he financed them is the question. Since Governor Durkee is said to have owned Primary Lien Bonds at the time of his death, it is important to understand what he was doing and what his intentions might have been. Following his death, his Last Will and Testament was contested, and the whereabouts of his financing bonds has been questioned for over a century.

This quest was to understand the role of the bonds as financial instruments in building the transcontinental railroads, who owned them, how, why and when.

In the effort to identify ownership and purpose of the bonds, it was necessary to access Government Archives; the Library of

Congress, Special Collections; State Archives; Land Records and Museums. Further details were strewn across the United States from California to New York.

To view this extraordinary feat in its context of American development, the setting of Salt Lake City Utah, New York City and Washington DC has to be seen through the prospective of the years 1865 to 1900 when early communications, transportation, recording of documents, and statehood began to shape the nation.

Charles Durkee was the Territorial Governor of Utah. Salt Lake City, the Capital center, was an oasis of civilization located 900 miles from the next nearest city: Omaha Nebraska was on the shore of the Missouri River; San Francisco across the desert and over mountains.

Chicago was a city of prospect and a centralizing depot for distribution. Salt Lake City, if adequate, was provisioned by supplies delivered by mule and wagon trains across the Great Planes. Transportation for settlers arriving was by horse; stage coach or wagon train.

Mormon settlers had arrived in the area in the 1847 seeking a new territory from the Eastern states, forming their State called Deseret. Indigenous Indians, the Utes, were being displaced by the new settlers and an Indian war was in the progress in 1865. When Governor Durkee arrived with Franklin Head, the Federal Indian Agent, it was uncharted territory.

Mrs. Mary Enroth began her enquires and worked on the project for many years. Associated with the restoration of the Governor Durkee House in Kenosha Wisconsin, she has shown remarkable interest. And with good reason.

These records provided basic details on Governor Durkee's life and the subsequent estate litigation and court cases following his sudden and untimely death in 1870. The story of Governor Durkee's Bonds served to tell the story of American development.

In the 1860's most records were handwritten, with some documents printed as part of the Congressional record. Originals were either the actual document or letter press copies.

The primary objective of the research project was to investigate the relationship of Governor Durkee and the Transcontinental Railroads' First Mortgage Bonds while he was in Utah. And to explain their disappearance after his death while returning home to Kenosha in January 1870.

The Transcontinental Railroads consisted of six roads, the Union Pacific Railroad, the Central Branch of the Union Pacific Railroad, the Kansas Pacific Railroad, the Central Pacific Railroad, the Western Pacific Railroad and the Sioux City and Pacific Railroad.

Early investigation began with the National Archives in College Park Maryland (NARA) - the major repository of government records of all agencies and records dated back to the Revolutionary War. There, records were examined and recorded digitally.

The Department of Interior was immediately consulted, holding various records from the Department of Treasury, the State Department, the Railroad Commission and other agencies.

Of particular interest were the Ledger books which listed financial transactions. This provided details of the railroad finances and payments to the Treasury up to the Receivership of the Union Pacific Railroad. Here were tantalizing clues suggesting the expansion of America - a vision not fully materialized, in the building of a railroad system that would give it commercial potential.

There was an important meeting between Mr. Leonard Blaisdell, representing the Estate, and the Secretary of the Treasury in April 22, 1884. At this meeting, First Mortgage Bonds of the Railroads were purported shown in the Treasurer's Office to those in attendance...but later renounced. This was the basis of several court cases that followed involving the issue of the lost $64,000,000 in Paramount Lien Bonds, First Mortgage Bonds for the building of the Railroad.

The court records of Mr. Blasdell's Court of Claims case 18003 led to viewing original documents which were recorded and kept in the National Archives. Additional court cases ultimately led to the Supreme Court case filed in1965 obtained from Washington DC.

The Library of Congress was also investigated for records. This proved a wealth of information. Since the Government Printing Office at that time printed all Congressional Records including bills, reports, speeches and documents, the Library of Congress has digitized these records. The GPO provided much of the correspondence between various departments of the government and President, some found in printed format. All were culled, collected and imaged as support for this project.

This material revealed details on issues related to the Union Pacific and Central Pacific Railroads, including their payment of US Government Bond interest, payments, and the First Mortgage Bonds which had priority over all Governments subsidy bonds.
It was essential to understand the view, policy, missions and interests of the United States as the accounts unfolded to reveal details of operations, expenses, ownerships, failures and construction of the Railroads as they related to Durkee's bonds.

It was an officially sanctioned mission – but built with private and subsidized capital. Where the two imperatives transected was the core of the Durkee bonds question.

As research evolved, records of the Central Pacific and Union Pacific Railroads were investigated. Syracuse University Libraries Special Collections had the collection of Collis P. Huntington papers. Huntington was the Vice President and later President of the Central Pacific Railroad. His records included correspondence during its construction with Leland Stanford, Charles Crocker and Mark Hopkins. The papers discussed details of its construction as it proceeded across California, including the issue of financing, bonds and purchase and transportation of material rails and locomotives. This material had to be transported by ship around the tip of South America, the Horn then up the west coast of the Americas. This proceeded into the 1869, when the road was joined with the Union Pacific at Promontory Utah. Records were recorded digitally up to the 1906 from the collection.

The next investigation involved the Museum of Finance in New York City at 48 Wall Street. The Museum's special collections contained bonds of the various railroads. Of interest was a First Mortgage bond of the Central Pacific Railroad, the only bond in existence, dated 1867. This showed what the bonds looked like, their size and the Coupons. It was the kind of bond that existed for Durkee. These, and other bonds were digitally copied for this project.

Utah was the next site to examine. Governor Durkee's home town of Salt Lake City produced information covering life in Utah in the 1860's and its records unique to state and to its exposure to the Transcontinental Railroad. One repository was The Church of the Latter Day's Saints Library which contained records of Brigham Young, a man who was involved with both Governor Durkee and the Transcontinental Railroad. The Mormon community, to which Brigham Young was affiliated, had built a segment of the end of the Union and Central Pacific Railroads in Utah. Thus details the actual construction as well as negotiations for payment of 1.3 million dollars from the Union Pacific Railroad were available. A visit was made to Ogden Utah to view the Union Pacific Museum and its records, followed later that day with a visit to Promontory Point where the Union Pacific met the Central Pacific Railroads were joined to complete the Transcontinental Railroad in an historic and celebrated event.

Omaha Nebraska was the final visit to research records. The Court Records of the Land office were examined and a trip to the Nebraska State Archives in Lincoln was made where a major portion of the old records of the Union Pacific were housed. Copies of correspondence concerning Bonds, and Ledger books of transactions were copied.
Further, a trip to The Union Pacific Museum in Council Bluffs Iowa was made to review documents. In their collections were records of the bond coupon payments for the Central Pacific. Ledger books gave details of bond serial numbers and other details of bond- ownership.

A visit to the University of Iowa Libraries' Special Collections was made. Their additional collection of Union Pacific documents augmented the Nebraska State Archives with Ledgers, corporate records books and other documents on the railroad showing how it was extending itself financially into eventual Receivership in 1897.

The Material from the Utah State Archives contained information on the later Estate filing of Governor Durkee's will. In reviewing the material, there was reference to a Federal court case in Salt Lake City. On investigation, the court case actually was held in 1908 in San Francisco. The National Archives in San Francisco was contacted and a digital copy of all those records in the file were obtained. These records contained certified copies of the First Mortgages of the Union

Pacific and Central Pacific Railroads made in 1865 which gives the actual details of the 1st Mortgage Bonds.

In discussing this upcoming book with the Kemper Foundation and Mrs. Enroth, the legal files of the officiating Attorney involved in the Supreme Court Case was located, obtained and digitally imaged. These records provided additional information which covered the period after the 18003 court case, including documents and depositions to support the issue of ownership of the 1st Mortgage railroad bonds.

In the assembly of the materials we see multiple divergent items. The First Mortgage Paramount Lien Bonds that were issued at various dates. The ownership question will be debated and records discussed addressing possible outcomes based on archival records and their ensuing court cases.

The Joining of the Union Pacific and Central Pacific Railroads at Promontory, Utah May 10, 1869

Courtesy of the Utah State Railroad Museum at Ogden Union Station

Governor Durkee

The

Transcontinental Railroad Bonds

Devils Gate Bridge Wyoming, Union Pacific Railroad July 1869

Courtesy of the Utah State Railroad Museum at Ogden Union Station

Chapter 1

Life of Charles Durkee

Charles was born in Vermont in 1805 as one of five children. Of Scottish descent, his family had integrated in early colonial America as settlers of Connecticut serving variously as merchants, captains and militia in the Revolutionary War. His great grandfather served in the Woodbury Connecticut military; his grandfather in the Vermont militia and Revolutionary War, and his father worked in the new republic in its early formative years, all sharing in early American sentiments against class divisions and elite establishment.

Boyhood schooling for Charles Durkee was available in the district school of Burlington and grammar school in Cambridge Vermont. While higher education for him was expensive and unattainable, he worked assiduously on a farm as a young man and quickly learned the skills of management, trade and interpersonal exchange.

His manner was astute and diligent, with particular proclivity for sociability and public service. Gradually, it was said that he had a particular ability for conflict resolution.

Above all, it was clear he aspired to opportunity and mercantilist development. He earned a living, acquired property and began an enterprise as a shopkeeper in Richmond, Vermont. Success brought him to a larger mercantile shop in Barton, Vermont where he partnered with a prominent businessman Judge Dana. Judge Dana's daughter, Catherine Putman Dana and Charles Durkee were married in 1836 and settled in Chelsea.

Charles was a religious man and by the mid 19th century, was a strong member of the Methodist Episcopal Church community. In the sweep of early American religious awakenings, Durkee's principles led him to advocate education and a righteous liberation of all people on an equal basis.

Durkee left Vermont in April 1836 and with some investment money and commercial wealth attained, moved Westward to cultivate new opportunities in trade, agriculture, lumbering and mining. He and his wife Catherine set sail, and following a storm on Lake Michigan, they landed in Southport Wisconsin. There, he built a home on Pike River.

When Wisconsin officially became a territory in 1836, Charles began construction of his first home. He helped develop the settlement town of Southport, and quickly set up commercial enterprise that would prosper. Catherine died in 1838.

In 1840, Charles Durkee married Caroline Lake, daughter of a local business associate. Encouraging Durkee to address wider fields of territorial interests, she supported his many campaigns for national office. They had two children, neither surviving into adulthood.

Durkee immersed himself in the newly forming politics of his region including the creation of territorial legislatures in Iowa. As the elected representative from Milwaukee County, he dedicated himself to matters of establishing definitions of jurisdiction and political powers; aid to settlers with pre-emption bills; organization of working teams to improve the waterways -including a harbor, and other transportation systems in the new territory. In his next successful campaign to the territorial House of Representatives in 1838, he tended to the codification of the laws; militia and more census realignments.

In proselytizing opportunity and expansion as the American way, he discovered that his outspoken activism was a means of garnering public support. He used this aptitude to great advantage as he moved to establish land claims commercial growth in Wisconsin, enjoying leadership in the founding of the region's progress.

While appealing to the US Congress in Washington for bills of appropriation for building projects, he was bringing to the region the vision of a national citizenship and full statehood, advancing himself as its representative. Local communities grew in trade and population, with Durkee dedicating parks, lands and a cemetery for public spaces and civic pride. In 1836, he built with R.H Deming a private commercial store that prospered, he then proceeded to engage in building projects and construction that filled the town with his enterprise and business. His brother Harvey joined him in Wisconsin to manage vast claims of farmland and timbering operations.

Credit was accrued with success as settlers filtered into the region, such that his largess was able to garner a populist base, especially in offering more to the laboring settlers, like citing generous sized building lots for accommodations to mechanics and laborers, offering credit if not in cash then in other tender like labor-bartering.

By the 1840s, Charles Durkee expanded into agricultural pursuits; construction of brick buildings, the building of a world class hotel that brought in travelling visitors. He developed stores and homes that he rented out, bringing in a considerable revenue. By the end of the decade, he was on the committee to incorporation the city of Southport, and a major stockholder in various ventures.

His affiliations were many, including business partnerships that would service him well. Kerr and Company was one. Another was the Durkee-Truesdell and Company which became a big financial success, especially for Gideon Truesdell who was propelled, under the wealth and influence of Charles Durkee, into the mainstream of Chicago industry and finance.[1]

Durkee's early callings drew him into a mesomeric society and the arena of debating local topics of interest. Gradually, the principles of Fourierism emerged and a Ceresco was established which advocated the communistic society of equality and work. Subgroups like the Wisconsin Phalanx and the Lyceum groups failed, offering to Durkee before the end of the decade, the invitation to go twice overseas as their guest to the International World Peace Congress of nations advocating peace [and equality] in Paris and Frankfurt.

The question of slavery was gaining national attention and international debate. With Charles Durkee's proclivity to side with fundamentalist fervor, he became an anti-slavery proponent if not a "determined abolitionist." His expressed views were considered radical and extreme.

The Liberty Party, born less to create a political party as to advance an agenda of anti-establishment, called for a separate American government. Charles Durkee made it his platform.
This came at a time when settlers were struggling to create a tenuous hold in their new territories. Not all embraced his radical notions. Challenges of distance, education, transportation, as well as local armed conflict with Indian uprisings made it hard to earn a living and defend a homestead. Thus, while Charles Durkee was a principle stockholder in the local newspaper with much exposure, he failed to garner enough support to be nominated for the territorial delegate seat in Congress.
However, Charles Durkee was a force to reckon with: He split the parties and divided the vote counts that drew votes away from the Democratic candidate, Moses Strong.
Durkee's next political nomination for Governor against John Dewey failed, and it was now that he realized he had enough anti-slavery support and activist sway to merge the Liberty party with the Free Soil Party, merging Whig men.

Iowa was separated, Wisconsin divided, and the territory was admitted into the Union as the 30th State. For Charles Durkee, that statehood offered the road to national politics, requiring two Senators and three Representatives for Congress.

When Charles Durkee called for a convention in Wisconsin to discuss the direction of anti-slavery cause, he was sent to a national convention in Buffalo as one of 25 delegations. He was sent to the House of Representatives by the national committee as their electoral ticket member of the Free Soil nominee, having split the Democratic Party and overtaken William Pitt Lynde.

His term of office lasted two years, his position on abolition so extreme as to be liabeled "one of only a handful of individuals....[equal to] Wilmot, Giddings and Hale."

By early 1849, at a state convention of the Free Soilers in Madison, a platform was drawn for land reform; free trade; revenue by direct taxation; election of all federal officer by popular vote and the reduction of the army and navy. However, in offering to merge with other parties, the Free Soilers were inviting themselves to larger platforms in the greater political arena of the times.

As soon as Henry Clay's Compromise of 1850 encouraged disunion, the Free Soil party dissipated, its popularity vanishing. Durkee's nominated was entered rather as a "people's petition" and he was ushered back into Congress in 1851.

In Congress he proceeded with this his abolitionist views "unabashed" and was considered a "radical" by his colleagues. In public debate of record, he was accused of engaging in 'puerile' debate if not open anarchy.

However, it is clear he had his misgivings as he saw on the horizon a civil war of much distress and devastation. In a letter to his brother Harvey, he wrote "I have been conversant with the southern mind for 12 years, and though I have been uncompromisingly anti-slavery and outspoken in all my views, yet all this time I have never had an unpleasant discussion with a southern Senator...yet I clearly see a dark cloud is fast gathering over our beloved land: this country of ours is about to pass through such a terrible, such a scorching and devastating ordeal, as history nowhere has furnished a parallel."

His term in Congress ended, and Durkee returned to his home. He built a lavish house in Kenosha, formerly Southport, and continued his life as an entrepreneur. He dedicated his home and much funds to the Wisconsin State Historical Society. Following years of prosperity within territorial acquisitions rooted in mining and industry - including the gold rush and the growing food and shipping requirements of Chicago, it became clear that a transcontinental railroad was needed.

The Charles Durkee House.

Durkee returned to politics. From 1855 until March 1861 where he went to Congress as the Republican Party Representative. While there, Durkee was instrumental in the inception of a transcontinental railway, and his bills advanced motions to recognize and organize for that need.

His actions following the civil war were focused on the construction of the transcontinental railroad, using his many contacts, connections and credit to aid in that endeavor. He engaged with the local community, including the Mormons, using his own resources to meet the financing requirements of government subsidies. He was keenly interested in the pivotal juncture where the two great building projects joined the vast network of railroad construction, East and West, at Promontory, Utah.

In 1865, Charles Durkee accepted the governorship of Utah and dedicated his home and grounds the cause of education at Racine for a College.

As his term of office expired, the conditions of his death began with the event of a ride to Salt Lake City late December 1869. He was about to embark on a trip scheduled to travel East, supposedly to submit bonds. He died January 14, 1870.

His Will and the affairs of his estate were contested following his death, and subsequently by heirs and parties of other interests. Since the contests involved government actions, and reactions thereto following, the period is ascribed by social historians as an era redolent with the aftermath of the civil war. Its costs, financial crisis and disruption to trade - including the assassination of Lincoln, infused many with disaffection and an abundance of caution. This, as an industrial revolution offered new opportunities in wages and financial measures for growth to a young nation. It was also a time of un-mitigating immigration to a new America.

The lavish home of Charles and Caroline Durkee in Kenosha was used by the St. Matthew Episcopal Church and named the Kenosha Female Seminary. When the missionary Episcopal Bishop of the Northwest Territory, Bishop Jackson Kemper died in 1970, the Milwaukee Diocese under the direction of Bishop Armitage renamed the school Kemper Hall.

To this day, it is the site of the Kemper Center Foundation.

Chapter 2

Utah Territory

State of Deseret was the name given to the native region encompassing Utah, Nevada, parts of California, Colorado and Idaho. This name was changed as Utah boundaries were defined..

Utah's history was recognized in early Spanish explorations of the 16 and 17th century. As America expanded with the Louisiana Purchase and the Mexican American War of 1848, Utah became a Territory of the United States with the signing of the Treaty of Guadalupe Hidalgo in 1848, later as an Act of Congress.

As a Territory of the United States, Utah was founded as part of the Compromise Act of Congress, 1850. Originally, in deference to the US President, Fillmore was the name ascribed to the first capital city located 148 miles south of Salt Lake City. However, Salt Lake City was later designated as the official Capital City.

In the wave of colonists and European settlers spreading across America, Mormon pioneers were the first to settle the territory in 1847, arriving in the Salt Lake Valley under the leadership of Brigham Young. There, they sought freedom to pursue their religious practices which came under reproach in the traditional regions of early colonial America. With the settlement of Salt Lake City, the Mormons moved to create cities of Bountiful, Ogden, Provo and other settlements throughout the territory, extending into Nevada, Wyoming and Idaho.

Brigham Young was designated the first Territorial Governor. The territory prospered, however, its high percentage of practicing Mormons created a cultural condition of government that was inconsistent with the law of the land. The issue of Polygamy, the taking of more than one wife was without sanction in the United States Government. In 1852, this became a significant issue with the Church of the Latter Day Saints, a strict Mormon religion. This resulted in the delay of statehood until 1895.

Territorial Governors were instituted to bring the authority of the United States over the state. Brigham Young took a lesser role and acted as the President of the Mormons. The Civil War created a unique dilemma of political affiliation, Utah siding neither for the North or South.

Four Territorial Governors were appointed by the president prior to the appointment of Charles Durkee, whose acts attempted to align policy of the region with the main central authority of the government in as many ways as possible.

Utah flourished. Farming was bountiful, and its mineral wealth deposits of gold and silver provided sources of income for settlements.

Salt Lake City was a thriving metropolis by 1866 at the time of Governor Durkee. Business was established; the Deseret News published weekly papers, and buildings and public facilities and schools were in place.

The coming of the Transcontinental Railroads, the Union Pacific Railroad from the east and the Central Pacific Railroad from the west, offered considerable employment in construction, grading, tunneling and laying of track. In addition, the Utah natives were offered the opportunity to sell food and other comedies to the tail crews as they were stationed in or near the territory.

After the joining of the railroads at Promontory, Brigham Young embarked on the construction of the Utah Central Railroad from Ogden to Salt Lake City.

After 50 years of waiting, and following a provision in the state constitution prohibiting polygamy, Utah became the 45th State of the Union on January 4, 1896. President Grover Cleveland signed the proclamation giving Utah full State rights.

Chapter 3

Governor Durkee of Utah

In May 1836 the schooner *Van Buren* carrying Charles Durkee and his wife docked in Southport Wisconsin, now Kenosha. Almost immediately Charles Durkee put up a land claim.[2]

When Wisconsin officially became a territory on July 4 1836, Charles began construction of a small log cabin on the northern part of his property in Southport. Charles' Wife Catherine became ill in early August of 1838, and passed away.

Charles remarried in January of 1840. Caroline Lake was the daughter of Jared Lake, a business associate and good friend of Charles. The couple had two children. Charles Jr, born 1843, and Harvey born 1850. Charles Jr took ill in 1847 and died at the age of four. Harvey also took ill in 1853 and died at three.

In the spring of 1853, Charles purchased 900 acres from Samuel Stevenson in section 17, and added 600 acres from section 16 at $8 per acre, putting all under plow in one year. Later he sold this land in to Isaac N. DeForest for $25 per acre making a nice profit as a result.

Charles Durkee was elected to the House of Representatives seat in the first district of Wisconsin in 1848, and reelected to Congress in 1851. He was subsequently elected to the US Senate in 1855 at a time when Senators were elected by a vote of the state legislature

The Republican Party was just being formed, and Wisconsin played a pivotal part in the abolitionist movement. Durkee supported the Republican Party in the Presidential bid of Abraham Lincoln. He worked on the Committee of Revolutionary War Claims, and the Committee on Public Land Claims. He was a strong advocate for a Homestead bill.

Retiring from politics when the Civil War erupted, he returned to Kenosha (formerly Southport) and began again his life as a private citizen.

He expanded his property holdings. In 1861 Charles Durkee built a new home for him and his wife in Kenosha on the shores of Lake Michigan. The house is still standing and today used as facilities of the Kemper Center Foundation, its living quarters restored to the 1860's style of construction and furnishings.

To serve in Washington, Charles had left the Durkee Mansion in Kenosha to St. Matthews Episcopal Church to be used as a seminary. The seminary-school established dormitories and classrooms and was later dedicated and named as the St. Claire's School for Girls. When the First Bishop of Milwaukee, Bishop Jackson Kemper died in 1870, the Milwaukee Diocese under the direction of Bishop Armitage renamed the school building Kemper Hall.

When the Territorial Governor of Utah, Governor Doty of Wisconsin died in office June 1865, President Andrew Johnson, a long time friend of Charles Durkee, was informed that Charles would be interested in succeeding Mr. Doty. The appointment was confirmed.

Charles proceeded to Salt Lake City with Franklin Head, his brother in law, who had been appointed as the Indian Agent for the Territory. He left his wife Caroline behind. Over 540 miles they travelled, across Indian territories of Nebraska, Wyoming and Utah from Council Bluffs Iowa. The Transcontinental Railroad, they knew, was just starting construction in Omaha Nebraska.

Shortly after his arrival at Salt Lake City, a brass band and "large number of persons" turned out to greet him. William H Hooper, Utah's territorial delegate to Congress introduced the new governor to the people of Utah giving him a "healthy welcome" and leading the crowd in three cheers for Gov. Durkee

Charles Durkee began his duties as governor, and found the Utah territory to be an oasis of advancements in farming, mining and commercial enterprise, a stopping point for travelers to California and Oregon.

Charles developed a relationship with Brigham Young, President of the Church of the Latter Day Saints, of the Mormon Church. He served still as the principal civilian ruling organization for the majority of the Mormons. This accord between them allowed the Mormons to proceed with their civil government while introducing the aspects of a Federal Territory.

In October 1865 he took office, and began working with the Territorial Legislature. The duties of Territorial Governor were straightforward; to act as the principal representative for the Territory; communicate and propose legislation with the legislature, and make executive decisions concerning the welfare of the Territory. Amongst his duties were matters of regional development. He needed to provide for Salt Lake City to be a capital with modern housing and facilities. The closest city at that time was Denver a mining town, and Council bluffs Iowa -over 500 miles to the east.

The Montana Post of October 14, 1865 reported that Governor Durkee was the successor of Governor Doty. He was serenaded in Salt Lake City and responded with a short speech expressing his determination to labor for the good of Utah, promising to resign if he failed in his efforts, October 3rd.

Cleveland Daily Leader, in Nov 14, 1865 Reported

> ".. The United States officers in the territory need the utmost wisdom and judgment, the best blending of moderation and firmness, the most spotless private lives and thorough knowledge of human nature. The new Governor, Ex-Senator Durkee is such a man and his appointment at the present time is especially fortunate."

Later on May 18, 1866 Durkee wrote to President Johnson requesting a leave of absence to visit Pahranagat, for his health. There has been news of a discovery of silver. He requested authorization to investigate the mining discovery found there.[3]

Charles had actually traveled to Pahranagat in April, the first of at least two visits in 1866

Charles was quoted as saying "The supposed wealth of our southern mines" as he passed through the Mormon settlements on his way south.[4]

Executive Office Utah
Territory
January 13th 1866

William H. Seward
Secretary of State

I have the honor to acknowledge
receipt of my Commission —
Governor of Utah Territory,
accompanied with a communication
from F. W. Seward — Assistant Secretary
State,

Very Respectfully your
Obedient Servant,

Charles Durkee

Governor Durkee's acceptance of office Governor of the Utah Territory

(National Archives Washington DC)

Durkee apparently liked what he had found. While there he made an offer of $8000 for 500 feet of the "Green Monster claim" and almost immediately began making plans to return to the district for an extended stay[5].

In a deposition by Franklin Head as part of the estate inventory, Head stated that the claim was 1100 feet in length. By the time he made his second visit however, Congress has settled the

question of the districts, placing Pahranagat in Nevada by adjusting the states boundaries one degree in longitude to Nevada. [6]
.

While Durkee was in office, the state boundaries became officially fixed, Nevada claiming one degree of longitude, Wyoming a Territory, and additional land ascribed to Colorado and Idaho.

It became the ambition of his administration to develop the resources of the territory for people to develop and grow in the region.

In his annual message to the Territorial legislature that year Durkee advanced the prospect that at least some of those resources were within the numerous mines of coal, lead and precious metals that "have been discovered in various parts of the territory". He suggested that many of these mines are surprisingly rich and that their discovery had just commenced. Durkee then urged the legislatures that any measures "you may be able to adopt the profile that promoted the region for development which would be beneficial to our people[1].

As governor he supported legislation encouraging business and commercial activity, especially for the greater utilization of the Colorado River. He instituted a revised code of Civil Laws. He emphasized the importance of schools and Indian treaties. His concept was to use the Colorado River to transport Utah products to markets in California. He pressured the legislators to maintain a Treasury surplus. He worked to allow settlers to obtain homestead grants.

Charles Durkee had to fit into the different culture of the Church of The Later Day Saints, Mormons and work with Brigham Young during some difficult times.

There had been conflict with the Mormons about security of the settlers and the influx of 'Gentiles' either passing through or settling in Utah. The Mormon society was well structured, with community responsibility taken as a part of their culture.

Charles Durkee had to skirt the Mormons, providing guidance as Territorial Governor while encouraging the state to prosper commercially.

But it remained a thorny issue: The Montana Post of Feb 1 1868 reported that in Durkee's message to the Legislative Assembly of January 13 was brief and did not address the issue of Polygamy.

Later in January 1868 Governor Durkee wrote to Secretary of State Steward saying that his doctor recommended he travel to San Francisco and the Pacific for his health. He said that he would be leaving early March for about 2 to 3 months.[7]

 In his trip to San Francisco, he noted that the Central Pacific Railroad had been completed to the Nevada State line. There, he met with Governor Stanford and Judge Charles Crocker of the Central Pacific in Sacramento and made arrangements for the railroad to come to Utah. Charles offered assistance. "He is one of our sort," the Judge observed.[8] Crocker was anxious to have the railroad pass to the north of Salt Lake "since the south was a morass of sinkholes and mudflats"[9] It was important to gage the sediments in the Salt Lake City. Crocker dispatched a Sacramento businessman, named Richardson to Salt Lake City on a sort of quiet political reconnaissance.[10]

The Central Pacific Railroad was getting anxious about the coming construction in Utah. They dispatched former Governor of California Leland Stanford to Salt Lake City to also act as liaison, "he is the most able-bodied and as a former governor he would have diplomatic standing both with the Territorial leaders and Brigham Young."[11]

Durkee returned to see Governor Stanford. Stanford regarded Durkee as an excellent intermediary for construction and the provision of Tie contractors on the Bear River and for buying coal properties. He would use Kerr and Company.

"We hope," said Hopkins, "they will be able to get a Mormon or Gentile force at work there. Perhaps let a contract go to Brigham Young and his representatives for 50 or 100 miles from Salt Lake westward towards Humboldt Wells"[12]

In Governor Durkee's Message to the Legislature of the Territory of Utah, January 1869, he authorized taxation at the rate of ¼ % of property value to support Public Schools. He recommended a resurvey of public lands to allow for new settlers, and asked for a definition of the amount of interest charged on loans to be 10%. He made a revision of the liability of Limited Partnerships to an amount agreed upon up front. He provided for the ability to place a lien of property by contractors, and he proclaimed the Indian incursions a problem in Utah as having been greatly reduced. Further, he courage the support of the indigenous tribes, and welcomed the Transcontinental Railroad to Utah. The finances of the Territory, he claimed, were in excellent shape.

In early 1869 Charles Durkee returned to Kenosha to record his Will and appoint Power of Attorney to his longtime friend and former Senator, Hon. James Doolittle. His Will was recorded February 12, 1869.

At the joining of the Central Pacific Railroad with the Union Pacific Railroad at Promontory Utah, Governor Durkee was not present. He was 87 miles away at Salt Lake City. At 12:32 p.m. Salt Lake City received the signal that the rails were joined; and immediately flags were unfurled, brass and martial bands in various parts of the city began playing; and artillery salutes were fired from the Court House, City Hall and from Arsenal Hill as a signal to the people of the city that the long awaited event had been consummated.[13] On the stand to speak to the crowd were Governor Charles Durkee, George A. Smith, John Taylor, William Hooper and Mayor Daniel H. Wells. The ceremony lasted several hours and consisted of band music, prayers and the promised speeches. In the evening the celebration continued with fireworks, large fires on the hills and illuminating banners. The people of Salt Lake City celebrated, but they looked eagerly to the day when they would hold a similar celebration welcoming the rails of the Utah Central Railroad to their city.[14] Work on the railroad was not completed however, and many improvements were necessary yet for the Government to approve the road.

Later in a delicate balance between local culture and national presence, Durkee evoked a national unity. The Fourth of July Celebration of 1869 was recorded by the Desert News[15] as:

"Impatient youth could not wait for the advents of the memorable fourth to commence it celebration. Four hours before the third had glided into an ocean of the past the sounds that are heard on the morning of the Fourth were stirring the drowsy atmosphere of an early night.

"As they filled into the New Tabernacle and took their seats the moving picture was intensely interesting, the thousand's of beaming faces ever-changing and the sparkling with joy, life and buoyancy; the magnitude of little national flags, fanning loyalty to the current veneration of our dear "stars and stripes"

The stands were occupied by Presidents Young and Wells, Elder Orson Platt, chaplain of the day, Elder John Taylor Col. F.H. Head, Orator Gov. Durkee and General Cheltenham. Col. D McKenzie then read the Declaration of independence, in an effective manner with sonorous and distinct elocution, followed by music by Capt. Parkman's band. The Marshall announced his Excellency Gov. Durkee for a speech who spoke as follows.

Governor Durkee gave a speech:

"Ladies and gentlemen, I have seen it announced through the press that I would deliver an address here today, let me disabuse your minds of this subject the committee called upon me and requested some remarks. I do not promise to do so but I promised to be here and I view this as a privilege to briefly utter a few of my sentiments. We have Orators here prepared to enlighten you on the condition of the country, and on the history of the past and on other topics of interest suitable to the occasion. What I may desire to say is with regard to our glorious Fourth of July, the anniversary of our nation's birth. You just heard the Declaration of Independence. It was a liberal war which followed in a progressive element in the British people rising against aristocratic ideals, they threw off this tyranny and declared their independence. This was a great era of American history, and advancing civilization and in the cause of Christianity for delivered the masses and gave the freedom of speech and of the press: and to the people of the right to govern themselves, where they were capable of exercising such a right. I do not wish to eulogize this government over all others. I believe it is the best, where all people are enlightened and prepared to sustain it. There may be other governments more despotic, better suited to the people where they prevail. Here the people are sovereign. This is an ideal that it would be well for all of us to fully comprehend: We should understand the duties and responsibility of sovereigns. Meet together once a year and have a celebration, and to let that be all there would be of our citizenship, would amount to no more than to have a little religion which we keep in the bandbox through the week and brought out on Sunday to air. We must study to the on to understand our duties and responsibilities as sovereigns and as citizens and as parts of this great machinery of government.

"Let us resolve today, in the sight of God our everlasting Father, to be more united in the cause of duty, of benevolence of charity, of industry, and maintenance of the principles of civil and religious liberty; and no matter who man may be, whether Methodist, Baptist, Mormon, or anything else who lives according to these principles he is a true man; those who live them are true Saints and doers of the Almighty's will and they have revelation, joy and peace. I have spoken longer that I intend I thank you for the attention."

Chapter 4

Mining The Green Monster

Missionary William Hamblin was scouting new areas for Mormon settlement in 1863 in Meadow Valley. A Paiute Indian showed him some rocks which he called "panagari" or "panacker." The next year Hamblin brought established claims on the "panacker ledge.' Samples of the silver ore was sent to Salt Lake City, and it was deemed worthy of more exploration.

C.W. Sales wrote from Meadow Valley on the fourth of May, 1865, to report discoveries by his party. Sale described the area they had traveled, gave the location of their claims, and sent samples of the ore. The ore was highly enriched with silver and consequently Sale was encouraged by these promising indications[16].

The Pahranagat mining district was formed in 1865, and William H. Raymond moved a Mill from Los Angeles to process the ores. As the ores dwindled, Raymond went into partnership with another Pahranagat Valley miner, John H. Ely, and they moved their mill to Meadow Valley. There, they established a site near Panaca, which processed ores from the Panacker ledge. This would became known as Bullionville.

Utah's Territorial Governor, Charles Durkee found his own interest in Pahranagat not in any official capacity, but personal gain. Utah's appointed governor showed little interest in defending the boundary concerns of his Mormon Constituents.[17]

In his annual message to the Territorial legislature that in 1866, Durkee stated that "Within the past year numerous mines of coal, lead and precious metals, have been discovered in various parts of the Territory." He suggested that " Many of these mines are surpassing richness and their discovery has but just commenced." In his message, Durkee never mentioned Pahranagat by name.

Less than four months later Durkee made the first of at two visits to Pahranagat in 1866. His initial tour occurred sometime in April, with Durkee touting "the supposed wealth of our southern mines" as he passed through Mormon settlements on his way south giving the impression to the Mormon that "he was going to Pahranagat on a mining excursion."[18] When he returned he exhibited "two shining silver lumps." One of which weighed forty ounces and contained about four ounces of gold."[19]

Governor Durkee apparently liked what he had found at Pahranagat. While there July to October, he made an offer of $8000 or 1100 feet of the "Green Monster claim" and almost immediately began making plans to return to the district for an extended stay.[20]

He later wrote President Andrew Johnson that Pahranagat was removed from the Utah jurisdiction, and to go there again required a leave of absence from the Governship. He wrote "It has been my purpose to spend two or three months this coming summer at Pah Ranagat for the benefit of my health, being somewhat affected with Rheumatism." Pahranagat will be transferred to Nevada. I therefore solicit your permission to carry out my design."[21]

Charles Durkee writes his old associate and Senator from Wisconsin, James Doolittle concerning a bill in Congress which would provide for the annexation by Nevada of a strip of land on the western side of Utah.[22] "It is generally conceded that the proper and peaceful solution of the Mormon Problem consists in introducing the development of our mineral resources, a population of "Gentiles" who will ultimately outnumber the "Saints". Governor Durkee recommended withdrawing the Legislation

The "Green Monster" did not live up to Durkee's expectations. A report to the Secretary of the Treasury by Rossiter Worthington Raymond 1869 stated "the mineral deposits of Pahranagat may be classified as follows: Veins running northeast and southwest in the quartzite, examples Green Monster, Penobscot. The veins in quartzite are narrow and resemble the foregoing, Several tons of ore have been extracted from the Green Monster and are said to have yielded $150 silver per ton; but there is hardly any ore now insight It is not known whether these veins of Quartzite descended into the underlying Limestone." [23]

Raymond reported that by 1868, investors had poured nearly one million dollars into the Pahranagat District, producing only about twenty thousand dollars worth of bullion. Even Governor Durkee's "Green Monster" lode quickly played out as did most of the other strikes, leaving Raymond to lament that developments in the district mining which "have been conducted with such conspicuous absence of skill and common sense."

It was established that to file a claim conveyed perpetual title and all that was required to hold possession was to make a pile of stones on the claim. [24]

The Green Monster mine yielded primarily silver, but also lead, copper zinc and antimony. The mine is presently listed under the Bureau of Land Management control. The ore was classified as Galena, an ore of silver and lead sulfides, valued at 150 dollars per ton, in 1866. The ore was in a fissure vein.[25] [26]

Chapter 5

Black Hawk War

Franklin Head

Utah Superintendence, Great Salt City, April 30, 1866

Sir: Black Hawk, a somewhat prominent chief of the Utah Indians, has been engaged for more than a year past in active hostilities against the settlements in the southern portion of this territory. His band consists at first of but forty-four men, who were mostly out laws and desperate characters from his own and other tribes. During the summer and autumn of 1865 he made several successful forays upon the weak and unprotected settlements in San Pete and Sevier counties; killed in all thirty-two whites, and drove away to the mountains upwards of two thousand cattle and horses.

Forty of his warriors were killed by the settlers in repelling his different attacks. His success in stealing, however enabled him to feed abundantly and mount all Indians who joined him, and the prestige acquired by his raids was such that his numbers were constantly on the increase, despite his occasional losses of men. He spent the winter near where the Grand and Green rivers unite to for m the Colorado. On the 20th instant he again commenced his depredations by making an attack upon Salina, a small settlement in Sevies county. He succeeded in driving to the mountains about two hundred cattle, and killing two men who were guarding them, and compelling the abandonment of the settlement.

His band from what I consider entirely reliable information, now numbers one hundred warriors, one-half of whom are Navajoes from New Mexico. I am very apprehensive that unless Black Hawk is severely chastised, an Indian war of considerable magnitude may be inaugurated. He has never yet met with a serious reverse, having always attacked small settlements or unprotected families. He has thus acquired a considerable reputation among the various Indian tribes, and I fear may of more adventurous will join him from bands now friendly. The ill-feeling engendered by the death of Sanpitch, and by the nearly starving conditions of the Indians on the Uintah Reservation, concerning which I had the honor to address you on the 23d instance, will tend to promote this result.

In view of the circumstances, and for the purpose of preventing accessions to the ranks of the hostile Indians, I have, after consultation with Governor Durkee, desired Colonel Potter, commanding the United States troops in this district, to send two or three companies of soldiers to that portion of the Territory to protect the settlements and repel further attacks. I have sent Indian runners to have an interview with Black Hawk and to urge him to meet me for the purpose of establishing a permanent peace. I have little hope, however, that he will do this, at least before he is defeated, with the loss of some portion of his warriors, as he has heretofore been boldly defiant, rejecting with scorn all overtures of peace. Colonel Potter has telegraphed to General Dodge for instructions in reference to my application. I should be much pleased to have an expression of your views as to the policy to be further pursued in this matter.

Very respectfully, you most obedient servant,

F. H Head

Superintendent

Atonga, an American native warrior also called Black Hawk, started an Indian War in 1865 with Northern Utes and their allies. A series of raids were made on cattle and horses owned by the Mormon Settlers of Utah. The Livestock were sold in a native American trading network covering the territorial regions Utah, Colorado, New Mexico, Nevada, Arizona and Wyoming.

Joseph Smith Jr., founder of the Mormon Church, said that he considered the Native Americans as Lamanites and hoped that they "may come to the knowledge of their fathers, Ancient Israel, and believe the gospel and rely upon the merits of Jesus Christ"[23] The animosity between the Utes and the Brigham Young's clan of Mormons was only somewhat tempered.

Early in 1865 there was a Smallpox epidemic among the Utes in Manti Utah south of Salt Lake City.

At a crucial meeting aimed to pacify the Ute's, a young warrior chief, Yene-wood, was yanked off his horse. Dishonored, the matter festered and failed to quell animosities.

The next day on April 10th 1865, Peter Ludvigson, one of the settlers at Nine Mile was killed. A month later John Given and his family of 6 were killed. By the end of 1865, 32 white settlers had been murdered in Sevier and Sanpete counties, and over 2,000 head of horses and cattle stolen.

---

[2] Utah's Black Hawk War, by John Alton Peterson, University of Utah Press,

[3] Cook, Book of Revelations of Joseph Smith

A Ute Warrior and his bride in 1874
by John K Hillers
(Library of Congress Photograph Collection)

Brigham Young assumed control and attempted to broker a peace, the conditions were firm.: The Utes would assign their lands in the territory --except for the Uintah Basin; and cease all hostilities. In return, they would receive payments from the government; a vocational school; grist mill, saw mill and supplies and food.

The Indians signed the Treaty with the Mormons. All but Sanpitch, father of Black Hawk. In the ensuing weeks, hostilities continued. Setters were murdered and over 300 head of cattle stolen.

In October 1865, Franklin Head assumed his position of Indian Agent for the Utah Territory.

The Mormons, in an effort to mitigate further loss, had started to consolidate their farms in two counties; secure their cattle and take arms. Many were newly arrived from Europe and did not know how to defend themselves.

A new attack occurred at Manti on April 10 1865. Black Hawk led sixteen Utes to drive off a cattle herd outside Manti. A shooting battle occurred with the Utes, one killed and the rest fled back to Manti. The Utes rounded up forty cattle and drove them toward Salina Canyon. There they combined with members of Jake Arapeen's Utes totaling 60 warriors. They held up in Salina Canyon.
The territorial militia, known as the Nauvoo Legion followed them into the Canyon. It was an ambush and only two survived. Black Hawk retreated of Castle Valley.

In March 11 1866 Governor Durkee and Franklin Head met with Brigham Young asserting their authority to direct Utah's Indian affairs. They agreed to send runners to Sanpitch and arrange an immediate meeting to make a peace treaty.[27]

Warren Snow of the Nauvoo Militia captured Sanpitch and eight warriors, charging them with aiding Black Hawk. Governor Durkee and his Indian Agent Head made a trip to Kanosh's camp intending to obtain the freedom of Sinpitch, but their effort was contradicted and their interference viewed as federal intervention. Richard James an interpreter went along before joining the ranks of the raiders.

In April 18, 1866 Sanpitch was killed. April 1866 saw further unrest between the Mormons and the Paiutes. A local militia from Fort Sanford was killed and the people of Circleville rounded up the local tribe and killed most of them.

The situation had only worsened. Franklin Head wrote to the Government for more troops.

In a letter by Head to the commissioner of Indian Affairs, he requested "one or two companies" of Federal Troops."[28] General John Pope replied that "there were no troops to be spared for such service" and that " the Sup. Of Indian Affairs will have to depend on the local Militia to compel the Indians to behave in Selina."

If nothing else, it gave Governor Durkee and Superintendent Head the oversight authority to manage the Nauvoo Legion in fighting Black Hawk and his band.[29]

Hostile armed attacks continued.

In June, a band of Black Hawks Braves approached a herd of 350 cattle near Scipio. They killed the herd boy and shot James Ivie. Stealing additional horses they moved the herd into Scipio Gap and into Sevier Valley.

The settlers chased the Utes as Black Hawks moved to attack the local town. Scipio ranchers sent for the Nauvoo Legion and tried to stop the escape of the settlers and herds. At the river the militia engaged. The ensuing fight saw Black Hawk in the foray, wounded.

Following the battle, the Mormons adopted a philosophy of fortifying the larger towns with a Fort and abandoning outlying settlements.

By May, it became clear to Durkee and Head that the native American Indians were destitute and starving, especially the Utes of Uintah Reservation were. They resolved to borrow several tons of flour and supplies from Brigham Young and distributed them to the Indian camp.[30] Head hoped this act of friendship would persuade the Utes to return to the Reservation. Management and control proved elusive

In July 2 1866, Governor Durkee and Franklin Head approved the Indian Reservation at Spanish Fork, and requested funding.[31]

The skirmishes continued, and the Militia called out. They discovered a Ute camp and attacked the marauding band, killing all who resisted. Over 100 men, plus militia surrounded them, killing ten warriors and wounding a great many more.

Durkee was outraged. In his address to the Territorial Legislature, he stated that the Utah's militia practices were "not in accordance with the Territorial Organic Act", especially the "Provision therein, that the Governor shall be Commander in Chief of the Militia".[32]

Later Governor Durkee repeated his efforts "to have this militia disbanded or its control turned over to him".[33]

Chief Sinapitch agreed to help hunt down anyone with connections to the Black Hawk raid. Those who were captured were tried and executed. The Utes, including Sinapitch were allowed visits with their wives while in captivity. But it was not without rancor and retribution.

Gradually, with Black Hawk wounded and the Mormons fully aware of Indian attacks, the Indian raids seemed to dwindle.

Disgruntled individuals wrote to the commissioner of Indian Affairs in Washington DC. They complained that Head had kept an interpreter who worked with Black Hawk; and that Head had made profits off purchasing and selling Indian supplies.

Governor Durkee wrote "I have been shown by Superintendent Head a telegram relative to certain charges against him. I Have known him personally for several years, and know him to be a man of strict integrality. He had accompanied him often in visits to Indians.[34]

Senator James Doolittle of Wisconsin also supported for the integrity of Franklin Head.

"I have heard mention of some legislator from all parts of the Territory give in the highest terms the reputation of Mr. Head stating that Indians have never before received so many presents of goods and provisions-have heard Indians say the same in all parts of the Territory.

I am sure that these charges are entirely false. Some of the former agents of the government by their plundering of the Indians at the Uita Agency had seriously brought in an Indian War. Have understood that they intended to get Mr. Head ... because of the expense of some of their relative charges .. form present maters. Posing making charges under such circumstances. I did not consider worthy of belief. The Indian business of the Territory is ... in a manner creditable to Mr. Head and to the Government and no charge should be made, certainly not in the interest of parties working against time. Have an ...that Mr. Giggs (one of the complainants) while U. S. Marshall of Utah was a defaulter to the Government and that his bail was ...[35]

It is due Mr. Head from his reputation and position that ample time be afforded his defense.

As Indian Agent Head was responsible for ordering such items as flour, Beeves, calico cloth and brass kettles, beaver traps and chains, to supply the various reservations."

In January 1868 Head lobbied the Commissioner of Indian affairs to designate the tribal lands of the Shoshone to establish an Indian reservation in the Valley of the Mill River. It was a favorite hunting place of the natives.

Governor Charles Durkee and Franklin Head were also appointed by the Secretary of Interior as Commissioners to appraise the value of the land contained in the Spanish Fork Indian Reservation. The reservation was surveyed and accepted by the Surveyor General.[36]

On 19 August 1868 – Black Hawk and a delegation of three Chiefs of about thirty of their men met with Superintendent Head and Dominick Huntington and held Treaty talks. At this time Black Hawk surrendered. This became known as the Treaty of Strawberry Valley, and lead to the end of the Black Hawk War. Two years later, Black Hawk died of tuberculosis, September 1870.

Head had acted as the Indian Superintendent of the Utah Territory and enabled the return of "Mormon and Gentile" communities to greater security and peace of mind.

Head was determined, above all objections, to sustain a steady supply of food and goods to the Utes on Reservations.

Chapter 6

The Trip Home

Charles Durkee's Mission as Territorial Governor of Utah was coming to an end. He anticipated travelling to his home in Kenosha Wisconsin and probably to Washington DC and New York to finish business.

Two days before Charles Durkee was to travel East, he decided to visit a local individual located just twelve miles out of Salt Lake City. He set out to do so. But it was late in the afternoon on the last day of December 1869 when he started out in a buggy for this purpose. The night came on quickly. It was dark and cold, and he lost his way. Finding no shelter, he claimed that he was obliged to spend the night on the open prairie. The next day he made his way back to Salt Lake City in a condition that was described as "frost-bitten." One reference – author unknown, says "Nothing very serious, however was apprehended from this night of exposure."[37]

On January 2nd, 1870 Charles Durkee took his departure from Salt Lake City for Wisconsin, accompanied by his wife and F. H. Head, formerly the Indian Agent for the Utah Territory.

On the first day of his journey the "cold" he had taken during his night of exposure on the prairie was "fearfully" developed. His situation seemed to demand medical attention and a telegram was from the train station at Cheyenne Wyoming for a physician to meet the party at the train depot in Omaha.
The physician examined Charles and recommended a day or two rest at Omaha, after which he thought the Governor would be able to proceed on his journey.

The day after his arrival at Omaha however, it became clear that Durkee had developed pneumonia and on the succeeding day his condition so deteriorated that a decision was made to telegraph his brother Harvey Durkee of Kenosha to come immediately. He had been at Omaha for several days. His brother reached Omaha by January 10th, 1870.

Governor Durkee's health deteriorated and he became delirious, leaving no hope of recovery. He admonished his wife Caroline to "beware of the Executors" of his Will and guard his papers. In lucid moments he expressed his desire to see once more the shores of Lake Michigan and meet his old friends and acquaintances where he had spent so many happy years of his life. To die among his old neighbors was his repeated wish.

As Durkee realized he was dying as he said goodbye to those around him "Give my love to everybody." Later, as witnessed, he said "I have been happy in this world and am now happy in leaving it." Shortly before dying he wrote "She the star I missed from Heaven, Long time ago."

Charles Durkee died on Friday, January 14, 1870 in Omaha, Nebraska at the age of sixty-four. His remains were brought to Kenosha and interred in Green Ridge Cemetery. Part of his obituary read

> *"He leaves no children to mourn their loss and the sympathies of his early friends are grieves to his widow to sustain her in her affliction of an irreparable loss. The remains of Governor Durkee will arrive in this city on Monday, and his funeral will take place on Tuesday next."*[38]

Charles Durkee's Will, which he had recorded in the Kenosha Court House the previous year, was probated. In it he designated his executors as "Harvey Durkee, of Kenosha, aforesaid, and Franklin H. Head, late of Kenosha. They were assigned

> "...all my real and personal estate rights and credits, with the right to sell, dispose and convey the same without order of any court or officer, in such amounts, and on such terms, as they may deem for- the best intentions..."[39]

> "Second. Whereas my beloved wife, Caroline Durkee, has now settled upon her an annuity during her life of six hundred dollars annually, and she has a life lease of my homestead in Kenosha City,...plus sum of one thousand dollars.."[40] from investments.

> Fourth. Out of said assets my acting executor will pay to the board of officers of the free schools of Kenosha City, Wisconsin, five thousand dollars, to be, by said board, expended in and towards procuring a telescope for the use of the free schools of said City of Kenosha.."[41]

> Signed and sealed at Kenosha, Wisconsin, this 12th day of February, A. D. 1869.[42]"

The Will was Probated, and an inventory of Charles Durkee's estate submitted to the court in April 1870.

The initial Inventory listed assets of Kenosha as $838.84; not including the real estate. There was a discrepancy in that Charles Durkee's Assets were chiefly outside Wisconsin and not listed.

The Governor Durkee Obituary of Wisconsin listed his lifetime accomplishments and focus.

"Obituary. *Milwaukee Daily Sentinel*, (Milwaukee, WI), Monday, January 17, 1870; Issue 13; col. A.

"The death of Governor Charles Durkee has cast a gloom over this city and state. He was one of our earliest settlers, and came from the state of Vermont in 1836, and set led here. He was a man of energy, good business capacity, and tales of a high order. He purchased considerable property here, and commenced early to build, which he pursued extensively to the advancement of the best interests of the place. Through his influence the city continued to grow and its business increase.

He built a large and commodious public house which was called the Durkee House, but is now called the Halliday House, and is one of the finest public houses upon the lake shore. Few men have done so much business, dealt so honorably with so many persons and made so few enemies as Charles Durkee. He was never *led*, but always forward in all plans of mercy, benevolence. He was early in the cause of freedom and temperance, and an earnest advocate of the same.

In 1836, the first year he came to this city, he was elected a member for the first Territorial Legislature. In 1850 the people of this district elected him a member of the House of Representatives at Washington and re-elected him again in 1852, where he served two terms, to the entire satisfaction of his constituents. In 1855 he was elected a member of the United States Senate where he served with distinguished ability.

After his term expired he moved to Dane County, where he purchased a farm, and left political for agricultural pursuits. In 1865, upon the declination of Governor Doty, as Governor of Utah, he was appointed by President Johnson to fill the vacancy, where has resided for the past four years.

For a few years his health has been declining, and for the past six months, has had little hope of ever returning to his home, and among his friends. He resigned the short time left of his term, and started for Wisconsin, and reached Omaha, where his symptoms became worse, and where death relieved him of his pains and trials on the 14th ult. His wife and sympathizing friends watched over him, and everything was done that could be done to restore him again to his friends, or make his paths pleasant. He leaves no children to mourn their loss and the sympathies of his early friends are give to his widow to sustain her in her affliction of an irreparable loss. The remains of Governor Durkee will arrive in this city on Monday, and his funeral will take place on Tuesday next.

Kenosha, Jan. 15, 1870."

Six months later, Franklin Head went to Salt Lake City to submit a revised inventory of Durkee's estate, and to collect cash and Notes from Kerr and Company.

It is nowhere recorded what the purpose was of Durkee's journey East.
However, it was earlier implied that he was intending to bring his career as Governor to a close, citing general age and rheumatic ill-health.
No record of an official retirement came forward at the time of his death, perhaps since the matter was moot.
Some observations can be drawn from his actions prior to his death however.
While his health was cited as his reason to go to California, just 18 months prior, it is known that in California, Durkee met with Governor Stanford; Judge Crocker and Hopkins to discuss the Transcontinental railway coming to Utah. Also discussed was the matter of working with Bingham Young, the Mormon leader. The day-trip intended for Salt Lake City (resulting in his overnight incident) was scheduled on New Year's Eve. Perhaps a celebratory event, or perhaps the turn of a new calendar year for business purposes, even for collection purposes.
Clearly, his planned journey East had been previously arranged. (Some preparations were underway.) And it had been scheduled for the start of the new year. For Governor Durkee to be accompanied by his wife on such a long and arduous journey suggested an anticipated stay of some duration. Further, the attendance of a former Indian Agent whose expertise was unique, suggests some business-related quest.

Was it his intention, perhaps, to market his Paramount Lien Bonds dated 1865 and later– Or cash in the 'Coupon' segments stamped "due and payable in the City of New York"?

Accounts from various people associated with his trip stipulate that he had a "Tin Box" with him containing valuable papers. Some of these papers were used to collect his notes with Kerr and Co, as well as others in Salt Lake City; and at his property in San Diego.

One witness John T. Dewees, who had met with Durkee at Cheyenne, Wyoming while Durkee was travelling East, offered the following insight in a DEPOSITION in 1901 (20 years later). Dewees claimed that Durkee had bonds with him.

> "Those []'bonds were usually $1000 bonds; did you handle all the bonds in Governor Durkee's possession, and are you sure they were all $1000 bonds."
>
> "...there were a large amount of bonds in his possession, but a large number of them for $2500 to $5000, were also there. (US Government subsidy bonds)[4]
>
> Subscribed before me this 25th day of November, A.D. 1901."

It should be noted Government bonds only came in denominations of $500, 1,000, $5,000 and $10,000 only.

---

[4] John T. Dewees, who had met Durkee at Cheyenne, Wyoming while Durkee was travelling in January 1870, offered the following insight in a DEPOSITION in 1901. Relating to Durkee's final trip home in January 1870. John T. Dewees "Subscribed before me this 25th day of November, A.D. 1901.", Appendix *III*

Chapter 7

The Estate

In May-June 1870, Franklin Head traveled to Salt Lake City Utah to settle some matters of the Charles Durkee estate.

He possessed several Notes contained in a "Tin box" ~in the possession of Charles Durkee on the return trip home from Salt Lake City at the time of his death.

Franklin Head provided a listing of the property owned: Most notable was $43,000 owed by Kerr and Company for transactions within the partnership; 20 acres of property in San Diego California; Mining property claim in Pahranagat Nevada; and various other small debts in Salt Lake City. Franklin Head submitted a revised inventory and collected cash and Notes from Kerr and Company.

In May 1871 Caroline Durkee assigned a portion of the estate to Harvey Durkee for a sum of $16,000.[5] This occurred following Franklin Head's trip to Utah. She reserved the house estate; half the Mining claim in Nevada; half the proceeds of the property in San Diego. All other property, rights and credits and assets belonging to the estate which was not included in the second inventory.

---

[5] The Caroline Durkee Harvey Durkee see Appendix IV

The second inventory included four promissory notes, one against J. W. Kerr of Salt Lake City, dated December 30 1869, for the sum of $43,000. (Franklin Head had himself established these transactions of Notes on behalf of Charles Durkee prior to his leaving Salt Lake City in 1869). This Note was written up on the day before Durkee's incident of night exposure, leading to his death.

Another Note submitted by Franklin Head was against Pardon Dodds, for $1,000 and various other Notes amounted to $770. In addition $1,245 was on account against Harvey Durkee, and $434 cash in hand of F. H. Head.[6]

The assignment of Caroline's share of the estate is vague in the benefits to Harvey, but it may be thought that he was considering the ownership of any Paramount Lien Bonds.

A suit was filed against the Will of Charles Durkee by a potential heir to the estate.

Omission was cited as a reason for the contestation in the listing of assets which did not include $100,000 in government bonds; neither a large amount of railroad and municipal bonds; nor a stock of the Union, Central and Southern Pacific railroads, as well as some other property.[7]

The complaint stated that the estate should have been probated in Utah where other relatives were entitled under state law to receive a portion of the estate. The complaint stated that other funds and assets were obtained in Utah and were not recorded. The Estate, the complaint said, held an additional value was now estimated at worth over $500,000[43]

---

[6] Sale of Charles Durkee Estate by Caroline Durkee, May 1871, Filed in Kenosha Probate Court. See Appendix IV

[7] Review of the stock subscription of the Union Pacific does not list Charles Durkee, and the Southern Pacific Railroad was not fully formed at the time of his death.

In another newspaper article of July 1887, Judge Gresham of Kenosha, ruled that Charles Durkee had conveyed to his executors Harvey Durkee and Franklin Head all his property valued at between $400,000 and $500,000.[44]

The Probate Court of Kenosha Wisconsin, by Judgment dated March 21 1882, stated that it had awarded the residue of Charles Durkee's estate to his sole heir and widow, Caroline, and that it had not assigned any of the residue to Harvey Durkee.[45]

Chapter 8

The Transcontinental Railroad

Transcontinental railway was envisioned in the early 1850s. Congress saw a need to cross the continent for expansion, trade and development of resources. Especially after the 1849 gold rush in California, and for opportunities presented by lands obtained in the Louisiana Purchase. Expeditions of the Army including cartographers, geologists and surveyors looked at potential routes across the continent. Reports came back in 1856 and 1857 showing the results of those expeditions.

For a new nation needing trade to grow, development across an uneven economic landscape presented challenges. While European Imperial economies were globally connecting domestic markets with Trade Agreements, America was beset by well-vocalized social movements; presidential elections and currency liquidity issues, such that greater cohesive plans for improvements were often pushed down because of regional disparities and local disputes.

In 1862 Congress passed an initial Transcontinental Railway authorization by legislating the Act of 1862, entitled "An Act to aid in the construction of a railroad and telegraph line from the Missouri River to the Pacific Ocean and to secure to the Government the use of the same for postal and military and other purposes."[46] This provided for the funding of a railroad to be built by private corporations from the Hundreds Meridian of longitude to San Francisco. The Union Pacific Railroad Company was to build from Council Bluffs Iowa to the Western boundary Nevada.

The Union Pacific was authorized to issue 100,000 shares $1000 each capital stock as initial funding. "The first meeting of said board shall be held in Chicago at such time as within one to three months after passage of this Act."

The Central Pacific Company was authorized to build from Sacramento California Eastern boundary of the state.

As shown in Section 2 of the Act, there was made provision for "a right of way through public lands be granted to the companies for construction of the road and telegraph line and the right to take from adjacent public lands for stone and timber and other materials for construction. The right-of-way for the road extended 200 feet in width on each side and included all necessary grounds for stations buildings workshops and depots. Section 3 the act authorized five alternate sections (one square mile) per mile on each side of the road within the limits of 10 miles as a land-grant to help finance a road."

In Section 4 of the Act, there was "authorized after completion of 40 consecutive miles of any portion of the said railroad and telegraph line ready for service the President would authorize patents conveying the right and title to the said company on each side of the road."

In Section 5 of the Act, financing was specified. "The US government would issue bonds of the United States of $1000 each payable 30 years after the date bearing 6% of and an interest rate interest paid payable semi-annually to the amount of $16,000 per mile for each section of 40 miles and to secure repayment the United States hereafter the amount of said bonds. The payment constituted *de facto* a First Mortgage on the whole line of the railroad and telegraph."

Under section 9 of the Act, authorized was the "Leavenworth and Western Railroad Company of Kansas, the Kansas Pacific Railway, the Sioux City and Pacific Railway and the Western Pacific Railway."

In giving competition to the plan between the two railways as to the place where they should meet, it stipulated that the Central Pacific Railway Company was authorized "to continue construction of the railroad and telegraph line to the territories United States to Missouri River until it met the Union Pacific Railway."

Under Section 11, the US government increase the number of bonds threefold for the most mountainous and difficult construction "to wit this amounted to $48,000 of subsidy bonds for those sections and for sections the on the mountain's condition is extended deeper into the continent from both directions double the amount of bonds was authorized. This amounted to $32,000 per mile."

Under Section 17, a time plan for payment was provided. The US government required the entire railroad to be completed before 1876. The government reserved on each part of the appropriated funds installment that "25% to remain in the U.S. Treasury undelivered until the road and all parts thereof provided for the act are entirely completed and 15% them to be and remain with the treasury until the whole road provided for this act is fully completed."

The initial Act did not get enough public and financial to support the construction of railroads in any large measure.

Amendment of July 2, 1864

The Civil War, incited by a northern immigrant-activist movement, disrupted the union in such disproportionate measure of risk and valor as to draw vast manpower and capital away from its principal objectives of growth, and the continent of America remained a wilderness without transportation until legislation in 1864[47].[48]

Congress quickly regrouped. The first major section of the Revised Act of Congress passed both chambers and allowed railroads to purchase land owned by others within 100 feet of the proposed railroad right-of-way. This allowed the railroad to proceed through areas settled, and to pass into towns.

Under Section 4, the amount of lands granted the railroads were increased significantly. Iron and coal deposits were not considered as mineral lands, which would later allow the railroads to supply fuel for a growing nation.

Section 17 repealed a prohibitive provision that required the need to retain government bonds.

The most significant section was Section 10. This authorized the issuance of the railroad company to offer First Mortgage Bonds on their respective railroad & telegraph lines not to exceed the amount of bonds of the United States. This put the US subsidy bonds in second position and allowed railroads to seek private financing support the construction of the railroad.

The amendment was passed not quickly enough on July 2, 1864, allowing the railroads to seek private funding in the form of railroad bonds; land the land bonds, and increased stock subscriptions.

The Union Pacific Railroad

The Union Pacific Railroad in accordance with the July 1, 1862 Act of Congress was organized on September 2, 1862. The railroad was chartered to extend from Council Bluffs Iowa to the California state line. The organization was provisional requiring a subscription for $2,000,000 in stock [8]which did not occur until October 1863. The Act of Congress did not provide sufficient investment to encourage strong financial support. Congress revised the act on July 2, 1864 to allow the provision of a private mortgage and issuance of first mortgage bonds equal to Government Bonds.

The funding of the road by the US Government and the issuance of First Mortgage bonds of $16,000 per mile, augmented to 517 miles on the Plains; then at the rate of $48,000 per mile for 150 miles through the Rocky Mountains; then bonds of $32,000 per mile for the remainder of the distance. In addition, the railroad received 12,800 acres to the mile on the main line of the road. The company was authorized $100,000,000 of Capital stock of which $8,500,000 had been paid for work already completed. [49]

The company had anticipated $29,328,000 in US Bonds and $29,328,000 in First Mortgage Bonds. The actual authorized amount of Bonds was $27,236,512.00. In evaluating the Ledgers of the Boston office for 1869, the Union Pacific was issuing bonds to serial numbers 29,000 or $29,000,000.

---

[8] A stock subscription is an obligation to buy the stock paying only a portion up front.

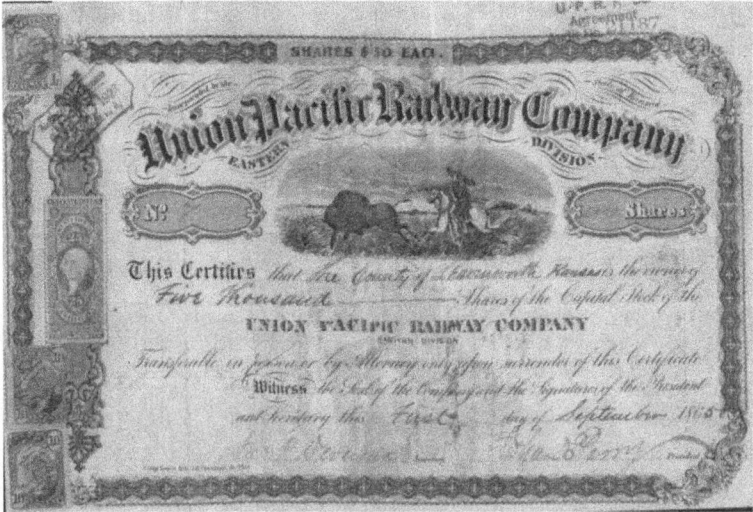

**Union Pacific Eastern Division Stock. Part of the First Issue, 1865
The railroad company became the Kansas Pacific Railroad in 1870.**

(Courtesy of David Beach, of cigarboxlabels)

This was later adjusted to achieve the distance to the meeting point, East and West joining at Promontory Utah. A separate financial agreement between the Union Pacific Railroad and the Central Pacific Railroads to sell or lease a portion of the line was made so that the endpoint of the Central Pacific was just 5 miles outside of Ogden Utah, providing an improved meeting junction for the railroads.

The directors of the company were Oliver Ames of Boston; Sidney Dillon of New York; Gordon Dexter of Boston; John Cisco of New York; Thomas Durant of New York, and several others. Oliver Ames was President, Thomas Durant Vice President and John Cisco was Treasurer. Ames' brother, Congressman Oak Ames was designated Trustee for the First Mortgage Bonds. (See Appendix I)

The road progressed across the plains and into the Rocky Mountains under the former General Grenville Dodge, and railroad construction was able to meet schedule. Herbert Hoxie had won the initial contract for 247 miles across the plains of Nebraska. The contract proved to be embroiled in conflicts of interest, and the Union Pacific switched to Credit Mobilier. Grenville Dodge was able to manage operations and made an extraordinary effort to meet the tight schedule of construction.

In Testimony before Congress, Benjamin Ham, auditor for the Union Pacific Railroad stated that there were 29,000,000 of Bonds issued and executed by the company. 1,600,000 were retired by order of Congress and surrendered and cancelled. They lost (Union Pacific) $250,000 in bonds which were regularly having their coupons paid.[50]

The Hoxie Contract and Credit Mobilier

Herbert Hoxie, an associate of Dr. Durant, Vice President of the Union Pacific Railroad was awarded a contract to build the first 100 miles of the Union Pacific from Omaha.

Hoxie submitted the only bid contract for construction. The bid was accepted on 23rd September, 1865. By October, the bid was increased to cover 247 miles for $12,350,000.[51]

Four days later he signed the contract over to Durant and four other men, Cornelius Bushenell; Charles Lambard; H. W. Gray and H.S. McComb. The contract was assigned to a company called Credit Mobilier formerly called the Pennsylvania Fiscal Agency chartered in 1859.[52]

Credit Mobilier was formed from the Pennsylvania Fiscal Agency for the purpose of acting as a contracting and processing entity for the Union Pacific. The organization was structured to allow contracting of the railroad; handling of stock, bonds and other financing, and the purchase of materials.[53]

On March 1864 the company officially became Credit Mobilier.[54]

Credit Mobilier became the primary construction agent of the Union Pacific. The Railroad and Credit Mobilier acted in concert with

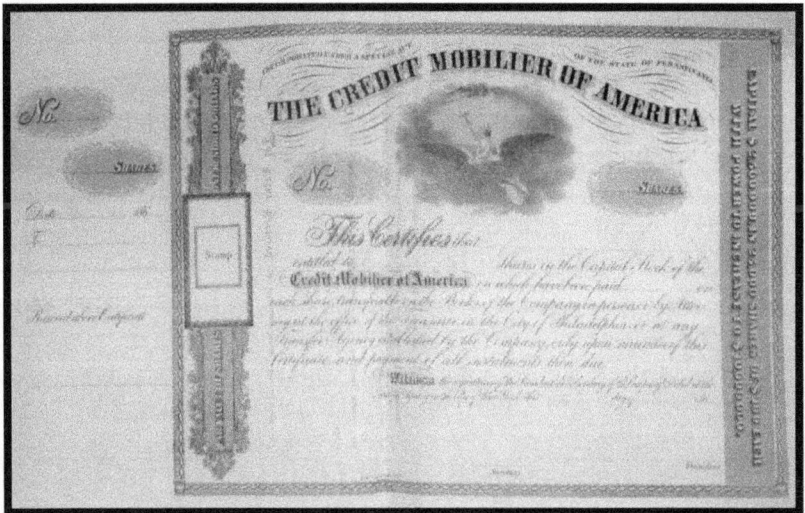

Credit Mobilier Stock The company formed in 1864 as a conduit for construction of the Main Line of the Union Pacific Railroad
(University of Iowa Library Special Collections, Union Pacific Railroad Collection)

each other. Many of the stockholders in Credit Mobilier were directors and stock holders of the Union Pacific. The Union Pacific made contracts with Credit Mobilier and were paid by check to build the Union Pacific Railway as intended by the mandates to build a railroad. Credit Mobilier used these checks to buy stock and bonds in the Union Pacific at par value, believing it to be in keeping with Section 10 of the

Revised Act of 1864 as reinvestment in the railroad , by example.[9]

The Union Pacific made contracts with Credit Mobilier and were paid by check to build the Union Pacific Railway as intended by the mandates to build a railroad. Credit Mobilier used these checks to buy stock and bonds in the Union Pacific at par value, believing it to be in keeping with Section 10 of the Revised Act of 1864 as reinvestment in the railroad, by example.[10]

They sold the bonds on the open market, avidly sought by investors. These construction contracts brought high profits to credit Mobilier, rewarding the owners and the principal stock holders of the Union Pacific. But they were criticized by many for their profits as reflected in the figures of Record Books of the Board of Trustees of the Union Pacific Railroad , 1867.[55]

Unaccustomed to universal industrialized costs of modern capital instruments of free market capitalism, opponents said that the western transcontinental railroad plan was an unprofitable venture, a "railroad to nowhere" paid by the United States Government.

Clearly it was a time to advance the interests of the united and commercially integrated America.

---

[9] Union Pacific Railroad Ledgers, Boston, 1869. Nebraska State Historical Society, RG 3761, Union Pacific Collections The ledgers showed no transactions to credit Mobilier on the sale of bonds. The Union Pacific for the most part discounted the sale of bonds by 15% on the books.

[10] Ibid

Central Pacific Railroad

The Central Pacific Railroad was one of the two primary Transcontinental Railroads stretching from Sacramento California to Utah.

Theodore Judah, a storekeeper in Dutch Flats California, received communications from Daniel Strong who showed him a route through the Sierra Nevada Mountains - along the old immigrant trail near Donner Pass – that would be ideal for track. The route had a gradual rise and would work for a rail line. Judah and Strong drew up a letter of incorporation for the Central Pacific Railroad Company. They sought investors and convinced businessmen that a railroad was possible across the mountains to the east.

Several businessmen backed the venture, including Collis P. Huntington a hardware wholesaler, and his partner Mark Hopkins of Sacramento; Charles Crocker, a dry goods merchant, and Leland Stanford, a wholesale grocer -later Governor of California. These four men would become known as the "Big Four."

The Pacific Railroad Act was passed on July 1, 1862 which authorized funding for the Transcontinental Railroad with US Government Bonds and Land Grants. Although the Pacific Railroad eventually benefited the Bay Area, the City and County of San Francisco obstructed financing during the early years of 1863-1865.

When Stanford was Governor of California, the Legislature passed on April 22, 1863, "An Act to Authorize the Board of Supervisors of the City and County of San Francisco to take and subscribe One Million Dollars to the Capital Stock of the Western Pacific Rail Road Company and the Central Pacific Rail Road Company of California and to provide for the payment of the same and other matters relating thereto" (which was later amended by Section Five of the "Compromise Act" of April 4, 1864).

On May 19, 1863, the electors of the City and County of San Francisco passed this bond by a vote of 6,329 to 3,116, in a highly controversial Special Election.

Bond of the Central Pacific Railroad and the Western Pacific
Railroad Issued by the City & County of San Francisco

(Courtesy of the Bruce C. Cooper Collection of US Railroad History)

Kansas Pacific Railroad

The Kansas Pacific Railroad Company was first chartered by the Legislature of Kansas as the Leavenworth, Pawnee and Western. The company was reorganized by acts of Congress as the Union Pacific Eastern Division Railroad by Congress in March 1869.[11] The Road extended from Kansas City Kansas to ultimately Denver Colorado, a distance of 643 miles. The name Kansas Pacific was not adopted until 1869.

The original intent was to build from Kansas City Kansas to Fort Riley and then join the Union Pacific in Fort Kearney Nebraska. This was to provide the US Government transportation routes into Kansas which had been scenes of ongoing conflict between Union and Confederate sympathizers earlier.

The Kansas Pacific received subsidy bonds of $16,000 per mile and a grant of public lands to 12,800 acres per mile constructed. The road received subsidies for 394 miles west from the Missouri River for a total of $6,303,000. In addition, in the provisions of the Congressional Act July 2, 1864 it was authorized that the railroad issue $6,303,000 in First Mortgage Paramount Lien Bonds which were positioned ahead of any government subsidy.[56] With the aid of German and Dutch investors the extension of the line into Colorado began in October 1869. The Road was completed by on September 1, 1870.

Central Branch of the Union Pacific Railroad

This road was originally organized under the corporate title of the Atchison and Pike's Peak Railroad Company February 11, 1859. It was provided as one of the branches of the Union Pacific in the Act incorporating that company.[57]

The main line of this road extended from Atchison to Waterville, Kansas for 100 miles. Being under the mandate of the 1862 and 1864 Congressional Acts, it received federal bond support for $16,000 per mile. The company was also authorized to issue $1,600,000 in First Mortgage bonds. Although a division of the Union Pacific Railroad, the road operated independently and had corporate offices in another location in New York City. The corporate officers and board of directors was not related to the Union Pacific Railroad.

The Atchison, Colorado & Pacific Branch ran from Waterville to Lenora for a length of 191.9 miles; Greenleaf to Washington for 7 miles; Downs to Bull's City for 23.6 miles; Yuma to Talmage for 29.8 miles – a total run of 252.3 miles. When the Atchison, Jewell County & Western road was extended from Jamestown to Burr Oak for a length of 38.8 miles, the total length of lines operated by the Central Branch Union Pacific Railroad in June 1, 1882 amounted to 386.1 miles.[58]

The company changed its name to Central Branch Union Pacific Railroad in January 1867, better reflecting its purpose. However, while owned by the Union Pacific Railway

Company, it was operated by the Missouri Pacific as its "Central branch Division.[59] [60]

Construction began in 1865, and the line was completed from Atchison west for 40 miles January 1867, the balance of the 100 miles to Waterville, in January 1868.

It was a feeder line and had revenues of $453,000 with a net earnings of $124,000 for 1882. This did not include payments to the US for the Government bonds and Paramount Lien bonds, each would amount to $96,000.

The Central Branch of the Union Pacific Railroad was one of the pioneers in opening Kansas farmland for settlement, offering a means of transporting grain and cattle back to eastern markets.

The Western Pacific Railroad

In 1864 under the Pacific Railway Act of 1862, rights were assigned to the Western Pacific for a connection from Sacramento to San Francisco. The Western Pacific Railroad was created in December 1862 by Timothy Dame, Charles McLaughlin, Peter Donahue and others. Designed as an offshoot of the San Francisco and San Jose Railroad to connect with the Central Pacific through Stockton to Sacramento California, the idea was to connect with the main Central Pacific to the East.

They were intending to couple with the San Francisco and San Jose Railroad to complete a railroad connection directly to San Francisco. The intent was to build a line from San Jose north to Niles Canyon, to Stockton and Sacramento.

The City and County of San Francisco issued Bonds to the Western Pacific as part of an issue which included the Central Pacific Railroad. This amounted to 200 of $1000 Gold Bonds paying seven per centum. The City and County required $1,000,000 in capital stock as security, combined from both the Western Pacific Railroad and the Central Pacific Railroad.

With the passage of the Railroad Act of July 2, 1865 the Western Pacific also received government bonds and could issue First Mortgage bonds for road. The first twenty miles had been completed in 1866 from San Jose, but funding and rail purchases caused a halt to construction.

Chapter 9

Financing the Railroads Mortgages and Bonds

The Congressional Act of July 2, 1864 authorized the builders of the Transcontinental Railroad to receive US Government 6% bonds for sale and issue First Mortgage Paramount lien bonds to the same amount. These bonds were gold bonds paying 6% interest twice yearly for 30 years. The railroads in question were the Union Pacific, the central Branch of the Union Pacific, the Kansas Pacific, the Central Pacific, Western Pacific, and the Sioux City and Pacific railroads.

In order to issue bonds, an underlying mortgage had to be issued and recorded for the lands across which the railroad was being built. The mortgage included the railroad, all the singular franchises owned possessed or acquired or which "shall be hereafter owned possessed or acquired by the said party of the first part for the purposes of building, and operating said railroad and telegraph above specified and designed and also all the rails, depots, yards, engine houses, car houses, station houses, warehouses machine shops workshops and fixtures of said party of the first part necessary to said railroad and telegraph line, or the running and operating of the same." [12]

The mortgages covered all possessions of the railroad except the land sections beyond the rail lines granted by Congress which was covered by land grand bond instruments. Mortgages were issued by all six of the Transcontinental Railroads in slightly different legal language.

---

[12] Union Pacific First Mortgage dated 1865, see Appendix I

Buried in the legal language were two important factors, the duties of the Trustees, and the procedure of foreclosing on the railroad if certain provisions were not adhered to specifically, payment of the interest 'Coupons' when due.

Bonds were elaborately engraved with details of the railroad's responsibility. The bonds were Bearer Bonds. The bonds came with a 'Coupon" sheet for payment twice yearly. Each coupon had the bond's serial number and the date at which it was payable. The coupons had a value of $30 payable in gold. These bonds did not have a recorded owner, and could be exchanged or sold, and interest coupons redeemed without question.

Bond coupons at the time were also referred to as "Call Bonds". Normally, bonds issued at this date had "Bond Books" which recorded the owners. This appears to not have been done for the Union Pacific and Central Pacific Railroads. Records reflected payment of coupons by serial number but not owner.

Collis Huntington expressed concern about the bonds from his New York offices as the Central Pacific was approaching the Nevada line, following the first segment across California.

In correspondence he asked that the bonds be revised to say "Registered Bonds' and to be issue as the railroad proceeded into Nevada.[61] The Central Pacific issued a second First Mortgage bond to cover construction in Nevada and Utah. This resulted in a new series of bonds, "E, F, G, H, and I" issued with new serial numbers. [62]
The First Mortgages of the Central Pacific and Union Pacific were found and transcribed. The specifics of the default requirements were altered, and affected the ability of the bondholders to hold the railroads accountable for payment of the Coupons. [63]

Union Pacific Railroad First Mortgage:

An Indenture was made on the first day of November, 1865 between the Union Pacific Railroad Company, or body corporate created by and under an Act of the Congress approved July First, 1862, entitled "An Act to aid the construction of a railroad and Telegraph Line from the Missouri River to the Pacific Ocean and secure the government the use of the same for postal, military and other purposes" (party of first part), and Edwin D. Morgan of the City of New York and Oakes Ames of Easton, in the state of Massachusetts (parties of the second part.)[13]

The mortgage promised to pay the holder "semi-annually 6% in lawful money of the United States." Their advertisement in January 1868 offered the bonds at a discount so that the interest was equivalent to "9% and payable in gold." In reality the bonds were discounted by 15% in 1869[64] [65]

If they defaulted on payments of coupons or bonds, at the time or place that they are due, they "shall continue for 6 months the Trustees on request in writing of holders of a majority of such bonds, then in force and so in default may and shall forth with enter and to be possession, of all and singular the said mortgage property rights and franchises and use operate and manage the same for the benefit of the Bond holders."[14]

The primary Trustee was brother of the President of the Railroad, and the mortgage required a majority of the bond holders to respond in writing. The Union Pacific Railroad had 29,000 bonds printed and on the Books. This resulted in a deferral of actions until the 1890's when the entire railroad was placed into receivership.

---

[13] Union Pacific Mortgage, Appendix I

[14] Ibid

Also, bond holders had problems with the corporate seal on the later bonds and there is much correspondence about bonds being returned for corrections so that they would be legally transferable.[66]

Central Pacific Railroad First Mortgage:
The Central Pacific Railroad Indenture was entered July 25th 1865. It was "between the Central Pacific Rail Road Company of California…and D. O. Mills and Wm. E. Barron of the City of San Francisco and the said State of California.." [15]

This initial mortgage was on the line extended from Sacramento California to the Nevada state line crossing the Sierra Nevada mountain range. The mortgage authorized the issuance of 6% Bold First Mortgage Bonds in $1,000 increments. These were Bearer Bonds with coupons payable twice yearly. Payment were in gold coin, and the Board of Directors were "further ordered and directed that the said 'first mortgage bonds' should be executed and issued for four several series A through D, and to include the remainder of said bonds authorized to be issued."[16]

Further, only 50 bonds were required to be in default. This was a more stringent requirement. "If a default shall be …by themselves or their agents or servants in that behalf, may upon request of the holder or holders of not less than fifty of said bonds… etc." [17]

.

---

[15] Central Pacific Mortgage , Appendix I, National Archives San Francisco Ca

[16] Ibid

[17] ibid

First Mortgage Bond of the Central Pacific Railroad Series D.
This is one of 3 in existence.

(The Museum of American Finance, Wall Street New York City)

A second First Mortgage was issued in 1867/8 for the continuance of the Central Pacific into Nevada and Utah. This mortgage covered the issuing of Bonds Series E through I.

Sinking Fund

A Sinking Fund was a reserve of funds for the repayment of a bond issued. In the matter of the Transcontinental Railroad this was a means of paying a portion of the Paramount Lien Bonds when they came due. Between the Union Pacific Railroad and the Central Pacific Railroads there were three sinking funds. Each railroad had an internal sinking fund; and the US Treasury had a joint sinking fund authorized by the Thurmond Act.

The internal sinking funds were organized about the time of the completion of the Transcontinental Railroad in May 1869.

In records, there is evidence that an effort by the Central Pacific Railroad was made to also issue Sinking Fund Bonds.

The Union Pacific set up its sinking fund and issued Sinking Fund Bonds in December 1873. Issued were 16 million dollars of bonds at $1000 denominations at 8% interest due in 1893. The bonds were now "Registered". On inspection of the records of the Union Pacific Railroad at the Nebraska State Archives, there were three annotations of these bonds being cancelled. Numerically ordered, they offer an insight on how the railroad cancelled and stored bonds.

Sinking Fund bond of the Union Pacific Railroad
The bonds were issued to raise additional funds for the Union Pacific after the joining of the railroads. Union Pacific Railroad had reduced had exhausted the First Mortgage bonds.

(Nebraska Historical Society Archives Union Pacific Railroad Collection)

The bonds issued in 1873 are an indication of a cash shortfall of the Union Pacific as a result of the final construction costs.

Congress was aware that the railroads were not paying interest on the US Government subsidy bonds, and only making partial payments. The Thurman Act, signed into law May 1887, applied to the Union Pacific and Central Pacific Railroads only.

The Union Pacific Railroad was issued $27,536,512 US Government Subsidy Bonds; Central Pacific Railroad was issued $25.885,120 in Government Subsidy Bonds. The railroads were authorized to issue the same amount in Paramount Lien Bonds. The Western Pacific - absorbed by the Central Pacific Railroad received $1,970,560 in Government Bonds and issued the same amount in Paramount Lien Bonds.

Net Earnings defined as the Gross Earnings, minus the necessary expenses actually paid and amortized within the year while operating -including repair and upgrades, together with the sum paid in interest of the First Mortgage Bonds.

The services provided to the United States in the form of transportation of people mail and goods, was to be retained by the US Treasury, one half applied to the US bond interest and one half applied to a "Sinking Fund". This Sinking Fund was administered by the US Treasury, and to be re-invested in US Bonds.

The Central Pacific was also required to pay each year $1,200,000 or "as much as shall be necessary to make the five per centum of the net earnings of its road payable to the Sinking Fund of the US Treasury under the act of 1862." The total aggregate was to be 25% of the whole net earnings.

The Union Pacific Railroad was required to pay to the US Treasury Sinking Fund $850,000 or "as shall be necessary to make five per centum of their net earnings."

Section 6 of the Thurmond Act stipulated that no stock dividend shall be voted; made or paid in either of said companies when in default, either for payments or for the retiring sinking fund.

In passing the Act of 1887, Congress allowed the Treasury to invest in any of the First-Mortgage bonds of either of the companies (Union Pacific and Central Pacific). However, it required the transcontinental railroads to put money in a US Treasury Sinking Fund as Guarantor. This allowed the Treasury to purchase First Mortgage bonds in their own sinking fund portfolio. Before the end of February 1887, the Secretary of Treasury began purchasing first mortgage bonds. Initial bonds received were two Kansas Pacific Railroad bonds, three Central Pacific Bonds, two Union Pacific Bonds. [67] [68].

The railroads at this time had not been paying he interest payments for the Government subsidy bonds and their ability to make payment for the First mortgage Bonds was questionable.

In Section 4 of the Act, the railroads were required to pay 25% of net earnings into sinking fund accounts of each railroad.[69]

By 1882, the sinking fund amounted to $1,534,626 for the Central Pacific and $1,181,607 for the Union Pacific.

Whereas Section 3 of the Act required that the Sinking fund shall be "invested by the Secretary of Treasury in bonds of the United States, preferably 5% bonds" it was recommended and changed that the Sinking fund be modified to allow the Secretary of Treasury to invest in First Mortgage bonds. [70]

The Treasury and Department of Interior kept account books for their Sinking Fund, specifically for the Central Pacific Railroad and the Union Pacific Railroad. These records reflected Treasury transactions, investments, amounts, cost and bond serial numbers in some cases. By 1887, the Treasury was purchasing Central Pacific Bonds, although reflected were either Union Pacific or Central Pacific accounts. By 1887 the Treasury was paying 114% to 117% of par value for the bonds, plus commission. [71] [72]

In 1896 the US Treasury asked for sealed Proposals to Purchase First Mortgage Bonds[73].

This advertisement was for the Central Pacific's portion of the Sinking fund. They listed $1,541,000 of Central Pacific Bonds; $939,000 of Union Pacific Bonds; and $300,000 of Kansas Pacific Bonds. The bond dates of 1895 to 1899 indicated a spread of bonds across the issuing dates.

In addition, the railroad companies had their own in house Sinking Fund. Accounting of the Central Pacific 1882 lists as an Asset $4,947,000 in their company sinking fund.[74]
Bonds Issued by Union Pacific mileage charged [75]

Accounting of the Union Pacific Indicating Amount of Bonds to be Issued. This lists 28,880,000 authorization for First Mortgage Bonds.
(University of Iowa, Libraries Special Collections, Union Pacific Railroad)

Union Pacific Railroad was authorized to issued $27,236,512. Others listed more. [76]

Under the Act of 1864 the Union Pacific issued their own bonds at an amount of their own bonds to reflect an equal amount , which would be a prior lien:[18]

	Govt. Auth.	Actual Issued	Serial No.
Jan 1, 1866	$6,475,000	$6,480,000	1-6480
Jan 1, 1867	$1,598,000	$1,600,000	6481-8080
July 1, 1867	$1,920,000	$1,920,000	8081-10000
Jan 1, 1868	$5,999,000	$6,000,000	10001-16000
July 1, 1868	$8,837,000	$9,000,000	16001-25000
Jan 1, 1869	$2,400,000	$4,000,000	25000-29000

Union Pacific Railroad Bond Amount and Serial Numbers by Issuing Date

In actuality the Union Pacific Railroad had issued $1,600,000 more bonds than were authorized based on road length.

---

[18] Note: The bonds were $1,000 First Mortgage Gold Bonds in $1,000 denominations. The values noted for the Union Pacific should be listed as 1,000 increments the Sioux City Bonds were in $500 and $1000 increments

Ledgers of Union Pacific Boston Office: Transactions to Clark-Dodge $1,809,000 in First Mortgage Bonds, April 30, 1869.

(Nebraska Historical Society Archives Union Pacific Railroad Collection)

Chapter 10

Blaisdell and the Treasury

Leonard Blaisdell

Leonard C, Blaisdell of Champaign, Illinois, was married to Harriett L. Durkee, niece of Charles Durkee. Blaisdell, a lawyer by profession lived in Champaign Illinois.

Charles Durkee's Will was contested, starting a legal controversy in the Kenosha County Court which lasted until a Court Judgment was entered on the Will on March 21, 1882. The cause of this controversy was the fact that some 17 heirs-at-law thought that they had legal rights to part of Charles Durkee's estate.

Since Leonard C. Blaisdell was a lawyer, his relatives requested that he represent them. They cited Caroline Durkee, Charles Durkee's widow, for illegally assigning part of the Inventoried and residuary estate of her husband to Harvey Durkee.[77]

At this time, none of the heirs at-law had knowledge of Charles Durkee's acquisitions of Paramount Lien Railroad Bonds prior to his death, principally because he was still negotiating with E. H. Rollins and C. P. Huntington on their final distribution at the time of executing his last Will and Testament on 12th, February, 1869.

Caroline Durkee, supposedly suffering from mental distress at this time was institutionalized briefly in a Mental facility.

From the Probate Hearing on Charles Durkee's estate in 1882, Blaisdell obtained information concerning some Indemnity Bonds which Charles Durkee had executed and filed with the Secretary of the Treasury[78].

Blaisdell commenced making Inquiries of the Secretary of the Treasury concerning what he now believed to be Railroad Indemnity and Security Bonds.

When Blaisdell again made Inquiry in early 1884, The Secretary of the Treasury advised him to start legal action in equity against one of the Executors of the Will of the late Charles Durkee and report same.

Blaisdell immediately filed the suit in the Supreme Court of Cook County, in Chicago, and reported to the Secretary of the Treasury and the First Comptroller of the Treasury, Judge William Lawrence.

Blaisdell then received instructions by letters from Judge Lawrence dated 3 April 1884, and from Mr. Coon, Assistant Secretary of the Treasury, dated 12 April 1884, to come to Washington on April 22, 1884 for a conference with Charles J. Folger, Secretary of the Treasury and Trustee of the Statutory Trust.[79] [19]

The Meeting reflects who attended. Leonard C. Blasdell; Judge Folger, Secretary of the Treasury; Judge Lawrence, First Comptroller; Judge Brewster, Attorney General; Fred T. Frelinghuysen, Secretary of State; Amos Webster, Treasury Department; Charles V. Parkman, stenographer who recorded events of the conference; and others.

---

[19] Note a Statuary Trust is a Trust created by operation of law where a real property is held by trustees for immediate or eventual sale at their discretion. All income from the property prior to its sale, and all proceeds of its sale, are held in trust for the benefit of the trust's beneficiaries.

The Attorney General informed the Secretary of the Treasury that Leonard C. Blaisdell was a proper representative of the estate of Charles Durkee, and that the Trustee could legally do business with Blaisdell in connection with the bonds assigned to Charles Durkee.[20]

Little was resolved. Secretary of Treasury Judge Folger died in September 1884. Judge William Lawrence retired from his position as First Comptroller on March 25, 1885 to establish a Law practice in Bellefontaine, Ohio.[21]

Blaisdell testified before the Senate of the United States on March 19, 1896 that the greater part of Blaisdell's correspondence occurred in 1882. "During this time however while there was no satisfactory answer to my question, there was a manifested on the part of the officials with whom I corresponded a desire to encourage my further inquires." [80]
He went on to say "At this juncture, or the beginning of the Year 1883, it was officially communicated to me that one of the two or more bonds of indemnity signed by Charles Durkee was in behalf of Franklin Head and pertained to the Indian Agency: That such bonds had been duly cancelled".

Washington and Treasury on April 22, 1884 to look at the issue of Indemnity bonds and railroad bonds related to the Durkee Estate.

---

[20] Blaisdell Deposition See Appendix II

[21] Ibid

Head, Franklin H.
(PRINCIPAL)

DATE OF BOND	PENALTY	TITLE
3/31-1866	$50,000	Superintendent of Indian Affairs for the Territory of Utah.

Record of Bond of Franklin Head Recorded at the Treasury Department Index of Surety Bonds.

(National Archives College Park Md. RG39)

In the Memorandum of the Civil Court, Blaisdell gave the following account of what happened.

"Within a short time there came into the Treasury Building Judge Lawrence, First comptroller; Judge Folger, Secretary of the Treasury; Judge Brewster, Attorney General; Secretary of State Frelinghuysen, and several others, each bearing in hand a large bundle of papers."[81]

"Immediately Judge Lawrence began to interrogate me as to what Knowledge I had acquired relative to the subject-matter of the proposed investigation. After ascertaining that I knew practically nothing of Charles Durkee's ownership of Pacific Railroad or other bonds (at that time)....Then Judge Folger arose and stated that the business was that he desired to transact and the purposes to be effected, if found practical, in the joint meeting of officials present and myself (Blaisdell).

At about this stage of the proceedings Judge Folger turned his attention to the vast number of papers, files and records of various kinds that lay on the tables, picking up different ones in his hand as he continued his remarks to Judge Brewster. "These" he said, pointing to the first collection, "are the first mortgage bonds issued by the Union and Central , and other Pacific railroad corporations under the provisions of the act of 1864." .... He{holding some of them up in his hands, so as to been by all present}, "are assigned to one, sole, assignee-Charles Durkee."[82]

"Then, exhibiting some of the interest bonds, Judge Folger explained that these, as well as the first mortgage bonds, were issued in the form of call bonds, by the terms of which, on any default being made in the payment of the same on the demand of the legal holder or his legal representative, the right of foreclosure immediately vested in the holder." [22]

Blaisdell responded to the question of disposition of the bonds, "I should prefer to leave the whole matter to your discretion, Judge Folger." Judge Folger stated how he would, on the First of January (1885), do for the payment.

Because the principal and interest was so great and it would cause the failure of the Union and Central Pacific railroads. [23] Blaisdell replied "How will this do. Secure the entire principal of the Mortgages, and you take just as long time for the Government to pay the accrued interest as you desire?".

Later Secretary Folger directed Judge Lawrence "You, Judge, will see to it that Mr. Blaisdell is supplied with the proper certification of ownership of these bonds and a copy of the

proceedings and transcriptions between himself and the Government omitting nothing essential to the protection of the interests he represents."

---

[22] Note that this statement is in error, See the Union Pacific and Central Pacific Railroad Mortgages in Appendix 1.

[23] Ibid

Judge Lawrence replied that Blaisdell would receive the documents in about a month. Blaisdell returned in about five to six weeks accompanied by Hon. J. G. Cannon and requested the papers. He was met with a degree of indifference and ignorance and refused to reply for other people being in the room, and requested that Blaisdell return later in the afternoon. Blaisdell was put off. Judge Folger had retired on account of sickness.

Blaisdell was promised by them "as soon as the terms of the agreements made with respect to the Railroad bonds had been completed that he would supply me with certified copies of every transaction." Blaisdell then returned home to Campaign Illinois.

On a third trip back to Washington in January, 1885, Blaisdell met with Senator Cullom and received documents from the Assistant Secretary of the Treasury, Jonathan Tarbel. They received large bundles of papers brought by the clerks, hunting for relationships of Governor Durkee and the Paramount lien bonds. Blaisdell had to return to Chicago and left without reviewing additional documents.

The Secretary of State, Mr. Frelinghuysen, however having a personal knowledge of the proceedings of the Secretary of the Treasury, April 22, 1884, voluntarily prepared some State papers to be used in the case, to which he attached the great seal of State, affixed his signature, saying that the purpose of so doing was to enable me to save all the testimony I had received and to attach.

The Metropolitan National Bank Question

The Metropolitan National Bank of New York City was a pivotal reference in the Durkee lost bond question of the estate. In the Court Case 18003, it is stated by Jacob Souder that Newspaper articles made reference to the fact that bonds were deposited in the bank.[83]

According to Souder, on Governor Durkee's final trip home he carried a "Tin Box" with documents.

> "shortly before his death he called this party to his bedside, and said, "that he had had his suspicions aroused by certain things that had transpired within the last six months; that one of his intended executors if not both had evil designs on his estate, and that he had taken the precaution to put his more valuable papers and evidences of estate into a certain 'tin box' which he pointed out to the witness, and that he wished this witness to observe that it was 'sealed' and directed to 'The Metropolitan National Bank of the City of New York ;' that he charged it as his dying request upon this witness that she would keep watch over his executors, to see that this box was safely consigned to said 'Metropolitan National Bank, in said City of New York."[84]

It should be noted that in the second inventory of the Durkee estate, Head had visited Salt Lake City with documents to collect on Notes owed the Durkee estate particularly a deed to 20 acres of property in San Diego California along with Notes of considerable value from Kerr and Company. In the court case 18003, the suit of the Durkee heirs against the US Government to recover $64,000,000 in bonds plus interest, referenced is the meeting between Leonard Blaisdell, representative of the estate and the Secretary of Treasury, Judge

Folger, the First Comptroller of the Treasury, Judge Lawrence, and others.

In affidavits and testimony various witnesses state that the bonds and documents were in the Metropolitan Bank of New York City.

In testimony of the Meeting of Leonard Blaisdell concerning the meeting of 22 April 1884, he stated he witnessed the bonds in possession of the Treasury. This gives a specific date at which the bonds would have been transferred. These details came out well after the meeting.

The oral story states that the bank was taken over and the deposit box contents of Governor Durkee turned over to either the Sub-Treasury of New York or the Treasury Department in Washington DC.

The Metropolitan National Bank was caught up in the financial panic of May 16, 1884. There was a depression in the United States from 1882 to 1885. The National Banks of the United States had halted investments and called in outstanding loans. The New York Clearing House, forerunner to the US Federal Reserve Bank provided financial support for banks at risk of failure.

The investment firm of Grant and Ward, and the Marine National Bank of New York City had extensive financial problems. On May 14, 1884, the brokerage firm of Grant and Ward became insolvent. Ulysses S. Grant Jr., President and General Grant's son were principals, and later, President Grant was involved.

The company had over $750,000 in unsecured loans and unspecified accounts. The principal Ferdinand Ward, had invested heavily in real estate which failed to materialize. Mr.

James Fish was a Special Partner in the firm and President of Marine National Bank. Marine National Bank closed 14th May.

News spread quickly on Wall Street and a full bank panic occurred as depositors and investors sought to pull their money from all banks in a full scale banking collapse. Rumors of three other failing banks were circulating. Mobs crowded the steps of the bank, depositors demanding money and depleting bank reserves throughout the city. [85]

The Metropolitan National Bank was caught up in the depositors run, and closed its doors that same day. The directors reorganized the finances and brought in additional capital. Metropolitan National Bank reopened its doors the next day and did not go into receivership.

Souder states that "in the presence of this affiant and another witness, the Solicitor of the Treasury, during the month of August 1888, in his office, stated that papers of that character described in the above had been delivered by the said Metropolitan Nation Bank... presumably so, he judged from the circumstance of the assignment of said bank being found on the books of the Solicitor and containing, ostensibly, 'the assignment of all such matters as were designated' by the order of the Secretary of the Treasury of April 22, A. D. 1884." [86]

Bank Panic of May 1884
Harpers Magazine Metropolitan National Bank was one
of the banks impacted, but reopened its doors the next day.

Blaisdell later stated

> "Secretary (Treasury) made the proposition to receive
> from affiant (Blaisdell) such character of orders and to
> execute the same at once ; and that said Secretary left
> the room with the last words on his lips which affiant
> ever heard him utter, saying, "I will see that the order is
> at once transmitted to the Sub-Treasury in the City of
> New York."[87]

The Metropolitan National Bank was still in existence in 1906 when it changed its name to Metropolitan Bank. Later in1921 the bank merged with Federal Chase Bank of the city of New York, and finally changed its name to Chase Manhattan Bank in 1955.

As the Durkee Estate Court of Claims Case 18003 against the US Government for recovery of the $64,000,000 progressed, publicity in several newspaper articles were published. The Wichita Times did an exposé on March 19, 1899 titled "*The Great Bond Theft.*"

Blaisdell had difficulty obtaining Caroline Durkee's consent for him to make inquiries in 1884. Caroline Durkee on August 4, 1885 was adjudged insane and sent to the Northern Asylum for the Insane. She reentered the Asylum by proceedings in Kenosha County Court in January 5, 1886. Mrs. Durkee was restored to sane mind later in 1886.

In August 13, 1886 a suit is filed against Harvey Durkee and Franklin Head for mishandling the estate.

By December 9, 1887 Mrs. Durkee signed her Will in Chicago. The next year, in Sept. 29, 1888 Mrs. Durkee is again adjudged insane. Her legal guardian was Attorney, Mr. James Cavanagh of Cavanagh & Barnes, Attorneys, Kenosha.

Chapter 11

Court of Claims Case 18003

Leonard Blaisdell filed the Court of Claims Case 18003 in 1893. This was the first of a series cases regarding Governor Durkee ownership of the majority of the Paramount Lien Bonds, were assigned valuations.

Of the six Transcontinental subsidized railroads, namely the Union Pacific, Central Pacific, Western Pacific, Kansas Pacific, Central Branch of the Union Pacific and the Sioux City and Pacific Railroads, a combined amount was provided for $64, 623,512 US Government Subsidy bonds, and $64,616,000 of First Mortgage Bonds issued by the various railroads.

The Durkee Court Cases were based on the claim that the Government had taken possession of the First Mortgage Paramount Bonds in entirety from Governor Durkee's estate, either held at the Metropolitan National bank of New York, or, according to Souder, deposited with the U. S. Treasury in January 1, 1868 by C. P. Huntington of the Central Pacific Railroad and E.H. Rollins of the Union Pacific Railroad. [88]

The second point of the Case was that Leonard Blasdell, a relative by marriage to Governor Durkee's niece had investigated the whereabouts of the estate assets and particularly the ownership of the Paramount Lien Bonds. He contacted the Secretary of Treasury, Hon. Charles J. Folger and First Comptroller of the Treasury, Hon. William Lawrence. A meeting was held as stated by Blaisdell between Judge Folger, Judge Lawrence, the Attorney-General Judge Brewster, Secretary of State Frelinghuysen and others concerning the bonds on 22 April 1884. Blaisdell stated the Paramount Lien

Bonds of all six railroads were shown with papers assigning them to Governor Durkee.

The US Government was well aware of the financial shortfalls of the various railroads as the 30 year date of payment of principal and interest on all of the bonds came due in the 1890's. Supreme Court rulings (Reference) allowed the companies to defer interest on the government bonds, and only account payments for the services provided to credit against the Government debt.

In 1887, the 49th Congress passed legislation allowing the US government to investigate the Railroads for improprieties and to ascertain their well being. There had been several legislative investigations made as the bonds of the Government and Railroads payments were coming due, tailoring specific legislation as needed.

 The one overriding concern however, was the Government Subsidy of $64, 623,512 being lost if the roads went into receivership. At that time, the government wanted to know if the railroads could pay off their bonds as they became due.[89].[90]

Section 4 of the statute stated
> "Section 4. That whenever , in the opinion of the President, it shall be deemed necessary to the protection of the interests and the preservation of the security of the United States in respect of its lien mortgage, or ......may exist and be then lawfully liable to be enforced, the Secretary of the Treasury shall under the direction of the President, redeem or otherwise clear off such paramount lien, mortgage, or other encumbrance by paying the sums lawfully due in respect thereof out of the Treasury; and the United States shall thereupon become and be subrogated to all rights and securities theretofore pertaining to the debt...It shall be the duty

of the Attorney-General ….to take steps to foreclose any mortgages or liens of the United States on any such railroad property."

This legislation allowed the US Government to assume responsibility for the First Mortgage Paramount Lien Bonds in order to protect the Government Second position $64,623,512 Subsidy Bonds.

Six years later the Union Pacific Railroad was in receivership and the unwinding of the debt between the junior creditors and the many acquisitions of railroads and track made it necessary to invoke the position of the Government to assume responsibility for Union Pacific First mortgage bonds.

By now, the Union Pacific Railroad had merged with the Kansas Pacific, another subsidized railroad with outstanding First mortgage bonds of $6,303,000. Plus, another division of the Union Pacific Railroad was the Central Branch of the Union Pacific which operated a line from line from Atchison to Waterville Kansas and had outstanding First mortgage bonds of $1,600,000.

The Sioux Pacific Railroad had merged with the Chicago and Northwestern Railway Company in 1880 and their bonds were secure with the Chicago and Northwestern Railway Company.

The other major railroad was the Central Pacific Railroad. The Central Pacific Railroad had acquired the Western Pacific in 1868 and did not complete this road until 1869 after the joining of the Transcontinental at Promontory in May 10, 1869. Their bonds remained outstanding and were refinanced by the railroad.

In May, 1893 Leonard Blaisdell filed Court Case 18003 by mail from Champaign Illinois.

He listed 18 people who were directly a blood relative and took part in the case by providing him with a Power of Attorney. In many cases they also advanced Blaisdell money to pursue the court case. The original petition and later amended petition provided four sealed packages of exhibits and other exhibits or supporting statements from the following officials:[91] (See Appendix II for transcripts)

E. B. Daskam, Clerk, Treasury Department
A. U. Wyman, Assistant U. S. Treasurer
Wm. Fletcher, Clerk, Treasury Department
Amos Webster, Chief Clerk
Hon. Jos. Cannon
Hon. J. F. Outhwaite
Hon. W. M, Springer
Hon. Fred T. Frelinghuysen, Secretary of State
Dr. Thomas Robinson, Solicitor of the Treasury

Blaisdell later amended the Petition on April 25, 1895 to allow for mistakes in the initial filing due to his lacking of standing from Kenosha Wisconsin.

The thrust of the case was that the Government had under the direction of various authorities, collected the said Union and Central and other Pacific Railway companies the First Mortgage Liens on the railway companies, and were holding them "for the protection, security and benefit of the lawful and just holders of any mortgage lien debts of such companies respectively, lawfully paramount to the United States".[92]

These First mortgage bonds had been assigned to Governor Charles Durkee, and were not being released to the estate. The claim was that the monies for the First Mortgage Bonds being held in a Trust Fund in the Treasury.

Caroline Durkee had been re-adjudged insane again in September 1888. In July 1895 Caroline Durkee new attorneys, filed papers with the Court of Claims Case 18003, but her filing was without merit.

Leonard Blaisdell, in pursuing the Court of Claims case was given no recognition by the Probate Court in Kenosha Wisconsin. He enlisted the aid of John A. Kuykendall to go to Salt Lake City Utah and initiate alternate probate actions on the estate of Governor Durkee, and be assigned as the Administrator. With this authority, Kuykendall and Blaisdell now represented the 17 other potential heir of the estate.

Kuykendall obtained the papers sufficient for him to represent the Court of Claims case. In May 1896 Kuykendall was substituted in the court case and refilled the case in 1897 adding four more depositions, that of Leonard Blaisdell, F. Head, Charles Nimocks and Edward Durkee. The case proceeded with administrative delays. [93]

During this time the receivership of the Union Pacific Railroad and the debt renegotiation of the Central Pacific Railroad were being processed by the Treasury; Attorney General and Congress.

Kuykendall later withdrew the case without prejudice in a strategic maneuver filing instead in the Supreme Court of the District of Columbia, to force the Attorney General and Secretary of the Treasury to provide testimony concerning the Durkee Estate filings.[94]

In court records the Secretary Gage, he replied "I have to state that if Mr. Durkee was at any time owner of any of the bonds referred to, record thereof would not be found in the Treasury Department, but with the records of the Railroad companies, or elsewhere, the United States has had no control of, or interest in, the First mortgage bonds of the roads...

"And I have further to state that no moneys or bonds of any description have ever been deposited with or held in trust by the Treasury of the United States for any person or persons representing Mr. Durkee or his heirs, nor is there any legal or equitable basis for the so-called Durkee claim upon the United States."[95]

Secretary of the Treasury Gage and the Attorney General had intimate knowledge of the workings of the 1st mortgage bonds of the Union Pacific, in that they participated in the railroads reorganization and the payment of the Subsidy Bonds due the United States.

The case was attempted to be reinstated in 1904 but documents do not seem to indicate that it proceeded.

The Court of Claims had accepted the Attorney-General position that the case should be demurred. A demurrer admits the truth of the plaintiff's set of facts, but it contends that those facts are insufficient to grant the complaint in favor of the plaintiff. A demurrer may further contend that the complaint does not set forth enough facts to justify legal relief or it may introduce additional facts that defeat the legal effectiveness.

It appears that while Court case 18003 was proceeding, Jacob Souder a lawyer, inventor and friend of Charles Durkee was either participating or involved in it, to some extent.

Jacob Souder later in 1912 wrote the book "*History of the Pacific Railway Co's. First Mortgage 30 Year 6 Per Cent Paramount Lien Bonds*", "*Issued by and Assigned to Charles Durkee from 1865 to 1869*". The book offers a detailed account of the Pacific Railroads from 1865 to about 1906 covering many of the financial problems with the Treasury, and provides an accounting of Governor Charles Durkee and his estate after he died. It tries to provide justification of ownership of the

Paramount Lien Bonds and details many factors in the Court of Claims Case, including depositions provided by Blaisdell and others.

As of to date, some of those depositions submitted by Blaisdell and Kuykendall other material appear to have been removed from the National Archives Records. [96]

Chapter 12

Continuing the Fight

Durkee Court Case 1906

Suit was brought in the Supreme District Court of Columbia Washington DC, and the suit was found still pending 1906. The citation was made against the Union Pacific Railroad Company filed February 7th, 1903 by Lane and Rodgers, and with Mr. Wood.

The Court Battle

John A. Kuykendall continued in the pursuit of the Durkee estate through other venues. He initially filed a claim against the Union Pacific Railroad in United States Circuit Court of the District of Utah. On April 28, 1906, it went before Judge Marshal. The case was moved to the 9th Judicial Circuit Court of the United States, Northern District of California.

The case was filed against the Southern Pacific Company, the Central Pacific Railway, and the Union Pacific Railroad Company alleging that during the construction of the Union Pacific, Governor Durkee had acquired $9,000,000 worth of construction bonds and that later he took $27,000,000 of the First Mortgage bonds.[24]

The case proceeded with a number of witnesses and documents. Most notable were certified copies of the Mortgages of the Union Pacific Railroad and the Central Pacific

---

[24] The Durkee project was able to obtain the complete records.

Railroad, providing details of the actual documents and the conditions backing the First Mortgage Bonds. The case was again dismissed for lack of proof of ownership.

Leonard C. Blaisdell died about 1909, perhaps with the disappointment that he had been double-crossed by Government officials in whom he had placed his trust.

Three years later Caroline Durkee died at the age of 87 in Kenosha Wisconsin. Caroline had lived at her home and was cared for by her servant Miss Alexander for 22 years until her death.[97]

Miss Alexander had been with Caroline through her ordeals, including when her Will was written in 1887, and later, as the dispute unfolded over Charles Durkee's bonds.

Carline Durkee's Will[98] had three basic provisions, the first was the endowment of a bed at St. Luke's Hospital Free Hospital in Chicago; the creation of "Caroline Durkee endowment of the Chair of Chemistry Applied Natural Sciences" at Racine College; and the majority a donation to the Board of Trustees of Racine Collage to be held by them in Trust forever. The college was located in Racine Wisconsin just north of Kenosha.[25]

The Will created a direct line of succession of the estate of Charles Durkee.

---

[25] Will of Caroline Durkee, Filed in the Probate Court of Kenosha, 1887 Appendix IV

In 1912, Jacob Souder published his book on the First Mortgage Bonds of the Pacific Railroads. Souder had known Charles Durkee and been involved in the proceedings and court cases. He was an inventor and lawyer by trade with several patents approved in the 1890's.

He proceeded to pursue obtaining the records from the US Treasury. One missing link was proof from the Union Pacific Railroad that Governor Durkee had received the bonds.

In 1914 Souder wrote, using his daughter Lillie Souder as a go-between, to W. W. Durant, son of the late Thomas C. Durant, Vice President and General Manager of the Union Pacific Railroad. Durant had been with the railroad from its incorporation to completion. Thomas Durant and Charles Durkee had met in Utah on or about May 1869, when Durand was present with the completion with the Central Pacific railroad at Promontory Utah. Souder stated that Thomas Durant had shown him documents that evidenced a large number of the Union Pacific Bonds belonging to Durkee, and that there was a contract between Thomas Durant and Charles Durkee. He was shown the document in the early 1870's[1].

W. W. Durant was shown a book in which were the numbers of bonds which Souder claimed were the numbers of the bonds Charles Durkee, as Trustee, had deposited with the Secretary of Treasury. Souder said his daughter (Lilly) had been allowed to copy these numbers in the Treasury."

Lilly Walker (Souder) took the lead and communicated with W.W. Durant, trying to obtain original records of the meeting and bonds. Souder appealed to Durant, stating that there was a possibility that the papers would lead to moneys for both of them. In later correspondence Souder offered one half of any moneys recovered.

Durant's lawyer C Snyder wrote to Durant on March 25, 1914 advising that "Mr. Souder is on a fishing expedition".[1]

In this exchange, a picture emerged: It appeared that Governor Durkee had been given a note for $2,000,000 against the bonds he received, and that the Durant estate could make a claim against the Durkee estate.[99] It appears that Souder was trying to gain access to the contract to pursue his claim.

In August, Durant went through about 1500 pounds of records of Thomas Durant's files in several locations, and found reference to bonds... but no details.[100]

The communications continued until 1917 when it was dropped. Union Pacific considered this important and kept the correspondence which the company donated to the University of Iowa along with other documents. Also in those documents were four letters dated 1937 express concern about Souder's initial into the Durant papers. Obviously the Union Pacific had taken this inquiry seriously, and retained all the correspondence.

Today, these are the only records that reference Governor Durkee, his name absent from the files turned over to the University of Iowa Special Collections Union Pacific Railroad Collection, and the Nebraska State Archives Union Pacific Collection. This appears to be a topic that the Union Pacific Railroad wanted to preserve.

However, Legal action pursued in Utah which had established the estate representative in 1913 as independent of the estate of Caroline Durkee, Norman Haire applied to become the Administrator of the Estate of Charles Durkee, representing the "Legal heirs" of the Durkee estate, which had grown to 23 by this time.

Kuykendall worked with Norman Haire now the administrator of the estate, and filed a statement that he had expended over $100,000 in pursuit of the litigation since 1896.

Outside investors had contributed funds with the pledge of assets if recovered. Norman Haire was replaced by Lydia Haire by 1921, and action continued through to 1927 when a John Davis replaced her.

Davis entered into a contract with Henry Gantner of Fayette Missouri to pursue the Durkee claims and agreed to pay 40% of all moneys or bonds recovered and by 1934, but there is no further action recorded on the Salt Lake City group regarding the estate.

On January 26, 1914 Treasury Department issued a warning that "that certain persons are endeavoring, in various parts of the country, to sell shares or interests in an alleged claim of the estate of Charles Durkee, deceased, against the United States."[101]

The notification further stated "..promoters of the alleged "claim" are representing that the justice thereof was admitted by the late Secretary of Treasury, Franklin MacVeagh, and that he was about to direct payment of the same when he left the Department."[102]

Noted in the announcement that "the Pacific Railroads, deposited in pursuance of join resolution of Congress , April 10, 1869 (16 Stat,. 56), which authorized the President to require from the companies for completion of the roads. The bonds so deposited, amounted to $5,600,000, was returned to the companies on the completion of the roads. [103]

Racine College

Caroline Durkee had bequeathed the principal share of her estate to the Trustees of Racine College which potentially included the Paramount Lien Bonds owned by the Charles Durkee Estate. Thus started the line of succession to the college.

Racine College started in the 1850's on the shores of Lake Michigan just north of Kenosha, and evolved to a significant Liberal Arts institution. It experienced a decline in the 1900's while switching to a Preparatory High School for universities, and a military school and junior college.. The college closed in 1933, partly due to the Depression and declining enrollment. The title to the Durkee Estate passed to be retained with the Board of Trustees of Racine College and with the Administrator of the Estate, Judge Warren Knowles.[26]

Knowles had entered into a contract with Hammond, and George Manchester to investigate and recover the bond and Treasury funds of the Durkee estate. These two gentlemen backed out and a fourth party Arthur L. Smith of Brookline, Massachusetts, continued searching for proof of the Durkee fortune, as "part as his compensation the next twenty-five per cent of any sum so recovered." After Judge Knowles death in 20 April 1939, L.S. Doolittle was appointed administrator.
Smith diligently researched the documents and records up to October 1940.

---

[26] Warren P. Knowles was appointed Judge in Wisconsin prior to 1935, and died on the 20th day of April, 1939. L. S. Doolittle of River Falls was appointed administrator de bonis non with the Will annexed of the estate of Charles Durkee. Senator James Doolittle had been a close associate of Charles Durkee and his family had supported the Durkee estate. Later, Warren P. Knowles son became the 84th Governor of Wisconsin.

Smith wrote a letter to the court in 1942, stating that he did not have the resources to continue. He stated "Nine years of my life's work without compensation Over $50,000 spent by myself and associates in the investigation and prosecution of this matter (The Charles Durkee Estate).[104]

He further stated that he had been at the Attorney General's office two years ago, when "Saul Myers, as General Council; Hon. Selden Bacon, former Professor of Law at the University of Minnesota, Assistant General Counsel, and together with three other -prominent Attorneys, called on The Hon. N. A. Townsend, former Federal Jurist, now Special Assistant Attorney General and heard the five hour interview....

"This Washington Official admitted in the presence of these men...that (1) he had spent months investigating this Claim and found nothing to support the allegations. (2). That he had not had examined the records of the Interior or Sub-Treasury Department at New York. (3). That after I had explained what those records contained, he believed we were entitled to an executive order for the right of examination prior to filing (court case). They feel that we have a good claim and that it should be concluded."[105]

Mr. Myers died two days later. Justice Cotilleo, New York, Special counsel, died three weeks later; Mrs. Lillie (Souder) Walker, Chief witness, also died that month. Judge Knowles and Judge Belden had also died recently. George R. Manchester died shortly thereafter. The result was a lack of further evidence to examine.

No formal claim of the estate was filed with the Federal Government at this time.

Chapter 13

The Court cases of the 1960's

The estate remained silent until the 1960's.

The next major legal action was by Howard Foulkes, filing in the Court of Claims Case No. 401-64. He petitioned as Administrator De Bonis Non Cum Testamento Annexo of the Estates of Charles Durkee and Caroline Durkee, in November 1964. This was the case by Arthur Smith.

Foulkes asserted that "Charles Durkee, owned bonds in the above railroads, by virtue of cash purchases, construction contracts, sale of supplies and professional services rendered to said railroad companies."[106]

The plaintiff stated the belief that funds in excess of $187,500,000 were paid into the Sinking Fund and are presently carried as a trust asset in the records of the United States Treasury Department. No portion of these funds have been paid to the estate.

The defense moved for a Summary Judgment in its favor and dismissing the petition for the reason that there was no genuine issue as to any material fact and that defendant was entitled to Judgment as a matter of law. The amount of the claim was not conceded nor was it considered to be a material fact for the purposes of this motion.[107]

The Defendants argued that "(1.) The claim was barred by the statute of limitations and by laches. The petition fails to show that the claim accrued within the six year statute of limitations, 28 0.S.C. 2501. (2). The claim is barred by the doctrine of res Judicata, meaning that the matter cannot be raised again, either in the same court or in a different court."

Foulkes and his attorneys presented many of the assertions depositions presented in previous cases, but were dismissed by the court in the final ruling:

> This case comes before the court on defendant's motion for summary judgment.
> Upon consideration thereof, together with the opposition thereto, and without oral argument, it is concluded that plaintiff's alleged claim is barred by the statute of limitations, 28 U.S.C, §2501 and the doctrine of laches, and
> IT IS ORDERED that defendant's motion for summary judgment be and the same is granted and plaintiff's petition is dismissed.[108]

The case was immediately appealed to the Supreme Court of the United States, Case No. 955 in January 1966 in a Petition for a Writ of Certiorari to the United States Court of Claims. This was a petition arguing that a lower court has incorrectly decided an important question of law, and that the mistake should be fixed.

The Court of Claims granted the Government Motion for Summary Judgment even thought the opposition thereto showed convincingly that the genuine issues of material fact existed. The Government was holding trust funds composed of receipts from the retirement of the Bonds of the Pacific Railroads. The Government in its Motion denied that a trust existed but asserted if one did exist the trust had been repudiated.

After hearing and reviewing all the evidence the Supreme Court of the United States denied the petition on March 6, 1966.

The Kenosha Case

1967 U.S. Navy Captain (ret.) James McCrocklin filed suit in Milwaukee Circuit Court requesting s a full accounting of the bond proceeds. 1967 Racine College petitioned the Kenosha County Probate

In July 1967 James McCrocklin and the Board of Trustees of Racine College brought suit against the United States in the United States Court of the Eastern District of Wisconsin Civil Action No. 67-C-221.

Under date of September 13, 1967, the defense filed a motion to dismiss the plaintiff's complaint on the grounds of lack of jurisdiction, unconsented suit and improper venue. Venue and jurisdiction were dropped.

> "We believe the Administrative Procedure Act establishes the right of the plaintiff to sue the Secretary of the Treasury and the Treasury Department without the consent of the Government."

While these motions were pending, the defense filed a motion for summary judgment asking for dismissal of the plaintiffs' complaint under the doctrine of res judicata; collateral estoppel and laches.

It is these three charges that we primarily are attempting to answer in this brief. Plaintiffs have heretofore filed a brief on these subjects and are refilling this brief herein in rebuttal. They have cited the case of *Kuykendall v. Union Pacific and Foulkes v. United States*. Enough has been said as to why these cases do not establish grounds of application of the doctrine of res judicata.

The defense further in their brief refers to the case of United States v. Willard Tablet Co. 141 F2d 141 , to establish the fact that the defendants are in privity with the same defendants that existed in the Kuykendall case.

This we do not deny, but we reassert that Kuykendall did lack status and standing and that the plaintiffs in this action can in no way be barred or bound by the illegal acts of Kuykendall in being appointed as administrator in Salt Lake City and in bringing a suit against the Union Pacific Railroad Co. that he had no right to bring. Kuykendall who was not the administrator in this estate and had no right to bring suit.

Arthur L. Smith was not successful and the Board of Directors of Racine College was first notified of the size of the claim and the true nature in the year 1966 by Captain James W. McCrocklin and, therefore, cannot be charged with laches with failure to proceed to collect a claim that it knew nothing about.

As previously pointed out, the Board of Trustees of Racine College were not notified of their rights to this trust fund until 1966. The following citations prove that it was not necessary for them to be aware of this trust fund prior to this time. A *cestui que* trust does not lose or forfeit his interest in trust res merely because of delay in asserting ownership thereof In re Schulz Estate, 98 Atlantic 2nd 176, and It is not necessary that the *cestui que* trust be in existence.

"On or about 1963 I met James W, McCrocklin, U.S. Navy Captain (retired) and, on learning that he had done, considerable research for the Navy, I engaged him to go to the Archives in Washington to do some research on this claim, I had to cancel his working agreement for cause, and he continued to contact the President of the Board of Trustees of Racine College and the Chancellor to the Bishop, Mr. Boggs, in his attempts to get these members to allow him to present a claim on behalf of the Board of Trustees against the United States Government, he also promised large sums as bribes to Government officials.

"I now have a Bill before the Congress of the United States on behalf of the Estate of Charles Durkee. This Bill has now been held up two months due to two different suits filed in Federal Court in Milwaukee and a suit filed in the Probate Court In Kenosha, Wisconsin, claiming that he is entitled to twenty-five per cent of any money coming to Racine College from the Estate of Caroline Durkee. Neither suit has any foundation in law or fact.

A.
L, Smith Letter Sept 1967

"I, Howard T. Foulkes, Secretary and Treasurer of. the Board of Trustees of Racine Collage, do hereby certify that at a special meeting of the Board of Trustees of Racine Collage held October 17, 1967, pursuant to call, a majority of the Trustees being, present that following Resolution was unanimously adopted

"**Resolved**, that the Secretary is hereby directed to notify the Probate Court, Kenosha, Wisconsin, that James W. McCrocklin does not now nor has ever been authorized to represent the Board of Trustee a of Racine College in any capacity in its claim to the residuary estates of Charles Durkee, deceased, and Carolina Durkee, which estates are being administered by said Court, and that the Board of Trustees recognizes Howard T. Foulkes as the lawfully appointed Administrator of both estates and

Further Resolved, that the Board of Trustees approves and supports the procedure followed by Mr. Foulkes in which he has filed a claim for relief with the Congress of the United States, funds held by the United States which he claims properly be longs to the estates of Charles and Caroline Durkee and that Mr. James W. McCrocklin has no right or authority to represent Racine Collage in any capacity before the Congress of the United States in processing the claim of such estate[109]

"On September 9, 1967, John Reichardt, Comptroller of the Bureau of Accounts, Treasury Department, told James W. McCrocklin that there was over $125,000,000.00 in the Trust Fund at that time. If properly administered the Trust Fund would be worth over five billion dollars

"On July 14, 1967, a suit was filed in the United States District Court in Milwaukee, Wisconsin, for an accounting of the Trust Fund; however, an out of court negotiated settlement is desired.

Gerald T. Flynn Attorney for Claimant
310 Fifth St. Racine, Wisconsin

The Supreme Court and Others

In a legal disagreement agreement of Charles and Caroline Durkee Estates There were two factions. The Howard Foulkes and Arthur Smith group - who held initial contracts for the recovery of the Estate dating back to the 1930's; and the Racine College Board of Directors James McCrocklin group. Both groups intertwined in their quest to recover the estate over the next two decades.

On May 3, 1945 Arthur Smith had renegotiated the agreement with Howard Foulkes and the Board of Trustees of Racine College. Smith was hired, employed and retained to investigate, discover, negotiate for, secure or collect, or otherwise reduce to possession for the benefits of both parties the Bonds and Securities of the Durkee Estates.

Smith had been working on the estate legacy since the 1930's. As a third party, Smith was to retain as his compensation for the services to be rendered by him, fifty percent of any and all moneys, properties, both real and personal, stocks, bonds and other evidences of debt, and all the proceeds thereof which may "hereafter be recovered and come into the possession of the said Estates." The agreement also stipulated that he "will not assign, pledge or otherwise use this contract, or the rights arising out of it, or any rights he may have there under as a basis to exploit the public, and will not sell or offer for sale any interest in said contract to persons not already financially

Smith had been working on the estate legacy since the 1930's. As a third party, Smith was to retain as his compensation for the services to be rendered by him, fifty percent of any and all moneys, properties, both real and personal, stocks, bonds and other evidences of debt, and all the proceeds thereof which may "hereafter be recovered and come into the possession of the said Estates." The agreement also stipulated that he "will not assign, pledge or otherwise use this contract, or the rights arising out of it, or any rights he may have there under as a basis to exploit the public, and will not sell or offer for sale any interest in said contract to persons not already financially interested and that this contract and the rights hereunder shall not in any way be used for the purpose of obtaining money from the public."[110]

Smith continued to file reports and did not take serious action until 1964. He supported a claim introduced by Howard Foulkes, still Administrator of the Estate, filed in the Court of Claims Case 401-64 for the recovery of the sum of $187,500,000 allegedly carried as a 'Trust Asset' in the U. S. Treasury for the purpose of retiring certain bonds issued for the construction of the Pacific railroads. (This will be discussed in detail later). The Foulkes case was dismissed in October 1965; appealed to the Supreme Court of the United States in January 1966, and again dismissed without a full hearing.

On or about 1963 James W. McCrocklin, U.S. Navy Captain (Retired) was introduced to Smith, and, upon learning of his qualifications and previous work, including considerable research for the Navy, Smith engaged him to go to the Archives in Washington to do some research on this claim. In a new agreement between Arthur Smith now of Miami, and James McCrocklin of April 1964, McCrocklin was to receives 30% of any proceeds that Smith may receive as a result of a successful payout. McCrocklin's working agreement with Smith however was later cancelled.

McCrocklin proceeded to contact the President of the Board of Trustees of Racine College and the Chancellor to the Bishop, Mr. Boggs, in his attempts to persuade them to allow him to present a claim on behalf of the Board of Trustees against the United States Government. McCrocklin also promised large sums as bribes to Government officials.[111]

McCrocklin started working directly with the Board of Trustees for Racine College. Seeing the failure in the Foulkes Court of Claims he devised another approach

First he established in Probate Court an additional inventory covering the Paramount Lien Bonds. Then he filed a suit in the 9th District Court of Wisconsin for the claim of the estate.
Foulkes Countered by putting forth a Resolution with the Board of Trustees of Racine College to recognizes Howard T. Foulkes as the lawfully appointed Administrator of both estates, and,
Further he wanted to stop any interference by McCrocklin in his attempt to initiate Congressional action to obtain payment of the estate from the Treasury,. in any capacity before the Congress of the United States in processing the claim of such estate."[112]
In an additional filings of inventory of the estate in November 1966, all the Paramount lien Bonds authorized by Congress as a part of the estate, brings the Paramount Lien Bonds into the estate inventory as listed by the FIRST NATIONAL BANK OF KENOSHA, trustee.[113]

This also provided for another listing in the inventory as follows: "Trust Fund held by the Secretary of the Treasury as Trustee in accordance with the Act of May 7, 1878 (20 Stat. 26), the aforesaid Trust Fund being the funds received from the redemption of the Paramount Railroad Lien Bonds owned by Charles Durkee, deceased, as listed in the additional inventory of his Estate as filed and awarded to the Estate of Caroline Durkee by judgment entered the 21st day of March, 1882, by the County Court of Kenosha, Wisconsin, plus the interest accruing thereon in said Trust Fund in accordance with the act of September 11, 1841, (25 Stat. 465).

The Trust Fund Account Number 20X8881 and 20X1807 of the United States Treasury, Custodian, with Secretary of the Treasury, as Trustee. Value at date of Death, (February 21, 1911) $502,081,406.00 was identified[114]

The Probate Court ruled that the Trustees of Racine College, had remained, since November 6, 1912, as the sole and exclusive owner of all residue in the Estate of Caroline Durkee, "which residue included any interest which the said Caroline Durkee either had or might have had in and to Paramount Lien Bonds, Subsidy Bonds or Sinking Funds in the hands of the Treasurer of the United States."
"Believing- that the appointment of said administrator was in error and improper does herewith release and discharge the existing administrator, d/b.n.c.t.a. Howard T. Foulkes, and does find that the Board of Trustees of Racine College is the lawful owner and holder of all rights to the residue of said estate, including the bonds above mentioned and funds in the hands of the Treasurer of, the United States.

"Said Board of Trustees of Racine College are in no way to be bound or affected by acts of any kind or nature that may have been performed or attempted by various administrators or their agents heretofore acting in said estate since November 6, 1912." Thus we have a clearing of the legal ramifications of the various contract contingencies for a share of the estate proceeds.

Further, the Probate Court voided any contracts entered into by administrators with the promise of recovering the estate from the US Government any percentage of proceeds.[115]

Once the Durkee Estates were under direct control of the Board of Trustees of Racine College, Captain McCrocklin proceeded, through his lawyer and associates, to file suit in the U. S, District Court of Wisconsin, Case 67-C-221 On July 14, 1967.

The suit was filed against the Secretary of the Treasury William T. Howell, in his capacity as Deputy Treasurer of the United States; and the Treasury Department, and Howard Foulkes as Administrator, d.b.n.e.t.a. of the Estates of Charles and Caroline Durkee. The suit asked for an accounting of the Statuary Trust in the Treasury Department, including proceeds from Charles Durkee's Paramount Lien Bonds, there deposited.

McClocklin's lawyer Gerald Flynn of Racine Wisconsin prosecuted the case. The complaint was later amended on October 17, 1967, removing Howard T. Foulkes as a defendant to the action and added the Board of Trustees of Racine College as a party plaintiff in accordance with Rule 19 (c).
.
The complaint was the first complete airing of the issues. It provided depositions of many people involved with the case, and brought forward records of the Court of Claims Case 18003, as well as additional evidence. In total there were 106 exhibits, see Appendix III.

The case was well thought out and presented evidence in logical order starting from the 1860's and progressing to the meetings at the Treasurer's Office on April 22, 1884; and to the court of Claims case 18003 and following. The full details of the case were presented in the deposition of James McCrocklin. (See Appendix II.)

The action was based on the Secretary of the Treasury's arbitrary and capricious refusal to grant the Board of Trustees of Racine College's request for a Hearing Examiner in accordance with the Administrative Procedure Act, Title 5 U.S.C. (This request was contained in a Petition signed by Rt. Rev. Donald H. V. Hallock, DD.) However, by the ruling of the Probate Court of Kenosha citing that the administrators of the estate had not properly informed the Board of Directors of Racine College until 1966, the issue of Statute of Limitations and Latches and was moot.

In June 5, 1968, the Court granted defendants' (U S Governments) Motion for Summary Judgment based on laches and res judicata.[116]

The Case was immediately appealed. The U. S. Court of Appeals for the Seventh Circuit, No. 17155 reviewed the case over a period of a year and in a Judgment entered in the case in favor of the defendants, the decision was affirmed by the Court of Appeals for the 7th Circuit on May 19, 1969.

The Kenosha County Probate Court denied the admission of any additional inventory (the Bonds) into the estate of Charles Durkee in 1970.[117]

It appears that no further legal action was initiated after that date.

The court records were sealed for 20 years and then placed in the National Archives College Park Md. Attempts to gain access to these records have been hampered by any locator index. Freedom of Information Act requests have been made to both the US Treasury and the department of Justice, Civil Division and are in process to date.

Chapter 14

Fraud, & Funding of the Litigation

The pursuit for the Paramount Lien Bonds for the Plaintiffs continued. The cost of litigation required funds to pay for investigations, depositions, legal fees and expenses.

This began with Leonard Blaisdell and John Kuykendall in the Court of Claims Case 18003 of 1893.

Blaisdell asked for funds to pursue the case from the 17 or more potential heirs: This is evident in the Power of Attorney agreements signed by all.[118] He also arranged that they should receive a larger proportion of any proceeds received. As part of this agreement, he hired several investigators and attorneys on a contingency basis to investigate and provide data and statements, especially the interviews of Judge Lawrence, pivotal in the proof of the claim.

Kuykendall proceeded beyond Blaisdell when pursuing the case in San Francisco, and requested funds to support his effort, which, if successful would pay a significant reward. The costs to proceed in San Francisco required extensive funds for travel and legal representation.

In January 26, 1914 the US Treasury issued a warning that certain persons were endeavoring, in various parts of the country, to sell shares or interests in an alleged claim of the estate of Charles Durkee, deceased, against the United States.[119] "All persons were warned that money paid for a share or interest in this so-called claim will be money thrown away."[120]

The selling of portions of the claim proceeded until in 1927 when selling-parties George W. Stern and others were convicted of mail fraud in connection with their activities in promoting the Durkee claim. [121]

In December 1929 George R. Manchester expressed an interest in the estate to the Administrator of the estate, Walter W. Hammond, and arranged a contract to pursue part of the claim. Manchester was to receive 50% of assets recovered. He acquired two partners, most notably George R. Boston for 15%, and Arthur L. Smith.[122]

In April, 1933, they were formally dismissed. Except Arthur Smith of Boston Massachusetts who was then designated as the researching party: Smith continued to research with his contingency fee providing regular reports to keep the contract valid.

In 1942 Louis A. George of 1359 Hancock St. Quincy, Massachusetts requested copies of Smith's reports and subsequently, a date of revocation to Mr. Doolittle was made, and a termination of Smith's contract was enacted. George had paid Smith money.

In May 3, 1945 an Affidavit and Agreement of Arthur L. Smith was written for and between himself and Howard T. Foulkes, - the new Administrator for the Estate with the Board of Trustees of Racine College: For Arthur L. Smith, it was ordered and approved and that agreement entered into by Arthur L. Smith and Saul S. Myers 25th day of Feb. 1938 was null and void. The new agreement was for Smith to receive 50% of all assets recovered.

Two weeks later Smith assigned a portion of his contract to Abraham Berkowitz, Esq., of Philadelphia, PA and Henry E. Alexander, Esq., 341 Madison Ave., New York City as being retained to do all legal work before Executive and Judicial branches of Federal Government, regarding the alleged deposit with US Treasury Department of First Mortgage Prior Lien Bonds of the Union Pacific and Central Pacific and other railroad companies, and to receive and share equally 15% of recovery. Foulkes was to receive a sum from Smith's portion.

> *"3 May 1945 the hereto annexed contract and agreement which was duly entered into on the 3 day of May, 1945 by and between Howard T. Foulkes as administrator de bonis non cum testamento annexe of the Estates of Charles and Caroline Durkee, Deceased, party of the first part, and the Board of Trustees of Racine College, party of the second part, and your deponent as the party of the third part.*
>
> *"FIRST: The parties of the first and second parts, and each of them thereby hire, employ and retain the party of the third part to investigate, discover, negotiate for, secure or collect, or otherwise reduce to possession for the benefits of the parties of the first and second parts,*
>
> *"In consideration of the services to be rendered by the party of the third part as hereinbefore mentioned it is understood and agreed that the said party of the third part shall retain as his compensation for the services to be rendered by him as aforesaid, fifty percent of any and all moneys, properties, both real and personal, stocks, bonds and other evidences of debt and all the proceeds thereof which may hereafter be recovered and come into the possession of the said Estates. The party of the third part shall have the right to transfer and assign to my attorneys, or to such persons who may, under his direction perform any services as herein provided, the v/ hole or any part of any moneys to which the party of the third part may hereafter become entitled as hereinbefore contained and set forth."[23]*

Smith also retained Damon, Hayes, While, Walk & Hoban, 33 North LaSalle Street, Chicago, Illinois for legal work assigning 50% of first 2 million dollars, accruing. The contract remained in place through the 1940's and 50's until Smith initiated the Court of Claims Case in1965.

Arthur L. Smith promised large returns to those advancing him money, much of it at the rate of $1,000,000.00 for each $10,000.00 advanced. These figures are cited in the records of Kenosha County Court which discloses notes from Arthur L. Smith to people who advanced him money.

"The sums exceeded $10,000.00; as affiants believed. That affiants further believe that Smith had collected money from a group in the City of Minneapolis, Minnesota, within the last two weeks and that affiants verily believe that the sums received by him from Minnesota people exceed $100,000.00."

It was at the time of 1963 that James W, McCrocklin, U.S. Navy Captain (retired) was introduced to Arthur Smith now of Miami; and when James McCrocklin signed an Agreement in April 1964 to research the estate for Smith who assigns or transfers 30 % to McCrocklin.

McClocklin's contract was cancelled for cause, yet he continued to contact the President of the Board of Trustees of Racine College and the Chancellor to the Bishop, Mr. Boggs, in his petition to represent the Board of Trustees against the United States Government.

As the Court of Claims progressed under the direction of Howard Foulkes, Administrator, and Arthur Smith, James McCrocklin worked with the Board of Directors of Racine College.

Following the failure of the Supreme Court Appeal, there now splintered two pivotal actions.

First the Board of Directors filed an action in the Probate court to declare that the estate had been settled in 1914 after the death of Caroline Durkee and that any contract for recovery of assets from the estates was declared null and void. The second was to reinstate the contract with McCrocklin for 50% of recovered assets. From there on, McCrocklin initiated with full legal challenges the suit in the 7th District Court of Wisconsin and later to the Court of Appeals.

The case was getting expensive.

To finance these actions McCrocklin sold 'shares' in the potential recovery to individuals.
In a contingency contract in November 1966, McCrocklin agrees to pay said Irving M. Berenson for his services, the sum of $100,000 plus taxes as legal fees, if the Trust Fund could be recovered.

In July 1966 "Upon receipt by the Trustee of Government bonds or other high-grade securities having a value of approximately $56,000,000 the trustee shall forthwith make a distribution to the following named individuals in the respective amounts and in the manor hereinafter set forth:

James W. McCrocklin	$ 19,500,000
Donald G. Rodebaugh	$ 2,500,000
Canton Sand and Gravel Co.	$ 2,000,000
Russell G. Johnson	$ 6,500,000
Walter H. Rohrbacher	$ 4,500,000
G. G. Albanese	$ 4,500,000
John J. Barone and	
Raymond D. Baldwin	$ 1,500,000
Etc."[124]	

None of the Agreements or assignments came to fruition. The investors who contributed to the recovery effort Fund are not found to have received any return on their investment.

Chapter 15

Paramount Lien Bonds. The Transcontinental Railroads

The concept of a Transcontinental Railroad was created by the Act of Congress on July 1, 1862. This was the culmination of studies and exploration parties investigating the feasibility of a railroad traversing from Iowa to San Francisco, California. The initial Bill provided for government funding to be placed in a First position and contained many provisions which hampered individual companies from raising capital and securing investors and stock holders. This occurred at a time of Civil War when the Government was facing many other pressing issues.

A second Bill, The Act of July 2, 1864 was passed towards the end of the Civil War. This allowed the interested railroads to issue 1st Mortgage or Paramount Lien Bonds for construction, placing investors in a financial position ahead of any government financing. In addition, land was granted to each railroad as payment which could also be 'sold' for financing.

Six railroads were authorized for funding and franchises to build segments of the railroad. The principal railroads were the Union Pacific Railroad - extending track from Council Bluffs Iowa to the California line; and the Central Pacific Railroad, extending from Sacramento California to the Nevada State line and beyond.

Other roads were the Kansas Pacific Railroad extending from Kansas City Kansas across the state to Denver Colorado (and ultimately connecting to the Union Pacific Railroad in Cheyenne Wyoming.) The Kansas Pacific Railroad was reorganized in 1863 and also called the Union Pacific Eastern Division. The Union Pacific Central Branch, initially reorganized in 1863 and also called the Union Pacific Eastern

Division. The Union Pacific Central Branch, initially incorporated as the Atchison and Pikes' Peak Railroad in 1859 was built from Atchison to Waterville Kansas, a distance of 140 miles.

The Western Pacific Railroad was to connect Sacramento California to San Francisco, skirting San Francisco Bay and through Niles Canyon to Stockton and Sacramento. The final road was the Sioux City and Pacific Railroad to connect Sioux City Iowa to the Union Pacific Railroad in Fremont Nebraska allowing another route to the Chicago area and also to the Dakota Territories.

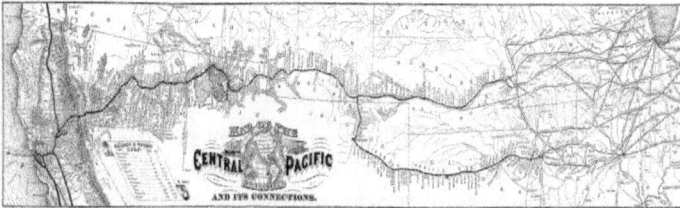

The Union Pacific Railroad 1865-1870

(Utah State Historical Society Records)

Union Pacific Railroad

The Union Pacific Railroad was incorporated in July 1, 1862 under the Act of Congress authorizing the Transcontinental Railroad. The company had offices in New York City and Boston. The first President of the company was John A. Dix, the Vice President, Thomas Durant.

On July 2, 1864 Congress passed additional legislation which allowed the Railroads to issue First Mortgage Bonds against construction; and to receive government lands as they crossed the plains. The Union Pacific Railroad issued its First Mortgage against the future property and railroad receipts by November 1, 1865, see Appendix I. Construction began from Omaha Nebraska and snaked westward along topography suited to track. The mortgage to lands given was supposedly
On July 2, 1864 Congress passed additional legislation which allowed the Railroads to issue First Mortgage Bonds against recorded in every county through which the railroad traversed.[27] By 1868 Oliver Ames was elected President of the Company and John Cisco as Treasurer. General Grenville Dodge was the primary construction manager.

Central Pacific Railroad

The Central Pacific Railroad was one of the two primary Transcontinental Railroads stretching from Sacramento California to Utah.

---

[27] No records could be found in several of the county courthouses, specifically, the Omaha Court house by the researcher.

The Pacific Railroad Act was passed on July 1, 1862 which authorized funding for the Transcontinental Railroad with US Government Bonds and Land Grants. Although the Pacific Railroad eventually benefited the Bay Area, the City and County of San Francisco obstructed financing during the early years of 1863-1865.

With Leland Stanford as Governor, the Legislature passed on April 22, 1863, "An Act to Authorize the Board of Supervisors of the City and County of San Francisco to take and subscribe One Million Dollars to the Capital Stock of the Western Pacific Rail Road Company and the Central Pacific Rail Road Company of California and to provide for the payment of the same and other matters relating thereto." This was later amended by Section Five of the "Compromise Act" of April 4, 1864. On May 19, 1863, the electors of the City and County of San Francisco passed this bond by a vote of 6,329 to 3,116, in a highly controversial Special Election.

Almost immediately, conflicts arose between Theodore Judah, the founder, and his business partners over the construction of the Central Pacific line. In October 1863, Judah sailed for New York to attempt to find investors who would buy out his Sacramento partners. He contracted yellow fever during this trip and died on November 2, after reaching New York City.

The first rail was spiked October 26, 1863. Samuel Montague replaced Judah and the Central Pacific construction worked on rail east from Sacramento. It was slow starting. But Charles Crocker resigned from the railroad's board, to form the new company called the Construction Finance Corporation, and completed the project in time under his management.

Huntington moved to New York and represented the company in the East, handling financing and purchasing rails, locomotives and railroad cars, and acting as political lobbyist.

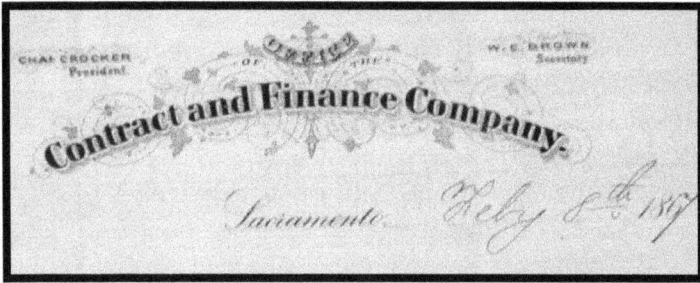

Contract and Finance Company Letterhead; The files of the
Huntington collection contained two references to the Company.

(Collis Potter Huntington Papers,
Special Collections Research Center Syracuse Library)

Crocker was in charge of construction. Stanford, who was
Governor of California in 1861–63, saw to the company's
financial and political interests in the West. The associates
subscribed some of their own funds initially, but most of the
capital for the actual construction came from public funds and
1st Mortgage Bonds.

The initial thrust of the construction was to reach the Nevada
state line across the Sierra Nevada Mountains. With the revised
legislation of July 2, 1864, government bonds and
Paramount Lien bonds, authorizing stock subscriptions, were
used to finance construction. A First Mortgage was issued for
the California portion of the road, Appendix I, and bonds were
issued in California and shipped to New York for sale. These
were four Series of bonds A through D.

As construction progressed Crocker and Huntington corresponded detailing the work progress; funding issues and the consideration of purchasing the Western Pacific Railroad to San Francisco. Communications were slow at this time in that letters were sent via Panama and there was about a two month lag between letters sent and returned. Often, letters crossed in the mail and correspondence referred to numbered letters. Original Copies of these letters are located in the Syracuse University Library Special Collections, and the Stanford University Library Special Collections.

The Bank of California played an important role in construction. Transfer of moneys between New York and San Francisco was slow, and in many instances advances from the bank were necessary to pay for workers and materials locally.
D. O. Mills, President of the Bank of California was one of the Trustees on the first mortgage of the railroad. Examples of these transactions are as follows:

> *"Hopkins to Huntington, February 16, 1866[125], yours to Stanford of January 14 is received in which you speak of using first mortgage bonds after first disposing of all the state aid bonds without waiting to retire or attempting to retire the 1.5 million convertible bonds. Now you say you think the holders of the convertibles do not desire to exchange them either for government bonds and or our first mortgage bonds more closely study of this question in your.*
> *"The convertible bonds will not be as high the government bonds with as some of the convertibles were held by O. Ames and others of our friends of influence you would prefer to avoid being that which would force on a question as to whether convertible bonds are a first second or third on the first 50 miles of our road.*
> *"Our view here as I have always understood Judge Crocker and all is that always been, that after the RRR shall have given the notice all convertible bonds which the holders elect not to exchange will occupy the position of third leave on the first 50 miles.*

"Still I consider it practically a question between the bondholders in which we have no interest unless it shall prove that convertible bonds have the effect of depreciating the market value of our first mortgage bonds which at some time price we have control are compelled to sell.

Stanford to Huntington, July 7, 1867, Enclosed please find F L Thirbaults certificate of mailing to your address 400 Bonds of the CPRR, No's 1001 to 1400 inclusive. The bonds go by the steamers mail of this date 1000 bonds preceding them by steamer.[126]

"Huntington to Crocker, January 1, 1868[127]*, New York, Mills (Trustee) signs Bonds in New York Mills* [128]*is going to Europe in the Spring and I will send a good man with him to take care of the bonds. You have been hurrying me to sell Bonds but it turns out that I am selling faster now than you can make them.*

I want in the next 3 months about $3,000,000 to use as collateral, but just where they are coming from I don't know. Mr. Barron is in Mexico, and I do not know just when he is coming back, I would send someone there with about $6,000,000 worth of Bonds and have him sign them and then send them to me in time to same time and expenses of sending a man to Europe to have Mills sign them.

The Western Pacific Railroad

In 1864 under the Pacific Railway Act of 1862 Congress assigned Rights to the Western Pacific for the connection from Sacramento to San Francisco.

The Western Pacific Railroad was created in December 1862 by Timothy Dame, Charles McLaughlin, Peter Donahue and others. This was an offshoot of the San Francisco and San Jose Railroad to build a rail line to connect with the Central Pacific through Stockton to Sacramento California; and to connect with the Central Pacific to the East. They were intending to couple with the San Francisco and San Jose Railroad to complete a railroad connection direct to San Francisco. The intent was to build a line from San Jose north through Niles Canyon to Stockton and Sacramento.

The City and County of San Francisco issued Bonds to the Western Pacific as part of an issue which included the Central Pacific Railroad. This amounted to 200 '$1000 Gold Bonds' paying seven per centum. The City and County required $1,000.000 in capital stock as security combined from both the Western Pacific Railroad and the Central Pacific Railroad.

With the passage of the Railroad Act of July 2, 1865 the Western Pacific also received government bonds and could issue 1st mortgage bonds for road. The first twenty miles had been completed in 1866 from San Jose, but funding and rail purchases caused a halt to construction.

On January 9th 1867, Leland Stanford wrote Collis Huntington about the purchase of the Western Pacific Railroad.

"I have made a proposition for the Western as follows, turn over to us the road free of encumbrance, about 250 tons of Iron, locomotives and cars together with about $50,000, the proceeds of the lands about $50,000, all the stock issued including that of the counties, we assume the Iron contract with Rensselaer, Iron work and the contract for 12 46 ton locomotives for 211 first mortgage bonds and allow them first mortgage and Gov. bonds on 1st twenty miles and 200 government bonds when the last should be xxx. on completion of road. I don't think that McLaughlin is in condition to accept it."[129]

Crocker again provided more details[130]:

and except for the $150,000 stock of the road owned by Santa Clara County, all the balance of the stock is to be transferred to us."

"McLaughlin contract with the W.P.R.R. Co. is to be cancelled by the Board of Directors and a contract entered into with us to build and start the road and give in therefore all the stock, all the Government Bonds and all the 1st Mortgage Bonds and all the lands and we are to release the W.P.R.R. Co. for, the CPRR Co's claim of 10% of Government Bonds.

We are to pay claims amounting in gold to about $60,000 now due and to become due within 60 days. Also claims of $17,000 gold in 6 months, also claims of $43,000 gold due in 12 months and claims of $31,000 in currency due in two years."

All in one breath by the principle leaders combining finance, steel, labor and terrain construction of track, the following efforts were achieved

Crocker, again on June 25 to Huntington[131] provided the following information:

"I enclose ____ Account of Griswold for 320 1ˢᵗ Mortgage bonds of the W.P.R.R. & McLaughlin's order to deliver the same to you.

You say that you were not prepared to say yes or no to the purchase of the Western Pacific, because you did not know the cost of construction and "many other matters". ...

"I am confident that the grading between here through Stockton and the base of the Coastal Range can be done for less than $1,000,000 and the bridging contract for $100,000. This would be 75 miles=$175,000 to make it ready for superstructure-five miles from there to summit at Livermore Pass not more than $40,000 of $200.000 to make it ready for the ties-15 miles over the Livermore Plaines at $2,000 per mile=$30,000-5 miles more to the present terminus in

Alameda leaving -$20,000 per mile =$100.000 or in all $505,000 for 100 miles of road, add $10,000 for superstructure-$1,000,000. We have in all $1,805,000 to do this we will have $1,600,000 US Bonds, $1,710,000 1ˢᵗ Mortgage Bonds, over $5,000,000 in stock, plus 20 miles of Iron, chains and spikes ready to lay."

Central Pacific had an excellent trade considering the position of Huntington to procure the capital when necessary. And it was an overarching success.

By September the Central Pacific Railroad had purchased the Western Pacific Railroad. The actual construction was put on hold while the Central Pacific continued construction towards Promontory Utah. Rails, fittings, engines and cars were diverted to the Central Pacific until the Western line was constructed. The initial bonds and mortgage were cancelled in March 1869[132].

By November, D. O. Mills, President of the Bank of California and William Barron as Trustees issued a new Mortgage for the road and forwarded a certified copy to Huntington in New York[133].

On October 29, 1869, Miller, the Treasurer of the company mailed 1000 Western Pacific Railroad First Mortgage Bonds to Huntington. As part of the process Huntington would exchange new bonds for Sterling Bonds issued some three or four years hence. The bonds were in two tranches, Series A for $1,970,000 maturing July 1, 1899; and Series B for $765,000 also maturing at the same date. [134]

This was the start of the final phase of construction of the railroad. The Western Pacific was redirected to Oakland where the Central Pacific had a loading wharf and could ferry passengers and freight directly to San Francisco.
This segment of the road proved to be providential. Just after the great earth quake of 1906, it served to move people and heavy supplies to and from the City of San Francisco. E.H. Harriman, the new owner of the Central Pacific as well as the Union Pacific, personally directed aid to the earthquake survivors, and provided free transportation.

Central Branch of the Union Pacific

The Central Branch of the Union Pacific Railroad was originally organized under the corporate title of the Atchison and Pike's Peak Railroad Company February 11, 1859. It was one of the branches of the Union Pacific in the act of incorporating that company.[135]

The main line of this road extended from Atchison to Waterville, Kansas 100 miles. This line was cited under the 1862 and 1864 Congressional Acts to received federal bond support for $16,000 per mile. The company was also authorized to issue $1,600,000 in first mortgage company bonds. Although a division of the Union Pacific Railroad, the road operated independently and had corporate offices at separate quarters in New York. The corporate officers and board of directors was not related to the Union Pacific Railroad.

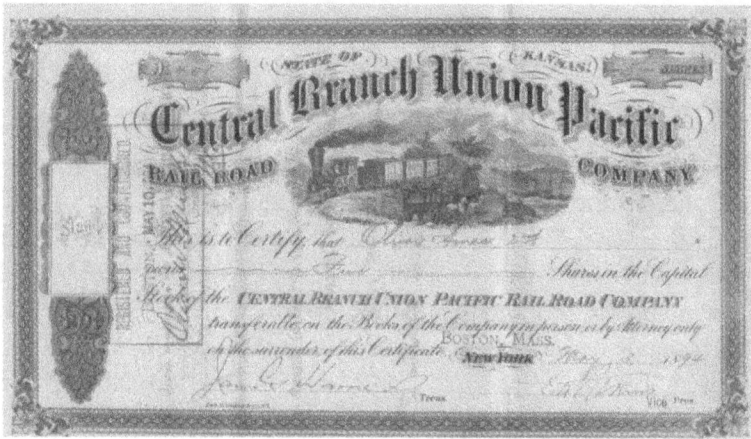

Central Branch Stock 1894: The Company was in Receivership and Trying to Raise Funds.

(Courtesy of David Beach Cigarboxlabels.

The Atchison, Colorado & Pacific Branch ran from Waterville to Lenora, 191.9 miles; Greenleaf to Washington, 7 miles; Downs to Bull's City, 23.6 miles; Yuma to Talmage, 29.8 miles; total 252.3 miles. The Atchison, Jewell County & Western road extended from Jamestown to Burr Oak, 38.8 miles. The total length of lines reported as being operated by the Central Branch Union Pacific Railroad in June 1, 1882 amounted to 386.1 miles.[136]

The company changed its name to Central Branch Union Pacific Railroad in January 1867, to better reflect its purpose.[137] While owned by Union Pacific Railway Company its was operated by the Missouri Pacific as its "Central branch Division.[138]

Construction began in 1865, and the line was constructed from Atchison west for 40 miles (64 km) in January 1867; later completing track for 100 miles to Waterville in January 1868.
The railroad operated as a feeder line and reported revenues of $453,000 with a net earnings of $124,000 in 1882. This did not include payments to the US for the Government bonds and Paramount Lien bonds, each amounting to $96,000.
The Central Branch of the Union Pacific Railroad was one of the pioneers for opening Kansas farm land to new settlements; and offering a means of transporting grain and cattle back to eastern markets.

Kansas Pacific Railroad

The Kansas Pacific Railroad was built from Kansas City Missouri to Denver Colorado stretching 672 miles. Organized under a charter from the Territory of Kansas as the Leavenworth, Pawnee and Western Railroad Company, the name changed to *Union Pacific Railway Company, Eastern Division,* June 6, 1863; and to *Kansas Pacific Railway Company* by authority of Act of Congress, March 3, 1869. Also covered by the mandates of Acts of Congress of July 1, 1862, and July 2, 1864.[139] Later the railroad incorporated the *Denver Pacific Railway* from Denver to Cheyenne Wyoming, completing a loop to the Union Pacific portion of the Transcontinental Railroad. The company received $6,303,000 in Government Bonds and also issued $6,303,000 in First Mortgage Bonds.

A railroad investor Jay Gould gained control of the railroad in 1874. Thomas Scott, Philadelphia, Sidney Dillon and Jay Gould of New York and Oliver Ames of Boston were directors of the company in 1876.

Gould arranged for the consolidation of the Kansas Pacific, Denver Pacific into the Union Pacific Railroad system in 1880 through stock exchanges. The Kansas Pacific reissued First Mortgage bonds in the 1880's which could replace existing First Mortgage bonds under new terms of payment. These did not extinguish the liability of the railroad to redeem those bonds.[28]

In 1873 America saw a financial panic from over investment in railroads and other risky bank loans. In 1874 the Kansas Pacific Railroad was unable to meet the interest on a portion of the First Mortgage bonds, land grant bonds, and the Leavenworth Branch bonds.[140]

---

[28] Overstamping: In a similar occurrence, the UP Sinking Fund Bonds (issued in 1873 due in 1893) were modified with an overstamping of the bond, citing new terms of redemption (altered to 1899.) This is likely to have occurred with the Kansas Pacific Bonds. (Overstamping examples are not found today.)

The company defaulted in the payment of interest on its bonds and was placed in the hands of a Receiver.[141]

Railroad investors Jay Gould and Sidney Dillon saw opportunity and gained control of the Kansas Pacific Railroad through stock purchases. Jay Gould gained chief control of the railroad in 1874, Thomas Scott of Philadelphia; Sidney Dillon and Jay Gould of New York and Oliver Ames of Boston were directors of the company in 1876.

Financial challenges remained. Through the intervention of Jay Gould, the company made overtures to overseas bondholders - an avid market for investments in industrial development.
The financial interest payments were deferred for the Coupons; Certificates for interest were issued to European bondholders who had the right to designate two members of reputable business firms in New York or St. Louis to the Board of Directors, and to exercise control over the finances of the company. The Board of Directors of the company formally agreed and pledged not to create any new floating debt without the consent of the two directors representing foreign bondholders.
Henry Villard, a German immigrant who became a railroad financer was appointed Receiver of the Kansas Pacific Railroad by the First Mortgage Bondholders overseas.

In 1880 the Kansas Pacific Railroad came out of Receivership with an increase in economic activity and was consolidated with the Union Pacific which changed names to the Union Pacific Railway Company. Consolidations, reorganizations and refinancing occurred in desperate attempts to offset receipts across an uneven landscape of economic progress.
The transitions of the Kansas Pacific Railroad into the Union Pacific Railway Company forced the Bondholders overseas to accept a mortgage secured by new bonds to the amount of $30,000,000 --many of them accustomed rather to discharge

matured indebtedness. Gould induced the shareholders of the Union Pacific and Kansas Pacific and the Denver Pacific to accept a stock redistribution. The Kansas Pacific Railroad was thereby continued as the Kansas Division of the Union Pacific Railway Company. In the process, Jay Gould and Dillon made a profit of over $10,000,000 in increased stock value.[142]

The transitions of the Kansas Pacific Railroad into the Union Pacific Railway Company forced the Bondholders overseas to accept a mortgage secured by new bonds to the amount of $30,000,000 --many of them accustomed rather to discharge matured indebtedness. Gould induced the shareholders of the Union Pacific and Kansas Pacific and the Denver Pacific to accept a stock redistribution. The Kansas Pacific Railroad was thereby continued as the Kansas Division of the Union Pacific Railway Company. In the process, Jay Gould and Dillon made a profit of over $10,000,000 in increased stock value.[143]

The Kansas Pacific Railroad remained in operation and effectively became part of the Union Pacific until the Receivership actions of 1893. The debt of the company was held separately during those negotiations however, and independently managed by a different Receiver when foreclosed.

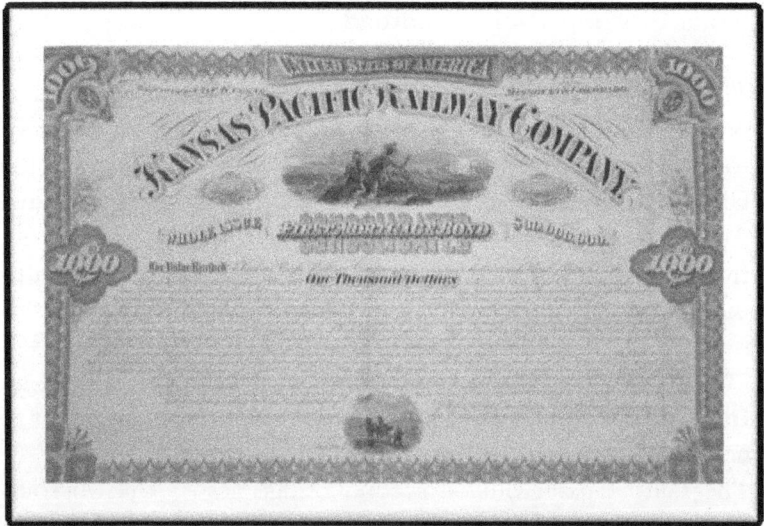

Paramount Lien Bond of the Kansas Pacific Railroad Issued May 1879: This was as a result of the reorganization by Jay Gould and the refinancing of the Road.

(The Museum of American Finance, Wall Street New York City)

Sioux City and Pacific Railroad

The Sioux City and Pacific Railroad was initially authorized as part of the Pacific Railroad Act of 1862 citing a network of roads connecting northern routes, including Chicago, to the Union Pacific Railroad in Nebraska. The July 2, 1864 amended Act of Congress allowed an independent railroad to connect from Sioux City Iowa to Fremont Nebraska; then to attach to the Union Pacific Railroad main line; and provisioned for it to issue Paramount Lien Bonds.

Further, the railroad was authorized to extend the Sioux City Iowa to Freemont Nebraska line and to also create an outlet to northern Iowa and new territories of the Dakota's.

The railroad later built a second bridge across the Missouri River servicing its outlet to Chicago: The principle function was to transport foodstuffs and beef to Chicago, then return iron and manufactured goods to the West from Chicago, connecting with the Pacific main line.

The railroad was authorized $16,000 in government bonds for each mile constructed plus the $16,000 per mile of Paramount Lien Bonds to finance the Railroad. The road's length was listed at 107.42 miles between Sioux City Iowa and Fremont Nebraska. A total of $1,628,320 in Government bonds were issued; plus $1,628,000 of Paramount Lien First Mortgage bonds were issues. (1,628 bonds). These bonds were due in 1898. The bonds were issued in denominations of $500 and $1,000. [29]

---

[29] Government bonds were generally issued in $500 and $1000 increments, National Archives Sinking Fund Ledgers

In the Fall of 1866, John I. Blair, an Eastern railroad developer sent a man to Sioux City Iowa to garner support for construction of the railroad. (At that moment, the line would connect Sioux City with the main line which ran through the Missouri Valley and give its connection to Chicago.) The City and County were asked to donate land for the tracks and depot. This, they agreed to do.

In 1869 John I. Blair was President of the company and member of the Board of Directors, with Oakes Ames of the Union Pacific, also a member of the Board of Directors. Blair's son, DeWitt C. Blair constructed the road.

Until 1883, the railroad operated a Ferry across the Missouri River. Blair Bridge was completed and opened successfully for the continuous running of the track across the river. The following year, in 1884, the Chicago and North-Western Railroad acquired the Sioux City Railroad which could now connect to Chicago.

In a controversial Congressional Hearing of 1887, John I. Blair was questioned about the construction of the railroad and its financial transactions.

Due to a previous Act of Congress - the Thurmond Act of 1878 wherein it was legislated that railroads deposit a certain portion of their net operating income into a Sinking Fund held Due to a previous Act of Congress - the Thurmond Act of 1878 wherein it was legislated that railroads deposit a certain portion of their net operating income into a Sinking Fund held at the US Treasury, the matter of a Sinking Fund was addressed: The Thurmond Act, which was amended in 1887, ten years later to allow railroad First Mortgage Bonds to be purchased as assets for the Sinking Fund, provisioned the Sinking Fund as Guarantor.

John I. Blair stated that the Books and financial records of the construction had been destroyed.[144] He cited the sale of the Sioux City and Pacific Railroad to the Chicago and North-Western Railroad, stating that the transaction included the stock, bond liabilities and all other liabilities. [145]

Included in the transfer of sale were 400 First Mortgage Bonds. It appeared that the railroad had been built with government financing and stock subscriptions; the bonds used in part, to pay dividends to the stock holders.

Northwestern Railroad Company, Mr. Blair had offered a resolution. However, in the Minutes set forth, it was shown that as a condition of the sale the Chicago and Northwestern Company, all financial obligations of the company were to be assumed and protected, excepting that of the United States Government.[146]

In a statement before Congress, Mr. David Litter, Springfield Ill, Council for the Chicago and Northwestern Railway Company, presented the case of the Sioux City and Pacific Railway transaction as follows.

> *"This road belongs practically to the Chicago and Northwestern Railway Company, which owns substantially all the stock; and while I am not prepared to give the names of the owners of the first mortgage bonds, I expect that if inquiry were made it would be found that many of those are the stockholders of the Chicago and Northwestern road who the first mortgage bonds of the Sioux city and Pacific."[147]*

Litter further stated that the Chicago and Northwestern Railroad had deposited into the Sinking Fund $716,000 in Sioux City First Mortgage Bonds as of 1896.

Litter testified that the Chicago and Northwestern Railroad was willing to pay the Government bonds in full and asked that a three-man committee should be set up to adjudicate the amount due.[148]

Ultimately the Sioux City and Pacific was placed in Receivership and auctioned. The First Mortgage bondholders were awarded the road with a deficit on the Government subsidy bonds.

Chapter 16

The Bond Failures of the 1890's

The Transcontinental Railroads were faced with a serious crisis. Over $180,000,000 ($180MM) in principal and interest - were due in the next 7 years.

The country was in an economic Depression. U.S. Government's Subsidy Bonds were placed in a position whereby the railroads could not issue new First Mortgage Bonds to clear the old debt.

Renegotiated debt allowed the Transcontinental Railroad to be funded by First Mortgage Bonds and U.S. Government bonds. These were now 30-year bonds with 'Coupons' payable twice yearly. The Government had issued $64,623,512. The railroads had issued $64,613,320 in First Mortgage Bonds. These bonds all became due starting in 1895 and running through 1899, payable mainly in gold.

In a Supreme Court decision allowed the railroads to defer payment of interest on the government bonds until the time the bonds became due. This put off the necessity of paying interest on the government subsidy loans until the bonds became due thirty years later.

Congress amended the agreements under the Thurman Act.[149] New requirements provided for the railroads to set aside 5 percent of net earnings; plus one-half of the sums owning from the US for government transportation, provided by the Acts of 1862 and 1864.

The Act also provided that the other half of the sums owing from government transportation should go into a Sinking fund for retirement of the debt to the 1st mortgage bonds..

In addition, if the 5 percent of the net earnings and the sums due for government transportation did not total 25 percent of net earnings, an additional payment (not to exceed for the Union Pacific $850,000) would be required to bring the companies payment up to the 25% net earnings.

The Sinking Fund, having some autonomy now, was amended by the Act of 3 March 1887 Chapter 345 Section 5 to allow the US Treasury to invest in any of the First-Mortgage Bonds of either of the companies (Union Pacific and Central Pacific). This allowed the US Treasury to purchase First Mortgage Bonds for their own at large Sinking Fund Portfolio.

Clearly, the railroads had developed a large debt to the government -along with other expenses which were maturing in the 1890's. Without significant increase in revenues to support the payments, the problem was becoming substantial. Moreover, as time passed, they did not invest in improvements and repair of track or engines and cars. The crisis came to a head in February 1893. The expansion of railroads - based on bonds and stock issues, and the ensuing railroad debt crisis of bonds becoming overdue, seemed insurmountable.

A major starting point of the crisis actually occurred outside of the United States in Argentina. Baring Brothers had encouraged investment in the wheat crop which failed that year. In addition there was a Coup de State in Buenos Aries.

This resulted Also occurring at that time was the impact of the 1878 Bland-Allison Act, followed in 1890 by the Sherman Silver Purchasing Act requiring the government to purchase silver and driving the supply of gold out of circulation. This caused the prices of other comedies to fall. Agricultural prices for wheat and cotton fell in 1892. As these factors came into play, the shortfall of gold-backed currency spread across the entire commercial sector resulting in a slow-down of transportation and resulting drop in railroad revenues.

The financial crisis manifested itself on February 23, 1893 just before the inauguration of President Grover Cleveland. The Philadelphia and Reading Railroad declared bankruptcy and was placed in Receivership.

As panic ensued, people started a run on banks by withdrawing their money and creating a liquidity problem, particularly with the gold supply. Concomitantly, a financial panic in Great Britain led to a decrease in American foreign trade with Europe, and overseas investors sold American Stock to obtain American funds backed by gold.

People in America attempted to redeem their silver notes with gold, but the statutory limit of the Federal gold reserves in the Treasury was reached. Interest payments for bond coupons and redemption in gold hit a predicament.

The Pacific Railroads were the largest debtors to the US Government. Their liability, principal and interest, aggregating to $115,348,287.73 induced them to publicly confess their inability to meet their obligations at maturity. The Commissioner of the Railroad concluded that the condition must be relieved by an increase in taxation through a readjustment of the public revenues.[150] in a run on gold in the U. S. Treasury as investors sought safety.

In fact, the Union Pacific Railroad and all its subsidiaries experienced a decrease in income due to the panic and reduction of business. Over the five previous years the income reduction had remained stagnant. This was similar for the Central Pacific Railroad which had been combined with the Western Pacific in 1869 and later leased to the Southern Pacific Railroad.

Even as the Union Pacific Railroad consolidated with the Kansas Pacific, and their debts amalgamated, they had only averaged $4,757,481 in net income; and the Central was $1,534,372. This was insufficient to maintain interest payments on the First Mortgage bonds and, ultimately, the payoff of the bonds, including the U. S. bonds which started to become due in 1896.

The situation was considered a disastrous failure.

Receivership.

The Union Pacific Receivership, October 13, 1893

The Union Pacific Railroad was placed into Receivership on October 13, 1893.

	1889	1890	1891	1892	1893
Liabilities	20,161,613	21,418,094	6,817,945	6,925,156	2,343,310
Assets	15,672,050	14,543,152	18,006,769	20,045,524	11,996,957
Profits	-4,489,563	-6,874,942	12,874,834	13,120,389	9,653,647

Profits Union Pacific 1889-1893[151] showing a decrease in revenues, they were able to supplement income by deferring major maintenance.

The Union Pacific had an extensive network of railroads at the time and a web of rail lines and affiliates which compromised over 7,681.72 miles and included 22 affiliated railroads. Numerous other business ventures including land, coal and water companies were also listed as their assets. In addition they held stock and bonds valued at over ninety million dollars. These were illiquid assets.

The problem was with the economic slow-down of the Depression of 1893. Many of the subsidiary lines were also operating at a loss such as the Junction City and Ft. Kearney RY($109,297); the Kansas Central RR ($71,800); the Oregon Short Line ($2,236,815), and others.[152]

Entering into Receivership, in a petition for Bankruptcy protection, the Receiver allowed the railroads opportunity to shed unprofitable lines; and align debt to associated other railroads. The intertwinement of finances was complex with many other companies; supplier banks; investment firms and bond-holders involved. The principal factor was the U.S. Subsidized Bond debt being placed in a second position to the First Mortgage Bonds. These two encumbrances influenced many of the other lesser debts involved.

The debate in the Receivership reached culmination late 1897. Many options to resolve the debt to the Government were debated, such as renegotiating Government debt for 10 years at a lesser rate under new notes.

The U. S. Government had the option to accept those agreements under Congressional Act of March 3, 1887. The Act, Section 4, authorized the President of the United States to direct the Secretary of the Treasury to redeem or otherwise clear off such First Mortgage Lien mortgages or other encumbrance, by paying the sums lawfully due in respect out of the Treasury.[153]

During the Congressional Hearings of 1896, most notably Hearings of the Committee on Pacific Railroads in the Senate, the receivers of the Union Pacific Railroad; Collis Huntington of the Central Pacific Railroad; and Leonard Blaisdell of the Durkee estate litigation, all gave testimony. [15430]

There were two propositions being considered: Foreclosing by the First Mortgage Trustees as receivers, and extending the US Government Debt at a lesser interest rate; or, paying off the U.S. Government debt. This involved detailed negotiations between the receivers and the Government through the Offices of the Attorney General.

Resolution was finally made in late 1897 whereby the Union Pacific main line was put up for auction. The auction was held in November 1897. The main line was sold to the purchasing Trustees of the Union Pacific Reorganization Committee under a decree of the United States Court for the District of Nebraska.

---

[30] It was during this period that Blaisdell had filed suit in 1893 (Case No 18003) citing ownership of the Paramount Lien Bonds issued to Durkee in 1866-69, his diseased relative. While his suit remained outstanding, he gave testimony with the Trustee of the Union Pacific, and Huntington of the Central Pacific at the Hearing. Blaisdell's claim was never disputed in the Senate.

This purchase price at the auction was older First Mortgage for $27,236,512. The entire indebtedness to the United States as of November 1, 1897 including the $13,645,250 in bonds at par was made available to the Secretary of Treasury for the Union Pacific Sinking Fund.

A secondary amount due the Government consisted of $27,236,512 (for the Principal of the US Subsidy bonds); plus interest on those bonds of $30,831,181; and interest accrued (four months) of $381,530 for a total of $58,448.223.

The cash and bonds in the Sinking Fund were credited for a value of $18,194,618 resulting in a Balance due to the United States of $40,253,605.

The Balance was required to be paid in four equal installments within thirty, forty, fifty and sixty days after confirmation of the sale. These payments were made.[155]

In essence, the negotiated deal enabled the railroads to retire the obligation to the Government for subsidy bonds authorized in the Acts of 1862, and 1864. This then allowed them to refinance a new first mortgage, and issue new stock. Also above all, the company was now viable under new management. January 31, 1898.

The new Union Pacific Railroad Company took possession of the properties which had been bought at the foreclosure sale. It found itself in possession only of the main lines which its predecessor had owned in fee simple, and one or two small branches. As of June 30 1898, that comprised of 1,849.29 miles of railway.[156]

The Union Pacific Railroad Company began its business on February 1898, with an authorized capital stock of $136,000,000 consisting of $75,000,000 of non-cumulative preferred stock; and $61,000,000 of common stock.

It also had an authorized bonded indebtedness of $100,000,000 consisting of 4 per cent interest, fifty-year First Mortgage Bonds.[157] By this way the Union Pacific could extinguish the original mortgage of 1865 (see Appendix I), and start with new financing without the encumbrance of Government obligations. The $27,236,512 of First Mortgage Bonds were guaranteed by a Trust Company, and arrangements made for them to exchange of old Paramount Lien Bonds for new bonds. Because the newly negotiated fifty-year First Mortgage Bonds of 1900 (which would become due approximately 1950) were exchanged for those Paramount Lien Bonds of 1866-69 (issued during Durkee's lifetime), it is entirely possible that the Union Pacific, and administering Trust Company Guarantor, has retained those records related.[31]

New bonds were to be issued in exchange for the old and for other reorganization purposes. The bondholders whose bonds and coupons did not provide interest beyond the due date, were induced to take out new bonds with the conditions of receiving (in lieu of cash) 100 per cent of their par value in new 4 per cent bonds, and a bonus of 50 per cent in new preferred stock for the exchange.[158]

A second foreclosure suit instituted by the United States against the Kansas Pacific portion of the Union Pacific was auctioned on 16 February, 1898 to Louis Fitzgerald and Alvin Krech as purchasing Trustees for the sum of $6,303,000, the value of the First Mortgage on that railroad. This amount was also the value of the U. S. Government subsidy bonds and was paid to the US Treasury. The Trustees assigned the Kansas Pacific Railroad, its franchises and property to the Union Pacific Railroad Company.

---

[31] Neither the Records of the Nebraska State Archives Union Pacific Collection; nor the University of Iowa Library, Special Collection Union Pacific, hold financial records after 1905.

The United States Government, in relinquishing interest due on the Government Subsidy bonds, established the right to have the preference at all times in the use, at fair and reasonable rate of compensation, of the telegraph line and railroad for the transmission of dispatches over the said telegraph line and transportation of mails, troops and munitions of was, supplies and public stores upon the said railroad for the Government whenever required.[159]

There was a deficiency of $6,588,900 still due the United States. In negotiations with the company, the United States obtained a decree directing the receivers to pay out of the moneys in their hands a sum of $821,898.[160]

To raise cash for the transactions, the old share-holders, or their successors, who responded to a cash assessment of $15 a share, were given about $9,000,000 of new preferred stock for this cash, and the $61,000,000 of new common stock for their old shares.

At this time E. H. Harriman had become the controlling factor in the reorganization of the Union Pacific Railroad Company. He directed many bold moves to modernize the road and it bring back to glory.

By 1899 company was going to be strong in earning power (it had already paid one dividend of 1½ per cent. on its preferred stock); the shareholders ratified a proposal to increase its common stock by $27,460,000, and to offer new shares in exchange for a like amount of Oregon Short Line stock. This offer was accepted by the Short Line shareholders.

By October, the Union Pacific share-holders were called upon to authorize another stock increase, namely $25,000,000 preferred and $7,718,600 common. The purpose of this was specific.

The old Oregon Short Line & Utah Northern had held, subject to a collateral trust mortgage, $13,827,200 of the of $24,000,000 of the capital stock of the Oregon Railway & Navigation Company. The Union Pacific exercised control of an additional 1,425 miles of the one; and 1,059 miles of the other, gaining an outlet to Portland, Oregon, and to the Pacific Ocean.

Further, through the ownership of $13,251,882 out of the $32,634,482 of the capital stock of the Union Pacific, Denver & Gulf Railway, the Union Pacific exercised actual control of that company's 1,463 miles of railroad, extending the Denver Pacific from Denver south-easterly to Fort Worth, Texas.[161] Through these acquisitions the Union Pacific gained an additional 3,950 miles of track and facilities and equipment.

E. H. Harriman expanded to the west and south the Union Pacific System and by January 1901, Kuhn, Loeb & Co., acting on behalf of the Union Pacific, purchased $75,000,000 par value of the Southern Pacific Company's stock. The total outstanding share capital of this company was $197,832,148. The major portion of the original purchase was obtained by the Harriman Syndicate from Speyer & Co. of New York City.[162] It consisted of the so-called Speyer and Huntington interests. Collis Huntington had died in August 1900, the last of the 'Big Four' of the Central Pacific Railroad.

An important question remains however, as to how this purchase was financed.

Within a few days after the purchases had been consummated (they were announced on February 1, 1901), the Union Pacific advertised a new bond issue of $100,000,000. These bonds bore 4 per cent. interest; matured at the end of ten years, and were convertible, dollar for dollar, into common stock of the company at any time before May 1, 1906. [163]

The end result was that the Union Pacific controlled the Southern Pacific Railroad and all its affiliates making it the largest railroad in the United States.

The plum was the old Central Pacific Railroad connecting Ogden Utah to San Francisco. This, coupled with the Oregon Short Line to Portland, and the Southern Pacific's rail lines to Los Angeles, created a rail empire controlling most of the rail traffic and shipping of goods across the United States.

Harriman went forward with a modernization proposal to bring the railroads up to modern standards of the time. By improving track, locomotives and cars, and increasing the weight of the rails, he was able to increase the productivity of the railroads to such a level as to make the railroads one of the most profitable industries at the time.

The Central branch of the Union Pacific Railroad had been one of the segments allowed to be foreclosed independently. The Central Branch was sold at foreclosure sale on May 23, 1898 by Simon Borg, and Gilmer Clap for $2,350,000. The proceeds of the sale was to cover principal of the First Mortgage Bonds and accrued interest thereon. The United States, holder of the subordinate lien on the road, received nothing. The Attorney General of the United States did not take any judicial action to retrieve the lost indebtedness.[164]

The Refinance of the Central Pacific Railroad

The Central Pacific Railroad pursued a different pathway. As the time came due for the principal of the First Mortgages and the US Government subsidy bonds to be paid, the Central Pacific negotiated with Congress to have legislation extend the payout of the Subsidy bonds, and to defer payments on First Mortgage Bonds. It was then able to reissue new bonds. Collis Huntington notified Speyer & Co of New York in April 1895 to "extend $2,995,000 of its First Mortgage 6% Gold Bonds, maturing July 1 1895, to the first year due for 2 ½ years at 5% principal, and interest payable in United States

Gold Coin."[165] Spreyer and Company agreed to pay at par any bond owner who did not want to extend, otherwise to enter Huntington's own bond account.

Central Pacific Refinancing First Mortgage Bond: Huntington sent a letter to Spreyer and Company to issue an interim bond to cover the First Mortgage Bonds coming due in 1895.

(Courtesy of David Beach cigarboxlabels)

Congress established a commission to conclude a settlement with the Central Pacific Railroad as a part of the Deficiency Appropriation Act of July 7, 1898. The commission considered both the Central Pacific mortgage debt as well as the Western Pacific Railroad which had been combined with the Central in 1869.

A settlement was made on February 1, 1899 with the United States for the principal and interest of the railroad's subsidy U. S. Bonds. The commission arrived at a sum of $58,812,715 being the amount necessary to reimburse the United States for monies paid for the bonds and the ensuing interest on the bonds not paid.

The agreement for settlements was that the company should sign twenty promissory notes dated February 1, 1899 payable respectively, on or before the expiration of each successive six month for ten years, each note being for the sum of $2,940,635. Said notes bore the interest rate of 3 per cent per annum payable semi-annually. The agreement had the condition that if default occurred in any payment of either principal or interest on any of said notes, or any part thereof, then all the said notes then outstanding principal and interest became immediately due.[166]

It was further provided that the payment of interest of said notes was secured by $58,820,000 of face value of a First Refunding Mortgage 4 per cent gold bonds, to be thereafter issued by the Central Pacific Railroad Company. The company was authorized to be issued bonds not to exceed $100,000,000 of refunding bonds. Those bonds were secured by the new mortgage on the railroads, equipment and terminals. The original mortgages were extinguished. (See Appendix 1 for original mortgage). The Refunding bonds issued were 4 per cent, 45-year gold bonds. Any bonds or funds held in the US sinking Fund were surrendered by the government to the Central Pacific Railroad.[167] Speyer and Company acted as the intermediary between the company and the government providing the appropriate legal documents. By accounts of the Treasury, the Sinking Fund contained $5,161,055 in bonds and interest as of July 1897.[168]

The agreement was submitted to the President and approved by him on the 15th day of February. It should be noted that Lyman Gage, Secretary of the Treasury, and John Griggs Attorney General signed the agreement.

By 1908 the Central Pacific Railroad paid off all the Government notes.[169]

In order to create the new First Refunding Mortgage gold bonds, it was considered expedient to promptly readjust the financial affairs of the company, and accordingly a plan was promulgated under date of Feb. 8 1899, and the line declared operative on March 28, 1899.

It provided for the retirement of all the outstanding securities of the company, both stock and bonds, and for the organization of a new company with a share capital of $20,000,000, 4 % cumulative preferred stock, and $67,275,500 common stock with authority to issue $100,000,000 First Refunding Mortgage 4 % gold bonds; and $25,000,000 Second Mortgage at 3% c. gold bonds.

Capital Stock. The preferred stock would be entitled to cumulative dividends up to 4 p. c. per annum, in gold, payable semi-annually, beginning from August 1, 1899, and before payment of any dividend on the common stock.

Thereafter, dividends up to 4 percent per annum could be paid on the common stock, the balance of dividends to be paid pro-rata upon preferred and common stock. The Preferred stock was capital to be used towards the common

stock upon liquidation or dissolution of the company. It was provided that no additional mortgage should be put upon the property, and that no increase in the amount of the preferred stock authorized. This would occur only after obtaining the consent of the holders of 75% of the whole amount of preferred stock, and a majority of the whole amount of common stock at the time outstanding.

FIRST REFUNDING MORTGAGE GOLD BONDS

These bonds were to bear interest from August 1st 1899, free of taxes, and run not less than 45 years. They were to be secured by a mortgage upon all the railroads, terminals and equipment owned by the Central Pacific Railroad Company, covering about 1,349 miles of first-track and about 365 miles of second-track and sidings, or secured by deposit as collateral security for least 90% of the present outstanding First Mortgage Bonds of the Central Pacific Railroad Company of California and the Western Pacific Railroad Company. That included 75% of the aggregate of all the now outstanding bonds of the Central Pacific Railroad Company and of all now

outstanding bonds of the divisional companies-by the consolidation, including First Mortgage Bonds of the Central Pacific Railroad Company of California and Western Pacific Railroad Company.

The US Government was to retain $47,056,000 of the bonds as collateral security for the $47,050,172.48 at 3 % interest on notes remaining in its possession, $51,253,500 to be issued in partial exchange for the outstanding bonds of the company; and the remaining $1,690,500 to be sold to a syndicate to provide cash requirements of the plan.

As the Government notes were paid, an equivalent amount of these bonds would be returned to the company, and the mortgage would provide them the means to reissue at the same or a lower rate of interest. . At no time was the total amount of bonds outstanding at any one time under this mortgage to exceed $100,000,000.

SECOND MORTGAGE GOLD BONDS.
These bonds were to run for 30 years, and bear interest from August 1st 1899, free of taxes.

Of these $13,695,000, these were authorized to be issued in partial exchange for the outstanding bonds of the company; the remaining $11,305,000 to be sold to a syndicate to provide cash requirements of the plan. The following statement shows the amount of cash and new securities offered to the holders of the company's outstanding bonds: *The Los Angeles Herald on July 18, 1899 reported that Speyer & Co., have placed Central Pacific bonds to the amount of $158,000,000.*[170]

They were to be secured upon the same property as the First Refunding Mortgage but subject to the lien thereof, and also "by deposit of all assets now or hereafter held in the sinking funds of the Company" and, by a Trust Deed upon the lands covered by the land-grant mortgage of Oct. 1, 1870. All income derived from the sinking fund securities or from the lands were to be applied primarily to the payment of the interest on these bonds, and afterward to the payment of any prior fixed charges; but so long as no default existed in respect to principal or interest on these bonds. The company was able to sell sinking fund securities and the lands and apply the
proceeds thereof to 'the retirement of these bonds when they can be purchased at not above par and accrued interest.' In the event the bonds could not be purchased at par and interest, the amount in the company's treasury available for that purpose would be applied as deemed necessary, for the retirement either of these bonds or of any bonds secured by prior liens upon the property. It was provided that no other new mortgage (except to refund the First Refunding Bonds or the Second Mortgage Bonds) was to be made upon the

properties covered by the mortgages securing the First Refunding Bonds or the Second Mortgage Bonds, so long as any of such bonds of either class - or any of the 4 percent gold bonds of the Southern Pacific Co., were outstanding; and that no other new mortgage was to be made by the company upon said properties except with the assent of the holders of 75% of the preferred stock and a majority of the common stock at the time outstanding.

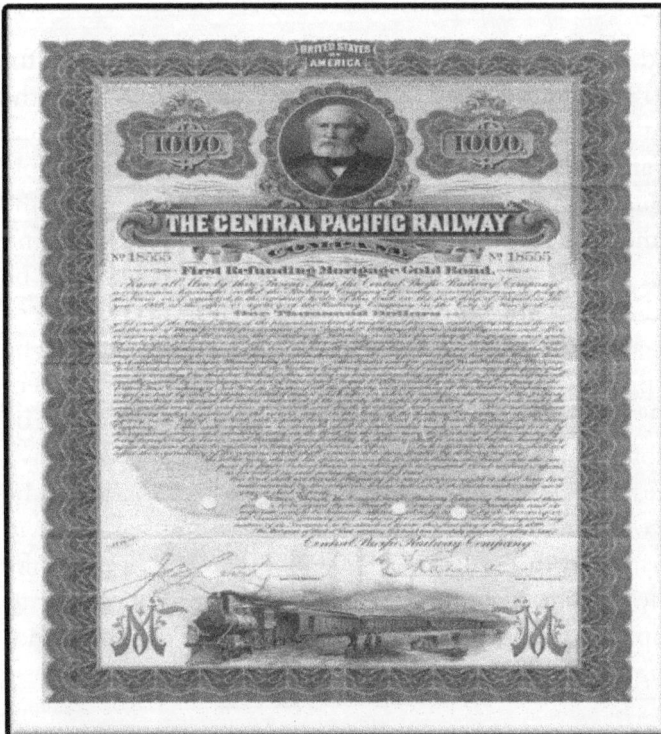

Central Pacific Railroad First Refunding Mortgage Gold Bond; Bonds were issued as part of the reorganization of the road in 1899.

(Courtesy of David Beach, of cigarboxlabels)

Distribution of Securities

Common Stock: It was provided that the entire issue of the new common stock should be sold to a syndicate and offered for sale to depositors of the old common stock at $2 per share. The Southern Pacific Co. offered to purchase all of the old common stock deposited under the plan, and to issue therefore share for share in its own common stock and 25% thereof in the new 4% gold bonds of the Southern Pacific Co.

Preferred Stock. The new preferred stock was authorized for the following purposes: $12,000,000 to be delivered to the Southern Pacific Co. in consideration of the issue of an equal amount at par value of the Southern Pacific Co.'s new 4% gold bonds. Such bonds, after providing for the requirements of the readjustment, was to be applied only to betterments and additions to this company's property; $3,000,000 was to be delivered to the same company in consideration of the issue of an equal amount at par value of its said 4% gold bonds, to be used to provide additional funds, if required, for the payment of the 3% notes to the United States, and thereafter to be applied only for betterments and additions to this company's properties; the remaining $5,000,000 was to be reserved to be issued from time to time to an equal amount at par value in consideration of the issue of $5,000,000 of the Southern Pacific Company's 4% gold bonds for betterments and additions to this company's properties (bonds to be issued at the rate of not exceeding $200,000 par value thereof per annum).

A year later in August 1900, Collis Huntington died at age 79. This was the end of the Big Four of the Central Pacific and the Southern Pacific Railroads and opened opportunity for new people to take charge.

EXISTING BONDS AND STOCK TO BE DEPOSITED.	EACH $1,000 RECEIVES.		
	Cash.*	New 4 p. c. First Refunding Mortgage Gold Bonds.	New 3½ p. c. Mortgage Gold Bonds.
Central Pacific RR. Co. 1st Mtge. Bonds, Series A........	$83 33	$1,000	$50
Series B, C, D, E, F, G, H and I........................	29 17	1,000	50
Western Pacific RR. Co. 1st Mtge. Bonds, Series A and B......	35 00	1,000	50
Central Pacific RR. Co. (San Josquin Vy.) Branch 1st Mtge. Bonds.	50 00	1,000	75
Central Pacific RR. Co. Land Bonds ....:	41 67	500	700
Central Pacific RR. Co. 50-yr. 6 p. c. Bonds......................	50 00	500	900
Central Pacific RR. Co. 50-yr. 5 p. c. Bonds	41 67	500	800
California & Oregon RR. Co. and Central Pacific RR. Co., successor, 1st Mtge. Bonds, Series A and B........................	29 17	1,000	200

* Interest from the due dates of the last coupons matured prior to Feb. 1, 1899, at the same rates up to the date when the new bonds begin to bear interest—namely, Aug. 1, 1899.

Notification of Payment of Coupons by the Central Pacific Railroad

In 1901 E. H. Harriman successfully bought a controlling interest in the Southern Pacific Railroad and tied it into the Union Pacific System.

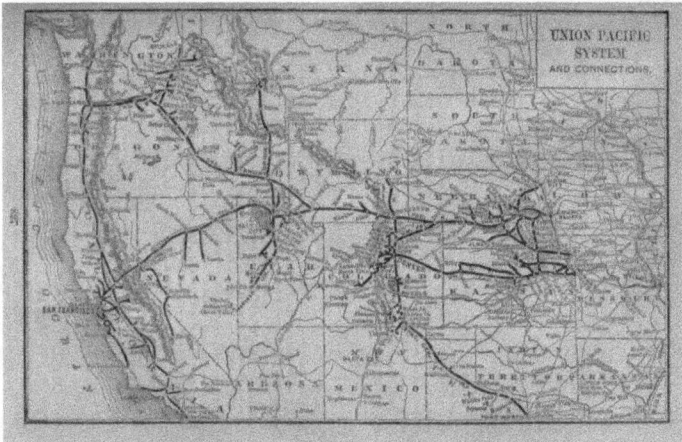

Union Pacific Railroad System as a result of the Harriman expansion

By 1908 all the government subsidy debt had been paid.

The Sioux City and Pacific Railroad

The Sioux City and Pacific Railroad had been purchased by the Chicago and Northwestern System. In January 1, 1898 the railroad defaulted on the Subsidy Bonds of $1,628,000. The First Mortgage Bonds also matured at that date. In legislation of June 6, 1900 Congress authorized the Secretary of Treasury; Secretary of Interior and the Attorney General of the United Sates to resolve the Government debt of the railroad. Pursuant to the legislation, government subsidy bonds were offered for sale on June 30, 1901, after public notice. The U. S. Government sold to the Chicago and North Western Railroad Company for $1,872,000 in cash and $250,841 of receipts earned by the Sioux City and Pacific Railroad Company for transportations services performed for the Government, totaling $2,122,841.[32] The total bond debt including interest was $4,180,018 which resulted in the Government losing $2,057,177 in interest paid on the subsidy bonds

This resolved the last of the Government's involvement with the Transcontinental Railroad financing

---

[32] Railroad Commission report   of 1901

Chapter 17

Kerr & Company and the Paramount Lien Bonds

During the course of the research on Governor Durkee, documentation relating to his Paramount Lien bonds ownership led to an examination of his business interests.

However, in the records of the Union Pacific Railroad housed at the Nebraska State archives; Union Pacific Collection in Lincoln Nebraska, and the University of Iowa Library, Special Collection in Iowa City Iowa there was no reference to Governor Durkee or his ownership of Paramount Lien bonds.

Neither was he listed in the Ledger books which detailed expenses and distribution of First Mortgage Bonds, although it is noteworthy that in 1866-68, the Union Pacific Railroad did give "Certificates" for First Mortgage Bonds[171].

Many bonds in those records were assigned to "Clarke-Dodge." This may have been a pseudo reference for Thomas Clark Durant, Vice President of the Union Pacific, and General Grenville Dodge, Chief Engineer.

Significant documents referencing Governor Durkee were found in the correspondence of Durant's son in 1914 to 1917 concerning bond records at the Union Pacific headquarters under his control.

The Central Pacific Railroad Archives, housed in the Syracuse University Library Special Collections, and the Stanford University Library Special Collections were examined for Paramount and Government bond transactions. There were no references to Governor Durkee.

Still, it is known in correspondence between Charles Crocker and Collis Huntington, that Governor Durkee was engaged in negotiations during his trip out to Sacramento California, later acting as a liaison between Brigham Young as the Central Pacific approached Utah.[172]

While there is no direct mention of Governor Durkee owning First Mortgage bonds in those letters, they do imply that he does, by assumption of his interests being served when acting as intermediary "for tie contractors on the Bear River and for buying coal properties".[173]

Durkee, it is known, had advanced considerable money into a joint venture business called Kerr & Company. Their partnership, during his lifetime, showed commercial ventures of multiple kinds including banking and finance; construction; dry goods shipping, supplies and provision. By the turn of the century, the company became a banking enterprise in late 1869 the assets of the bank were taken over by the First National Bank of Utah.

In the biography of Alexander Toponce, an entrepreneurial shipping contractor and partner to Kerr and Company during the construction of the Transcontinental Railroad, a narrative describes the transaction above mentioned.[174] The delivery "for tie contractors on the Bear River and for buying coal properties" was particularly mentioned. Toponce started out with the purchase of 79 wagons and six yoke of oxen for each wagon to haul Wells Fargo & Company cargo. Wells Fargo, knowing that the market for hauling cargo by wagon-train would be displaced by the Union Pacific Railroad coming West, offered deals. Toponce was able to buy the ox and wagon-train "Cheap."

Governor Charles Durkee; John W. Kerr and Bill Kiskaden had contracted to provide 100,000 railroad ties to the Union Pacific Railroad in July 1868. The ties were to be delivered to Hilliard, Wyoming, located about 15 miles east of Evanston Wyoming, a terminus of the Union Pacific Railroad. [33]

The railroad ties were cut on the headwaters of the Bear River between Montpelier and Soda Springs Idaho.

Kiskaden sold out his one third share of the venture to Toponce.

Toponce stated that the Union Pacific paid about 80 cents a peace for the 100,000 ties. Toponce also stated that they were paid in cash, and the balance in Union Pacific First Mortgage Bonds - due in thirty years. Toponce elaborated that the bonds were discounted at 15 cents on the dollar. They were left in the hands of John Kerr. Thus in 1868, by this accounting, the Durkee/Kiskaden/Kerr sale of ties to the Union Pacific resulted in a documented transaction that included Union Pacific First Mortgage Bonds.

Union Pacific contracts for ties were not unusual. Several records attest to similar transactions: One is registered in 1867 for 501 ties, paid for at the rate of $500.[175]

---

[33] Bill Kiskaden was the uncle of Maude Adams, a celebrated actress who was born in Salt Lake City Utah. By the 1890's Maud Adams advanced in a career to be one of the highest paid theatrical performers of her time.

Later in October 1868, Toponce received a contract from a Jim Noonan to haul 100,000 ties from Bear River up to Soda Springs to Corinne, Utah. Corinne was about 27 miles northwest of Ogden. The contract was written with the Central Pacific Railroad, probably initiated by Governor Durkee. The delivery date was to be before "Iron of the Railroads crossed Bear River." The ties were held up by the ice freezing over Bear River and were not moved until April, just as the Union Pacific crossed the river. The ties did not arrive until May 15, 1869 - after the joining of the roads had occurred. The Central Pacific Railroad refused to take possession of the ties.

According to Toponce, all the bonds from both contracts were turned over to Charles Durkee, adding, "and the bonds have never been paid yet as far as I know."[34]

The Utah Northern Railroad was not started until August 1871, and built by volunteer Mormon laborers extending 75 miles north to the Cache Valley. For this route, the railroad offered rail competition to wagon hauling to Idaho and Montana via Corinne, north of Ogden. The Utah Northern Railroad was a narrow gage railroad of three foot width.

Here, the recollection of Toponce appears to differ with some factors of timing and funding. The Utah Central Railroad was the branch line from Ogden to Salt Lake City and critical to the development of lower Utah.

---

[34] *Reminiscenses of Alexander Toponce [1839-1923]" Autobiography at age 80, c. 1919.*: Century Printing Co., ©1923] [Salt Lake City, Utah

Brigham Young, as leader of a growing community of Mormons, had anticipated this spur of transportation when trying to lobby the Central Pacific to come south of the Great Salt Lake. Young organized the Utah Central railway in 1869, and started serious construction on the road immediately after the joining of the Central Pacific and Union Pacific Railroads.

As of 1869, after completing work on the Transcontinental, Brigham Young and the Mormon workers on the roads of both the Union Pacific and Central Pacific had not been paid.
Young sent Bishop Sharp to Boston to negotiate payment of over $940,000 from the Union Pacific. In negotiations, they finally agreed to accept $231,000 in Notes; $50,000 in cash; $10,000 in transportation of evangelized immigrant Mormons arriving to the United States; and $599,000 in Railroad material.[176] The latter the track; engines and cars were used to construct the Utah Central Railroad to Salt Lake City.

The Company issued a First Mortgage for bonds and stock to finance the completion of construction of the Utah Central.[177]

With 100,000 ties immediately available in Corinne - having been rejected by the Central Pacific, in place adjacent to the tracks of the Transcontinental Railway, it is clear that those ties were used to build rail track from Ogden to Salt Lake City. This is probably the actual use of the ties, and explains the fact that the Utah Central Railroad was completed by January 1870 in such short order. Governor Durkee while alive, might well have traveled on the railway section just completed for his trip back to Kenosha, just prior to his death.

Payment for those ties was therefore in all probability made in First Mortgage Bonds, consistent with the account of Toponce.

In addition to Toponce, others sources cite the existence of bonds in the possession of Durkee.

Another significant reference is made, years later, regarding Governor Durkee having First Mortgage Bonds. This is found in the deposition of John T. Dewees, former Congressman from Raleigh North Carolina, 1868-1869. Dewees lived in Washington DC, and gave two depositions concerning meetings with Governor Durkee.[178]

Dewees stated that Durkee was in a co-partnership with Kerr and that for some time had been engaged in furnishing railroad cross-ties to the Union Pacific and Central Pacific Railroad.

Dewees stated that he met Durkee on his way home to Kenosha in January 1870 in Cheyenne Wyoming. In that conversation, Governor Durkee had stated that besides receiving $50,000 from Kerr, he had a large amount of the said Construction Bonds amounting to many hundreds of thousands of dollars, and that he had also deposited a large amount in a New York Bank. He did not remember the name.

In a second deposition in 1901, Dewees stated that the Casemate Brothers of Paynesville, Ohio, also had the contract with the Union Pacific Railway Company to lay, construct, back-fill and surface the track lines, and furnish the ties from Omaha to the junction of the Central Pacific Railway. They also furnished ties for Union and Central Pacific Railway Companies. Governor Durkee, he said, was also furnishing ties to their subcontractors.

Governor Durkee at his times in Kenosha, had been deeply involved in the lumber and shipping business, and had full knowledge of the requirements of delivering timber. Also not mentioned, the requirements for additional construction lumber for railroad bridges and buildings were required.

Dewees also stated they were paid partly in money, and partly in Union Pacific First Mortgage Bonds; also in First Mortgage Bonds of the Central Pacific Railway.

At the meeting in Cheyenne Wyoming, Dewees further stated "I did not examine all the bonds Governor Durkee had; there were a large amount of bonds in his possession, but a large number of them for $2500 to $5000, were also there."[35]

Franklin Head, former Indian Agent and associate of Durkee, also sheds light on Governor Durkee's bond ownership.

In the deposition of Franklin Head at that Court of Claims he said that the firm "Was...also engaged in the Railroad tie and lumber and timber business. I think they had something like $20,000 in ties and the circumstance were these.
They had cut them up on Bear River and [were]expected to flow them down the river in time to sell them to the Union Pacific Road, but before they got them down, the road was finished and then there was no market for them, and they felt it was a slow asset."[179]

Clifton Finch of Denver, Colorado also deposed in the Court of Claims "That I distinctly recall the statement of H. M. Hoxie 'that Governor Durkee, of the Territory of Utah, not only guided the legislation creating the railroad corporations and business destiny of these Pacific Railroads, but, he also furnished the original cash required.' That I have knowledge and basis of fact, that Mr. Hoxie procured the original construction contract, and the Governor Charles Durkee also acted as his bondsman to the United States Government." [180]

---

[35] Government subsidy bonds were in the denominations of $500, $1,000, $5,000 and $10,000.

"Mr. Hoxie further stated that Governor Durkee had acquired many millions of dollars worth of construction bonds of the Union Pacific Railroad in lieu of cash for the supplies which he furnished to the construction companies thru his firm, John W. Kerr & Co. , Salt Lake City, Utah."

Finch had more to report about Durkee's concerns. "..while traveling with me in my private car between Houston and San Antonio, that that Attorney Robert Lovett Sr. stated that he was greatly concerned over the fact that [the] banker in New York had pledged as collateral for the contracts with the Cleveland companies the First Mortgage Bonds of their railroads, or as they were called in those days of construction, the construction bonds, which were issued under the Acts of Congress passed 1862-1864." [181]

Financial resources and cash were clearly within reach of Durkee for business transactions: William Kiskaden, earlier partner of Kerr & Company with Durkee, was a shipper of freighted gold and supplies from Colorado after the discoveries at Pike's Peak in 1859. He and John F. Noonan, a Kansas freighter who had a small bank in Salt Lake City, combined with John Kerr & Company to form a private bank and became its cashier. The assets of this bank increased from $165,000 in July 1866 to more than $400,000 in January 1869, (29 months). The bank was subsequently taken over by First National Bank of Utah.

In summation, Governor Durkee was in company with Kerr and Company at the time of its creation, and its construction and various operations. Especially in the delivery of railroad ties and lumber from the Bear Lake of Idaho to the Union Pacific Railroad, and the Central Pacific Railroad, wherein we find evidence of his disposition.

He received partial payment in Union Pacific Railroad Paramount Lien Bonds, which he retained. He had the opportunity to take a portion of the bonds to Kenosha Wisconsin when he went East to record his Will.

It appears that he did not travel East to New York or Washington DC. His lawyer James Doolittle, a Senator from Wisconsin until March 1869 could have taken possession of the Bonds and delivered them to Durkee's bank in New York, as a possibility.

Durkee's estate was not completely recorded, and it is clear he had a considerable fortune at his disposal. His transaction on the sale of farm land in 1866 had netted him over $225,000. He could have used part of these proceeds, or others unrecorded, to purchase bonds from contractors in Utah and Wyoming.

Chapter 18

The Mystery of the Bonds

In that Legal cases had been filed from 1893 to 1969 trying to prove the case of the missing funds from the Transcontinental Railroad Bonds, there is the question of accountability of the Governor Durkee bonds.

In researching the records of Governor Durkee, the Treasury, Congress, the Union Pacific and the Central Pacific, it is possible to establish certain basic facts which could lead to a conclusion.

Jacob Souders Book, *History of the Pacific Railroads Co's First Mortgage 30-Year 6 Percent Paramount Lien Bonds having Priority over the Subsidy Bonds of the United States,* presents a detailed chronology and record of the search for the First Mortgage bonds of Governor Charles Durkee from 1865 to the Court of Claims Case 18003. Souder was himself acquainted with Governor Durkee, and being a lawyer, was cognizant of the legal parameters as they unfolded in the case subsequently. From an historical point of view, Souder's book remains a contemporaneous record of the events and was well informed. It is a commendable work. However, possibly due to the passage of time, much elucidation can be added to those assumptions.

In that Souder's asserts certain findings, we are today able to verify them against original documents found variously in the National Archives files, Library of Congress, the Syracuse University Library's Collis Huntington Central Pacific Files, the University of Iowa Special Collections of the Union Pacific Railroad, the Nebraska State Archives Collections of the Union Pacific Railroad, the Church of the Latter Day Saints Library Collections of Brigham Young records and other repositories, such that we have a digital record of all documents pertinent to the Durkee mystery.

On the questions of enquiry, it is asked: Did Governor Durkee obtaining all the First Mortgage Paramount Lien Bonds of the six Transcontinental Railroads? Further, how did any funds arrive in possession of the U. S. Treasury?

The first issue was to search for the Paramount Lien Bonds in question. Did such bonds exist today?

The Transcontinental Railroads have left both an industrial legacy and a cultural narrative to the American story. For many, they are today a topic of great intellectual interest, from industrial technology to financial history. Yet, no door into 19th century bonds would be as revealing as the bonds themselves, including their financial structure; their meaning to society, their management, and the circumstances that gave them legal tender and comparative valuations. It therefore became immediately clear that insight into transactions required an intimacy with the character of bonds in order to understand how people responded to them, and why. Especially regarding the Transcontinental Railways.

Collectors of Bonds are an avid group of enthusiasts who show care and knowledge in the intricate details of bonds. Many of them were contacted with quiet questions. Further, searches for bonds led to remarkable repositories demonstrating responsible preservation and security of their archives. One bond of the Central Pacific Railroad was found at the Museum of Finance in New York City and copied.(See Back Cover). Thus, from their appearance, size and details, the shadow of the players was cast upon them.

In discussions with various bond dealers, it appears that Transcontinental Railroad bonds did not survive. There were two Central Pacific bonds in private collections and considered extremely valuable as collectibles.

The underlying mortgages of the railroads were also researched since they accounted for much documentation. Copies of the Central Pacific Mortgage and the Union Pacific Mortgage were found in a Durkee court case in San Francisco, long ago forgotten! These were copied from the originals at their Court House, notarized in 1906. The mortgages gave the exact conditions of ownership on the bond, and they listed the Trustees. The clues were shy, but promising to tell more.
At the same time developing was the second question. Did the bonds of Charles Durkee rest with the U. S. Treasury on April 22, 1884?

This assertion was s made by Leonard Blaisdell who visited Secretary Folger and First Comptroller Judge William Lawrence, that they did. Several questions remained.

On this examination, the main question was about the meeting itself, and what was asserted. How did the meeting occur? There are depositions from several people, including the Secretary of State[36] that the meeting did occur. Further, Blaisdell's correspondence with Judge Lawrence documents the meeting. That gave the matter significance.

Next, the matter of the bonds being presented by Secretary Folger at the meeting had to be explored. From the comments of Blaisdell and correspondence from Lawrence, bonds were presented, but how many?

Blaisdell stated that "all of the bonds were presented." This would require that 64,623 or more bonds, plus an equal number of coupon sheets to accompany each bond would have had to be visible in a furnished room, (not a vault?). The sheer size of "all of the bonds presented" would have been over 10 feet tall when stacked together. This in all probability did not occur. If it had, Blaisdell might have used different language to describe such a burden. Blaisdell's statement opened the door to some suspicions.

Then Blaisdell was shown a smaller amount of First Mortgage Bonds. Could Souder's book shed light on what he meant perhaps?

Souder offered a detailed explanation of how the Durkee bonds came to arrive at Treasury. He showed how Collis Huntington of the Central Pacific Railroad, and E. H. Rollins as Secretary of the Union & Kansas Pacific Railroads delivered '$64,616,000 First Mortgage Bonds' to the Secretary of the Treasury under power of attorney granted to Senator James Doolittle. Souder asserted that Huntington and Rollins had all Durkee's bonds with them, which ended up in the Treasury, in essence, by a default action of receivership…etc. etc.

---

[36] Fredk. T. Frelinghuysen Letter, See Appendix II

Clearly, this warranted further explanation, its veracity now questionable.

Souder said that this occurred January 1, 1868. (Perhaps a misprint?).If this occurred, then it should have occurred January 1, 1869, one year later: The Congressional Act that would support this claim was not approved until much later 1869.[182]

Further, as per the correspondence of Collis Huntington, we find that he was *not* in Washington DC at either date stated. Other details of that year were lacking in consistency, such as the dates, times and locations of the Western Pacific Railroad bonds being issued; allowances for delivery of bonds still being printed in San Francisco California.[183]

We find that the Union Pacific Railroad deposited with the Treasury the sum of $1,600,000 in First Mortgage Bonds late May 1869. In another document the Union Pacific states that they deposited $3,000,000 in bonds to the Treasury stated by the President and Secretary of the Company. [184]

The Central Pacific Railroad deposited $4,000,000. Further, they were personally delivered by Collis Huntington just after May 28, 1869.

How were the Bonds of Charles Durkee involved?

It is known that President Grant in 1869 felt that the railroads should provide security before getting any subsidy bonds from the government. Congress passed a Resolution known as the Act of April 1869: Railroads should deposit Securities with the US Treasury before any government subsidies could be given. For the railroads, this new requirement was problematic. Where should the security funds come from? The Union Pacific had little money, we find, approximately $600,000 as reflected in their accounts. Further, even with government subsidy bonds, they needed *cash* for construction, labor, supplies, services and ties for track.

At approximately that time, we find in records the Metropolitan National Bank of New York depositing with the Comptroller of the Currency $2,000,000 of the subsidy bonds, in exchange for cash. [185]

Clearly, the railroads are seen in desperate need of funds. While they do need the government subsidy bonds to finish up the Transcontinental, they are more in need of cash.

Thus, if they had asked the bank to convert their subsidy bonds into cash, that presupposes they had already somehow qualified to receive the government subsidy bonds, that is, by meeting the security requirements with the Treasury in advance of receiving the subsidy bonds.

Further, the problem for the research was that the Souder bonds transaction, as he described, could not have occurred: He asserted that Governor Durkee had an account and deposit box with the Metropolitan National Bank of New York, and the U. S. Subtreasury took possession of the papers, later, when the bank went into receivership, thereby allowing the Treasury to assumed possession of the papers of Governor Durkee.

In actuality the Metropolitan National Bank experienced a cash shortfall on May 14, 1884. Marine National Bank closed its doors at 11:30 of the 14th of May as part of the ensuing bank panic. The Directors of the bank reorganized the finances and brought in additional capital. Metropolitan National Bank reopened its doors the next day and did *not* go into receivership.[186] Metropolitan National Bank was still in existence while Court case 18003 was in progress, yet the bank records were never investigated. Actually the banks still in existence as Chase Manhattan Bank.

Moreover, that would have had to happened *prior* to 22 April, 1884 in order for Durkee's bonds to be in the possession of the Treasury when Blaisdell apparently saw them.

More importantly, then, were the circumstances and characteristics of Durkee's bonds, and how did Governor Durkee obtain First Mortgage bonds?

It is documented that he was in partnership with John Kerr and 'Kerr and Co.' They were supplying railroad ties and other materials. Documentation shows they received First Mortgage bonds of the Union Pacific Railroads as partial payment for services rendered. Not mentioned are other services that Kerr and Co. provided both the Union Pacific and Central Pacific Railroads.

In addition Governor Durkee had outside funds from Kenosha, and could have been purchasing bonds from other contractors who were partially paid in bonds, but not readily convertible on the frontier.

Transporting bonds to the East coast was a dangerous proposition in 1869. There were stage coach robberies and other mishaps. Governor Durkee traveled to Kenosha in January 1869 to record his Will and brought his wife back to Salt Lake City. This would have given him an opportunity to take back East bonds he had obtained, and to meet with his attorney James Doolittle, also a Senator from Wisconsin. In his final trip back to Kenosha in January 1870, it was stated in a deposition that he had bonds in his possession, see Dewees.[187]

The next question was a need to establish the nature and intentions of his ownership of the First Mortgage Bonds. This would have occurred in two ways. An 'assignment document' specifying his ownership, or the bonds had an ownership stamp or signature on the bond.

Ownership Statement Central Pacific First Mortgage Bond as writton on back of bond.

(The Museum of American Finance, Wall Street New York City)

In the ledgers of the Union Pacific Railroad for 1868, they list Certificates for First Mortgage Bonds.[188] This would have allowed the transfer of rights and could be collected at the Union Pacific Railroad Headquarters in Boston. The second was an actual stamp or signing on the bond. This was demonstrated on the Central Pacific Bond found at the Museum of Finance in New York City.

It would be a considerable effort to sign an ownership statement on each bond. It should be noted that Leland Stanford had to sign over 25,000 the bonds individually. The method of documentation of ownership would have been a stamp on the back of the bond, with the owner's name added. Considering the large amount of bonds in question, it would have been a large task.

How did the bonds get to the Treasury? There are several alternatives. Governor Durkee could have had Senator Doolittle deposit them with the Treasury between 1868 and 1869, perhaps to support the Union Pacific Railroads requirement to deposit security bonds with Treasury?

The circumstances of about mid-1869 were these: On May 1, 1869, the Union Pacific Railroad carried on her account books a balance of only $610,114[189]. When the Union Pacific Railroad was faced with a financial shortfall, in May 1869, Union Pacific officials like Thomas Clark Durant, Vice President of the Railroad, in Utah, made financial arrangements with the Railroad to use Durkee's bonds as collateral for the U. S. Treasury as required by the recently enacted resolution by Congress. Note in latter Souder's activities he searches for a contract between Durant and Durkee made in 1869. In turn when returning East, one of Durkee's intention was to visit the Union Pacific Railroad offices to collect bonds. By accounts, the Union Pacific finances had improved by the beginning of 1870's. The bonds then deposited with the Treasury were retained but they had an assignment to Governor Durkee on them. Those bonds were never returned. Thomas Durant died in 1885.

Redemption would be for Treasury to have returned the Securities to the Railroad Company. That is, with evidence in the records of Durant and Dodge: This may well explain the effort of Souder to examine their records, years later, held in the possession of Durant's son.[190]

On further elaboration, with the Railroad crisis of having to find securities before being able to receive government subsidies, It is entirely possible that Durkee offered the bonds or certificates owed to him by the Union Pacific for services rendered, valued roughly at somewhere between $500,000 and $2,000,000. Durkee would have made this offer to the Union Pacific, specifically, his friends Durant and Dodge in order to allow them to meet the requirement of the US Treasury and finish the railroad. We know that Durant and Dodge were in Utah for the joining of the railroads at Promontory in May, 1869 where they met with Durkee at this time. In accepting Durkee's 'assignment' of bonds owed him by the Union Pacific to meet their requirement with Treasury, they would have given Durkee a contract certificate of ownership receipt, if not an Assignment Instrument of Loan Agreement, - promising to repay him in due course for his Coupon Certificates, once released by Treasury… Jacob Souder and his daughter were trying to find these documents from Durant's son in 1914.

At about the same time the Union Pacific Railroad deposited $1,600,000 of First Mortgage bonds with the U. S. Treasury, yet they did not list them in their account books.[191]

The Treasury stated that later that they had redeemed the security bonds to the Union Pacific Railroad upon completion, but there is some question of this occurrence. Also, the Union Pacific had issued $1,600,000 of bonds not authorized. This was again observed in the account books as the issuance of bond serial number 28,999 to Oak Ames.[192]

The explanation that Governor Durkee had taken "Certificates for First Mortgage Bonds" from the Union Pacific Railroad, and that the actual bonds were in Boston Headquarters of the railroad is feasible. The certificates could easily have been confused with the actual bonds.

This provides a viable opportunity to occur in the time frame of 1869.

An alternative is that Caroline Durkee or James Doolittle had deposited the bonds with the Treasury for safe keeping and that the Treasury did not know what to do with them. This would explain Secretary of Treasury wanting to resolve the issue in 1884.

This is found in the results of the receivership of the Union Pacific Railroad and the reorganization of the Central Pacific Railroad authorized by Congress. The confusion arises from a provision of the Congressional Act of March 3, 1887. Section 4 authorizing the President to direct the Secretary of the Treasury to assume responsibility of the First Mortgage Bonds of the railroads in order to protect the U. S. Subsidy Bonds. This provision was not invoked.

Instead the Union Pacific Railroad was sold at auction to the Trustee of the First Mortgage bond receivership, the U. S. Government subsidy bonds paid, and the Union Pacific under the new reorganization allowed to issue new First Mortgage bonds, with the old First Mortgage bonds either being paid off, or the owners given new refinancing as First Mortgage bonds backed by funds of the railroad.

The Union Pacific issued $100,000,000 in new bonds, more than enough to cover the old bonds. The Central Pacific Railroad, through Congressional Action, agreed to pay the subsidy bonds over a 10 year period with payments every 6 months and issue new refinancing First Mortgage bonds which offered the old bond (Paramount Lien Bonds) holders the option of payment or exchange for refinanced bonds.

The payout of the old First Mortgage bonds had to come from the railroads not the U. S. Treasury.

If there were bonds to be cashed by the Treasury they had to be paid by the Union Pacific or the Central Pacific Railroads, in or about 1893 to about 1903.

The U. S. Government Railroad Subsidy Bonds came due at the same time. The U. S. Treasury issued a notice that the bonds were being "called" and instructions for redeeming the bonds. In the records of the Treasury Department, the bonds were very quickly redeemed and paid with records of those who redeemed they, the railroad involved, and the amount of the bonds.[193]

The records of the exchange or payout of the First mortgage bonds would be in the financial records of the Union Pacific Railroad. Since the bonds were 50 years bonds, they would have still been valid to 1950.

In 1937 the Union Pacific lawyers were worried about this fact.

The Union Pacific Railroad was preparing financial papers for the redemption of the Refinancing First Mortgage Bonds coming due in the future. In a letter to Averill Harriman, the President of the Union Pacific in May 1940, they state that "to take bonds in lieu of $14,098,000 old bonds (Paramount Lien Bonds) now in the treasury, and 4,300,000 not now being refunded.[194] Bonds as of 1940 were still in the Treasury.

The Court Cases

The court case brought by Leonard Blaisdell had problems. He did not have the authorization of the Kenosha Probate Court nor the support of Caroline Durkee. This created creditability issues for the court and also, before hand, with the Treasury in 1884. This continued into 1930s with the split in interests of the Caroline Durkee estate and other heirs based on the probate court in Salt Lake City Utah.

The Court of Claims case was dismissed on the basis of the claim of demurrer. That is, while the assertion of Blaisdell in the complaint may have be true, they did not provide sufficient evidence for the plaintiff to prevail in the lawsuit.

Blaisdell and Kuykendall sued the Secretary of Treasury Lyman Gage and the Attorney General in the U. S. Supreme Court of the District of Columbia in 1901. There, the Treasurer refused to cooperate and said that there were no records of any Durkee Bonds.

In May 1900 the Attorney General Hon. John W. Griggs submitted documents covering the aspects of the agreement of ending the receivership of the Union Pacific Railroad, including the allowance of the refinance of the First Mortgage bonds in existence. He was working with Secretary of the Treasury Lyman Gage in the negotiations and had certain knowledge as to the disposition of any first mortgage bonds of the Union Pacific Railroad[195]. Yet they both provided no information to the court case in sworn testimony. The Attorney General and Secretary of Treasury both had knowledge of the First Mortgage bonds and refused to provide that information.

The court cases continued to 1970 with more refusal by the Treasury Department to provide conclusive proof to the negative. They provided a defense of Statute of Limitations, Latches, Res Judicata, and Demurrer. The U. S. Government never put up a defense.

The case of the two treasury accounts of Trust Fund Accounts Number 20X8881 and 20X1807 has not been verified.

An alternative proposal to the Durkee bonds is that there were bonds about $500, 000 to $2,000,000 in value with coupons at the Treasury on April 22 1884.

They disappeared between that time and Blaisdell's return three months later. That would explain First comptroller Lawrence's evasiveness. They were either lost, mixed with other bonds or stolen. The bonds could have been redeemed when due and coupons cashed in between. The bonds were Bearer bonds, and the Railroad companies kept no records of ownership. Thus when cashed the owners were simply paid or given new bonds. If the funds were kept within the Treasury, they would have not been of significant amounts to have created any financial hardship on the Treasury to pay out. The issue would be the embarrassment of either the theft or mistake leading into the law suits.

End Notes of the Book

[1] Gideon Truesdell: Profiles of a Nineteenth Century Wisconsin Lumber Barron, by Robert W. Fay

[2] Charles Durkee, Pioneer, Politician, Philanthropist Thesis Arthur unknown

[3] Letter. Durkee to President Johnson, DSC 9835, May 18, 1866, NARA State Department Files

[4] Harrington was the initial discover of Silver in Pahranagat

[5] Second inventory of Durkee Estate, Kenosha Probate Court

[6] Deposition Franklin Head Court Case 18003, dsc304

[7] Letter. Durkee to Steward, Jan 27, 1868, DSC 9840, NARA State Department Files

[8] Empire Express, Building the First Transcontinental Railroad, David Howard Bain Page. 364

[9] Ibid Page 365

[10] Ibid

[11] Ibid page 489

[12] Ibid Page. 489

[13] Deseret Evening News, May 10, 11, 1869.

[14] Deseret Evening News, May 10, 11, 1869

[15] Desert Evening News July 6, 1869

[16] Daily Union Vedette, August 18, 1865, p. 2.

[17] Early Mining in Southwest Utah and the Southeastern Nevada, 1864-1873, The meadow Valley, Pahranagat, and Pioche Mining Rushes By John Michael Bourne Page XV

[18] Making Space of the Western Frontier: Mormons, Miners and Southern Piautes, By Paul Reeve Page 34

[19] Ibid Page 41

[20] Ibid

[21] Ibid Page 40

[22] Letter from Charles Durkee, F.H. Head and Amos Reed to Senator Doolittle, 4 December 1865, National Archives

[23] RAYMOND, R.W., 1869, USBM MINERALS YEARBOOK FOR 1868

[24] Early Mining in Southwest Utah and the Southeastern Nevada, 1864-1873: The meadow Valley, Pahranagat, and Pioche Mining Rushes By John Michael Bourne

[25] Ibid

[26] Other references are BROWNE, J.R, 1868, MINERAL RESOURCES OF STATES AND TERRITORIES WEST OF THE ROCKY MOUNTAINS, 1867 P. 339-340. .

[27] Utah's Black Hawk War, by John A. Peterson, University of Utah Press

[28] Ibid and Head to Cooley, 30 April 1866

[29] Ibid

[30] Ibid 260-61

[31] Letter Franklin Head to Hon. N Taylor, Commissioner ,Jan 20, 1868, National Archives Records of the Bureau of Indian Affairs.

[32] Utah's Black Hawk War, by John A. Peterson, University of Utah Press.

[33] Governor Durkee's Address to the Territorial Legislative assembly, December 10, 1866, in the governor Messages

[34] Letter, Governor Durkee Salt Lake City Utah to the Commissioner of Indian Affairs, July 25, 1868

[35] Letter Franklin Head to Hon. N Taylor, Commissioner ,Jan 20, 1868, National Archives Records of the Bureau of Indian Affairs

[36] Ibid

[37] Charles Durkee, Pioneer, Politician, Philanthropist, Thesis, Author unknown

[38] Milwaukee Daily Sentinel, (Milwaukee, WI) Monday, January 17, 1870; Issue 13; Vol. A

[39] Charles Durkee Will Probated in Kenosha Wisconsin, Spring 1870 See Appendix IV

[40] Ibid

[41] Ibid, The Telescope is still at the Durkee House in the Kemper Institute

[42] Ibid

[43] Milwaukee Sentinel, August 13, 1886

[44] Salt Lake City Herald, July 3, 1887, Governor Durkee's' Will,

[45] U S District Court, Eastern District of Wisconsin, Civil Action No. 67-C-221, Memorandum on Leonard C. Blaisdell.

[46] US 12 Stat. 489, Report of the Commissioner of Railroads, 1890

[48] 13 Stat., 356, Amendment of July 2, 1864, Report of the Railroad Commission of 1892

[49] Poor's Manual of Railroads, New York, H.V. & H.W. Poor, 1869

[50] House of Representatives Misc. Doc. 176 Part 1, 44th Congress 1st Session House of Representatives.

[51] Empire Express, Building of the First Transcontinental Railroad, David Bain, Page 199

[52] ibid

[53] Charter of Credit Mobilier, Pamphlet, 1866, University of Iowa Library Special Collections, Union Pacific Railroad Collection

[54] The Credit Mobilier of America, , 1864, University of Iowa Library Special Collections, Union Pacific Railroad Collection

[55] Record Book of the Trustees, Union Pacific Railroad, University of Iowa, Libraries Special Collections, Union Pacific Railroad Collection.

[56] Poor's Manual of Railroads, New York, H.V. & H.W. Poor, 1869

[57] Pacific Railroad Commission, Report to Congress, 1882

[58] Poor's Manual of Railroads. New York, H.V. & H.W. Poor; 1869

[59] Ibid

[60] Interstate Commerce Commission, 40 Val. Rep. 249 (1933): Missouri Pacific Railroad Company and Its Leased Lines

[61] Letter Collis Huntington to Charles Crocker, Syracuse University Library Special Collections, Collis Huntington

[62] Bond Coupon Books, Union Pacific Museum Archives, Council Bluffs Iowa

[63] San Francisco Court Case 1906, National Archives San Francisco Ca

[64] Poor's Manual of Railroads, New York, H.V. & H.W. Poor, 1869

[65] Union Pacific Railroad Ledgers, Boston, 1869. Nebraska State Historical Society, RG 3761, Union Pacific Collections The ledgers.

[66] Nebraska State Historical Society, RG 3761, Union Pacific Collections, , returned bond letters

[67] Secretary of the Treasury Letter dated February 24, 1887, alter amended by a letter dated March 29, 1887, National Archives, College Park Md. . RG 48

[68] Account Books for the Railroad Sinking Fund Accounts, 1879-1888, National Archives College Park Md. RG 50 Page 52

[69] Pacific Railroad Commission Report to Congress 1882.

[70] Ibid

[71] National Archives RG 50 Entry 173, Accounting Books for the Railroad Sinking Fund Accounts, 1879-1888. National Archives RG 50 Entry 173

[72] Ibid page. 11

[73] US Treasury Advertisement December 17, 1896.

[74] Pacific Railroad Commission Report to Congress 1882, page. 454

[75] Calculation Sheet on bond finances, DSC 823, Box 50, University of Iowa, Libraries Special Collections, Union Pacific Railroad Collection.

[76] *Souder* page 149 Table 8 Statement of 1895 Showing the Amount of bonds issued to the Several Pacific Railroad companies

[77] U S District Court, Eastern District of Wisconsin, Civil Action No. 67-C-221, Memorandum on Leonard C. Blaisdell.

[78] Ibid

[79] Ibid

[80] 54th Congress First Session Senate Document No. 314, Notes of Hearings before the Committee on Pacific Railroads.

[81] Ibid PAGE 413

[82] Ibid

[83] History of the Pacific Railway Co.'s 1st Mortgage 30 Year 6 Per Cent Paramount Lien Bonds , by Jacob Souder, 1912

[84] Ibid, Page 179

[85] New York Times, May 15, 1884

[86] History of the Pacific Railway Co.'s 1st Mortgage 30 Year 6 Per Cent Paramount Lien Bonds , by Jacob Souder, 1912Page 179 Sworn Statement of Leonard Blaisdell, 24th day of May, 1895.

[87] Ibid

[88] History of the Pacific Railway Co.'s 1st Mortgage 30 Year 6 Per Cent Paramount Lien Bonds , by Jacob Souder, 1912

[89] "Chapter 345. An Act authorizing the investigation of the books, accounts and methods of the railroads which had received aid from the United States, and for

90 United Statutes at Large, 49th Congress, 1885-1887, Volume 24

91 MEMORANDUM on Leonard C. Blaisdell, CIVIL ACTION NO. 67-C-221, UNITED STATES DISTRICT COURT, EASTERN DISTRICT OF WISCONSIN, JAMES W. McCrocklin, and THE BOARD OF TRUSTEES OF RACINE COLLEGE v. HENRY H. FOWLER, in his capacity as Secretary of the Treasury of the United States and Trustee; the Secretary of the Treasury; WILLIAM T. HOWELL, In his capacity as Deputy Treasurer of the United States

92 U. S. Supreme Court of the District of Columbia, In Equity, No. 22,296, Kuykendall v. Lyman J. Gage, Secretary of the Treasury, and Ellis H. Roberts, Treasurer of the United States. DSC 728

93 Utah State Archives, Durkee Estate Folder DSC 9499

94 U. S. Supreme Court of the District of Columbia, In Equity, No. 22,296, Kuykendall v. Lyman J. Gage, Secretary of the Treasury, and Ellis H. Roberts, Treasurer of the United States

95 Ibid, DSC 1744-1757

96 National Archives College Park Md. Record Group 123, Stack Area 16E3, Row 4, Compartment 1, Shelf 5, Box 1142. The author personally copied all the records of the case in 2014.

97 Deposition of Miss Eleanor Alexander, Hearing on Petition for Probate of Will Testimony taken April 20, 1911

98 Caroline Durkee Will, Appendix IV

99 Snyder to Durant March 1914, University of Iowa Library Special Collections, Union Pacific Collection.

100 Ibid

101 Press Release, Treasury department Washington DC, Dtd. January 26, 1914

102 Ibid

103 Finance Report, US Treasury, Vol. 28 Page 237, and Vol. 29 Page 193.

104 Letter, Arthur Smith to Judge Baker, Kenosha Court Dated June 8, 1942

105 Ibid

106 Court of Claims Case No. 401-64 Transcript

107 Ibid

108 Ibid

109 Enroth Papers

110 County Court in and for the County of Kenosha, State of Wisconsin, Deposition of Arthur Smith, May 3, 1945.

111 A. L. Smith Letter Sept 1967, Enroth Papers

112 Enroth Papers

113 STATE OF WISCONSIN: COUNTY COURT: KENOSHA COUNTY Additional Inventory by the First National Bank of Kenosha, Wisconsin

114 STATE OF WISCONSIN: County Court (In PROBATE) KENOSHA COUNTY, Estate of Caroline Durkee additional inventory

115 Probate Court Kenosha County Wisconsin Order relative to the Estate of Caroline Durkee, Dated January 15. 1968

116 U. S. Court of Appeals for the Seventh Circuit, No. 17155, McCrocklin and the Board of Trustees of Racine College vs Henry Fowler et al.

117 Enroth Files

118 US Court of Claims Case 18003 Powers of Attorney

[119] US Court of Claims, Case 401-64 Dtd 1965
[120] Ibid
[121] *Steam* v. *United States, 18* F.2d 465 (4th Cir. 1927).
[122] Time Line, Enroth Papers
[123] Enroth Papers
[124] Enroth Papers
[125] Hopkins to Huntington, February 16, 1866, Collis Potter Huntington Papers, Special Collections Research Center Syracuse Library,, Box 1, image no. 662
[126] Stanford to Huntington, July 7, 1867, Collis Potter Huntington Papers, Special Collections Research Center Syracuse Library, Box 1, image no. 617
[127] Huntington to Crocker, January 1, 1868, Collis Potter Huntington Papers, Special Collections Research Center Syracuse Library, Box 1, image no. 654
[128] Mills is the Treasurer of the Company and is not to be confused with D. O. Mills of the Bank of California
[129] 1867 Jan 9, Stanford to Huntington, Collis Potter Huntington Papers, Special Collections Research Center Syracuse Library
[130] 1867 April 10, Crocker to Huntington, Collis Potter Huntington Papers, Special Collections Research Center Syracuse Library
[131] Crocker to Huntington June 25, 1867, Collis Potter Huntington Papers, Special Collections Research Center Syracuse Library
[132] Stanford to Huntington 3/15/1869, Collis Potter Huntington Papers, Special Collections Research Center Syracuse Library
[133] Miller to Huntington 11/12 1869, Collis Potter Huntington Papers, Special Collections Research Center Syracuse Library
[134] Miller to Huntington 10/29/1869, Collis Potter Huntington Papers, Special Collections Research Center Syracuse Library
[135] Pacific Railroad Commission, Report to Congress, 1882
[136] Poor's Manual of Railroads. New York, H.V. & H.W. Poor; 1868-1924.:
[137] Interstate Commerce Commission, 40 Val. Rep. 249 (1933): Missouri Pacific Railroad Company and Its Leased Lines
[138] Poors Manual of Railroads, New York, H.V. & H.W. Poor, 1868-1924
[139] Poors Manual of Railroads, New York, H.V. & H. W. Poor, 1876-77
[140] Poors Manual of Railroads, New York, H.V. & H. W. Poor, 1874-75
[141] Ibid
[142] Ibid
[143] Ibid
[144] House of Representatives 53rd Congress Second Session Report 1290 page 30
[145] US Senate 50th Congress 1st Session Ex. Doc 51, Part 8, Testimony Taken by the Pacific Railroad Commission
[146] Ibid page 30
[147] Senate 54 Congress 1st session, Document No. 314 (Note Blaisdell's testimony is part of this document.)
[148] ibid
[149] (Pacific Railroads) May 1878, Chapter 96, 20 US Statutes at Large 56.
[150] Report of the Commissioner of Railroad, 1893, Page 6
[151] Poor's Manual of Railroads, New York, H.V. & H.W. Poor, 1894-1895
[152] Ibid page 848
[153] US Congress Act of 3 March 1887, Section 4

[154] Senate Document No. 314 54th Congress, 1st Session

[155] Report of the Commissioner of Railroads, November 1, 1899

[156] The Growth of the Union Pacific and Its Financial Operations: Thomas Warner Mitchell: The Quarterly Journal of Economics, Vol. 21, No. 4 (Aug., 1907),

[157] Ibid

[158]Neither the Records of the Nebraska State Archives Union Pacific Collection; nor the University of Iowa Library, Special Collection Union Pacific, hold financial records after 1905.

[159] Ibid

[160] Ibid

[161] Ibid

[162] Spreyer and Co. was the exclusive agent of Huntington and the Central Pacific Railroad.

[163] Ibid

[164] Report of the Commissioner of Railroads, November 1, 1899

[165] Sprayer and Co. Letter to CP Huntington, April 19, 1895, Syracuse University Library Huntington Collection, DSC 1942

[166] Railroad Commission 1899 page 9

[167] Ibid

[168] Estimated Interest on Bonds in the Sinking Funds of the Pacific Railroads, July 1, 1897, US Treasury Document, DSC 0046

[169] Report to Congress US Treasury 1908

[170] Los Angeles Herald, Number 291, 18 July 1899

[171] Union Pacific Railroad Ledgers, Boston, 1868. Nebraska State Historical Society, RG 3761, Union Pacific Collections, Page 292.

[172] Empire Express Building of the Transcontinental Railroad by David Bain

[173] Ibid Page 489

[174] It should be noted that this biography was independently delivered, without any connections of interest in Durkee's estate, and made years later, towards the end of his life, long after the Durkee case was filed at the Court of Claims.

[175] Nebraska State Historical Society, RG 3761, Union Pacific Collections Receipt found in Omaha Nebraska, 1867.

[176] Records of Brigham Young, Church of the Latter Day Saints Library, Salt Lake City Utah

[177] Salt Lake City-County Land Records Mortgage Book 2, Liber 1

[178] Deposition of John Dewees 25 November 1901, Washington DC Appendix II

[179] Deposition of Franklin Head in Court of Claims, Case No. 18003, 1896.

[180] Deposition of Clifton Finch of Denver, Colorado, Court of Claims, Case No. 18003, 1896.

[181] Ibid

[182] Joint Resolution of Congress date April 10, 1869, authorizing the President to require the deposit of 1st mortgage bonds to secure payment of subsidy bonds, this supported the President's personal direction..

[183] Letter Miller to Huntington, November 22, 1869, Collis P. Huntington Papers, Special Collections Research Center, Syracuse University Libraries

[184] University of Iowa Library, Special Collection Union Pacific Papers

[185] National Archives Records of the Comptroller of the Currency ,Rg 101, 1869

[186] New York Times, May 15, 1884

[187] Deposition of John T. Dewees See Appendix II

[188] Ledgers of the Union Pacific Railroad, 1866-1869, Page 292, Nebraska State Archives, Union Pacific Railroad Collection

[189] Union Pacific Railroad Account Books Boston Office, 1869, page. 54, May 1, 1869, Nebraska state Archives, Union Pacific Special collections.

[190] University of Iowa, Libraries Special Collections, Union Pacific Railroad Collection, Durkee File.

[191] Nebraska State Historical Society, RG 3761, Union Pacific Collections

[192] Ibid

[193] National Archives College Park Md. RG 60, Records of the Treasurer, Entry 198, Redemption of the Pacific Railroad Bonds, 1895-1903

[194] Memo, Tharske to Averill Harriman, May 10, 1940, Library of Congress Special collections, Averill Harriman Papers

[195] Senate Document 342, 56 Congress 1st Session, May 9, 1900, Letter from the Attorney General Transmitting response to Resolution of the Senate.

REFERENCES

History of the Pacific Railroad First Mortgage 30 Year 6%; Paramount Lien Bonds, Jacob Souder, 1914. Stoner & Hughes, Washington DC 1912. Bancroft Library, Berkley Ca.

Dark Genius of Wall Street, Edward J Renehan, Jr., Basic Book, 2005

Empire Express, Building of the First Transcontinental Railroad, David Howard Bain, Penguin Putnam books, 1999

Railroad 1869, Along the Historic Union Pacific, Edward Arundel Miller, Antelope Press, 2009

Railroaded, The Trans-continentals and the Making of Modern America, Richard White, W.W. Norton and Co. 2012

Union Pacific Vol I, 1862-1892, Maury Klien, University of Minnesota Press, 1987

Appendix I

- First Mortgage of the Union Pacific Railroad
- First Mortgage of the Central Pacific Railroad

First Mortgage of the Union Pacific Railroad
November 1865

This Indenture, made on the first day of November, 1865 between the Union Pacific Railroad Company, or body corporate created by and under an act of the Congress of the United States of America, approved July 1st, 1862, entitled "Am Act to aid the construction of a railroad and Telegraph Line from the Missouri River to the Pacific Ocean and secure the government the use of the same for postal, military and other purposes" party of first part and Edwin D. Morgan of the City of New York and Oakes Ames of Easton, in the state of Massachusetts parties of the second part.

Witnesseth:

Whereas, the said party of the first part is authorized by the said Act of Congress in incorporating the same, and the several Acts of Congress amendatory thereof, namely, the act approved July 2nd 1864 being chapter 216 and the act approved March 3rd 1865 being chapter 88 to borrow money for the object and purposes therein mentioned and to execute a mortgage to secure the payment thereof

and unto it the lien of is hereinafter contained which bonds and mortgage by said act of Congress are made the first lien, and unto it the lien of the government bonds is subordinate, and Whereas for such objects, and purposes said party of the first part is desirous of borrowing a sum of money which shall be equal to the amount per mile of three United States bonds provided by said act to be issued to sold company for each and every mile of its said railroad completed and to be hereafter completed and of securing the payment of its corporate bonds to be issued and negotiated therefore by a mortgage to said parties of the second part as trustees is hereinafter provided and set forth.

And Whereas, under and pursuant to lawful authority conferred by said several Acts of Congress, all of which are hereby declared to be taken as a part of this instrument the said party of the first part has determined to make execute issue negotiate and deliver under its corporate seal its corporate bonds, from time to time, and severally payable to bearer for the sum of $1,000 each thirty years

After the date thereof with semi-annual interest at the rate of six percent per annum from the date thereof to the amount equal and not exceeding per mile, the amount provided to be issued by the government of the United States, to aid in the construction of said railroad, each of said bonds so to be issued to bear date of the time of its issue and to be in form and be certified and have coupons annexed as follows:

United States if America

First Mortgage Bonds.
The Union Pacific Railroad Company acknowledges itself indebted to the bearer hereof in the sum of One thousand dollars which sum the said company promises to pay unto he holder in hand at its office in the City of New York thirty years after the date hereof and also interest thereon at the rate of six per centum payable semiannually from the date hereof in lawful money of the United States, until the principal sum be paid, on presentation of the annexed interest coupons at the office of the Company in the City of New York.

In testimony whereof the said company has here unto caused to be affixed its corporate seal and these presents to be executed by its President and Treasurer at the City of New York this day of --- A.D. one thousand eight hundred and -----.

_____Treasurer
_____President

We the undersigned trustees do hereby certify that the above bond is issued by virtue of authority granted to the Union Pacific Railroad Company by the acts of Congress of the United States, approved July 2, 1864 Chapter 216 and March 3 865 Chapter 88 and is of similar unto, except as to the date, and of like amount with the other bonds issued and to be issued under the said Acts of Congress. That the said Company has executed to us a mortgage dated November 1, 1865 purporting to convey to us, the entire railroad and telegraph line of said Company, with its equipment and appurtenances for the benefit of the holders of said bonds and to secure the payment thereof, that the said mortgage has been recorded in every count through of in which the said road has been permanently located, and a certified copy thereof filed in the office of the Secretary of the Interior at Washington and that the same is a first lien upon the line of the said Company road and that no more such bonds have been have been certified by us than are authorized by the said Acts of Congress.

_____Trustees

Coupon
The Union Pacific Railroad company will pay bearer at its office in the City of New York thirty dollars on the _____day of _____ being interest due that day on its bonds, now

_____Treasurer

And Whereas, said party of the first part is further determined under pursuant to authority so conferred by the Acts of Congress as aforesaid to execute and acknowledge under its corporate seal, and deliver to the said parties hereto of the second part, a mortgage conveying assigning, and transferring to them in trust all the corporate real and personal property franchises and effects, herein after specifically described as security for payment of the said bonds so to be issued and the interest to grow due thereon, and that said mortgage should contain all singular the covenants and conditions hereafter set forth and should bear date the first day of November, 1865,

Now therefore this indenture witnesseth that the Union Pacific Railroad Company, parties of the first part under and pursuant to its XXX

Several acts of Congress as aforesaid and for and in consideration of the premises, and for the purpose and with the intent of better and more effectually securing payment of said bonds to be issued aforesaid with the interest due, and to grow due thereon, and for and in consideration of one dollar lawful money of the United States of America, by said parties of the second part hereto fully and truly paid to the said party of the first part the receipt hereof is hereby acknowledged both bargained and sold assigned transferred and set forth forever, conveyed and confirmed unto the said Edwin D. Morgan and Oakes Ames the said parties of the second part, as trustees, and in trust, and to the survivors of them, and to their successors, or successors, all and singular the railroad and telegraph of said party of the first part heretofore constructed, or hereafter to be constructed from a point on the western boundary of the State of Iowa heretofore fixed by the President of the United States pursuant to terms and provisions of said acts of Congress to wit. At the city of Omaha, in the Territory of Nebraska, thence as provided in said Acts of Congress through the territories of the United States to the western boundary to the late Territory of Nevada, together with all its lands tenements here testaments, right of way and easements, acquired and appropriated for the purpose of a right of way XXXXX Telegraph line, and for depot engines houses car houses station houses, warehouses machine shops, structures erected and fixtures being necessary for the use of said railroad or telegraph and also all the singular the franchises o owned possessed or acquired or which shall be hereafter owned possessed or acquired by the said party of the first part for the purposes of building, and operating said railroad and telegraph above specified and described and also all the rails, depots, yards, engine houses, car houses, station houses, warehouses machine shops workshops and fixtures of said party of the first part necessary to said railroad and telegraph line, or the running and operating of the same. To have and hold all and singular the premises rights franchises lands and property, real and personal herein before and hereby assigned mortgaged, pledged, and conveyed or intended to be, and in every part and parcel thereof, with all the appurtenances unto the same, belonging, or in any arise appertaining, unto the said Edwin D .Morgan and Pales Ames parties of the second part and their survivor, successors or successors and his or their assigns in trust for the persons or person firm or firms, bodies, politic or corporate, who have heretofore, or who shall hereafter at any time become the purchasers or holders or workers of any or either of said bonds so to be issued as aforesaid, and subject to the terms provisions and conditions in said bonds contained and subject also to the provisions and conditions of the said Acts of congress, and also subject to the possession and management of said railroad and telegraph line and property by said party of the first part and its assignors, so long as no default shall be made in the payment of either the interest or principal of the said bonds so too be issued, or any of t hem, and so long as said party of the first part shall well and truly observe, keep and perform, all and singular the covenants, agreements, conditions and stipulations in this indenture contained and set forth, and which are to be observed, kept and performed by and on the part of the said party of the first part.

And the said Union Pacific Railroad company, the party of the first , covenants and agrees to and with the said parties of the second part that it shall and will pay, or cause to be paid, all taxes, charges rates levies and assessments imposed assessed or levied on which may hereafter be imposed, assed or levied upon the premises, lands franchises and property hereby mortgaged, conveyed and assigned, or intended so to be, and shall and will at its own proper cost charge and expense do or cause to be done, all the acts or things necessary or proper to be done or performed in order to preserve and keep valid and intact the lien or incumbrance upon, all and singular, the aforesaid lands and premises properties and franchises, hereby created, and further, that the said party of the first part shall and will not, at any time hereafter, or in any way or manner, interfere or avail itself of any extension laws, appraisement laws or any other laws of the States or Territories through which said road shall pass, now in force, or hereafter to be enacted and in force in the said States or Territories , which would alter affect or impair, or which are, or which may be designated, intended ,or construed to after affect or change the rights and interests of said parties of the second part, as herein declared, or which shall in any way impede or obstruct the made or manner of realizing perfecting, or enforcing the rights and interests of any of the owners or holders of said bonds so to be issued and as aforesaid or which shall effect, change or alter the time, place, mode means or manor of effecting, enjoying, or enforcing any of such rights or interests, as the same are herein declared and also that the said party of the second part shall and will at any time or times hereafter, and from time to time execute acknowledge and deliver, under its corporate seal, to the said parties of the second part, and the survivor successor or successors thereof all such other or further assurances , deeds, mortgages obligations, transfers, indentures and instruments in writing, and shall and will do and perform all such other or further acts as things, as shall or may be necessary or proper so as their council learned in the law shall deem necessary proper or, expedient for the bettor or more effectually securing upon the above mortgaged premises the payment of the said bonds so to be issued, and the interest due and to grow due thereon in the manner aforesaid, or for carrying into effect the true intent , design objects and purposes of these presents or making preserving continuing or keeping valid and effectual the lien, and incumbrance created or intended to be created, by the execution, delivering and recording of his indenture, upon the property, real and personal rolling stock equipments, franchises and effects herein before particularly described.

This indenture further witnesseth, that the said Union Pacific Railroad Company, the party of the first part by these presents further covenants and agrees, and with the said parties of the second part hereto and survivors or survivors of them and their and his successor or successors, as trustees in manner and form following that is to say First-that the said Union Pacific Railroad company the party hereto of the first part, shall and will well and truly pay the sin sums of money received in and by said bonds so to be issued, as herein provided together with the semi-annually interest to become due thereon, at the rate of six per centum per annum, at the times in the manner and at the place specified therein respectively.
Second- That no greater amount of bonds shall be issued or put in circulation under the provisions of the deed that the sum or amount authorized to be issued by the Acts of Congress aforesaid, nor shall any such bonds be issued before the same lawfully may be issuable in presence of said acts.
Third- If any default shall be made in the payment of any of said bonds or coupons at the time and place when the same shall become

payable, and such default shall continue for six months, thereafter, then the said trustee on request in writing of holders of a majority of such bonds, then in force and so in default may and shall forth with enter and to be possession, of all and singular the said mortgage property rights and franchises and use operate and manage the same for the benefit of the holders of all said bonds, and if such default shall continue for the space of one year from the time of happenings of such default then said trustees, upon the request in writing of the holders of a majority of all said bonds then outstanding may and shall offer for sale and sell,, all and singular the said mortgaged property rights and franchises, or so much thereof as may be necessary at public auction, first giving notice of such sale by advertisement in one or more newspapers published in the City of New York, for a period of ninety days and otherwise proceeding according to the statutes in such case made and provided, and as the attorneys of the said party of the first part for that purpose and by these presents duly authorized constituted and appointed   and shall make and deliver to the purchasers or punchers and said sale, a good and sufficient deed or deeds of conveyance in the law of the lands and real property so sold, in fee simple, and of other property rights franchises, and privileges so sold, by such full perfect and effectual title and the estate as the nature of things sold shall admit and allow, and all and all proceeds of said mortgaged property, rights and franchises which shall be realized by the management or operation thereof, on the sale thereof provided for in this third clause after deducting all necessary and property costs, expenses, charges and commissions of said sale and all the other expenses and disbursements of said trustees' in their proceedings shall be applied by said trustee in their payment of the moneys then owing for principal and interest upon such said bonds or shall then remain in force whether due or to become due, and without preference and the surplus, is any, shall be paid by them to said party of the first part its successors or assigns.

And in case of the said trustees entering and taking possession as aforesaid, then at any time afterwards but before such sale as aforesaid, upon the payment and satisfaction of all sums then payable on said bonds for interest, and all costs, expense
+ and charges incurred by reason of such entry possession and use, and the operating and using of the property by the said trustee they said trustees shall relinquish and said party of the first part to be held subject to these presents in like manner as if such entry had not been

made and when so ever the said trustees shall be in possession by means of any such entry they shall have full power to run and operate said railroad and to do and carry on the business of the Corporation party of the first part including repairs for the benefit of the holders of said bonds under the trusts by these presents declared in such manner as the said trustees shall deem discreet and advisable.

And for all services rendered by the said trustees in performance of any duty whatsoever under and by virtue of these presents they shall be entitled to receive from the parties of the first part, or from and out of said property or its proceeds a fair and proper compensation.

This Indenture further witnesseth that these presents are upon the express condition, that upon payments of all the bonds so issued and to be issued, in full and the interest due thereon, then these presents and the estate hereby granted shall cease and determine and the said party of the first part, its successors and assigns shall thereupon be immediately and fully reinstated with said premises, franchises and property hereby granted in law and in saerier. It is further agreed that no one of the said trustees, their successors or successors shall be answerable for thing short of gross negligence or willful default in the discharge of his duties.

And this indenture further witnesseth that this trust, and the security hereby intended, extends only to such bonds of the party of the first part, as shall be certified by the said trustees or the survivors of them and his or their successors or successors, and when all such bonds shall be satisfied and discharged the trusts herein and hereby created shall cease.

This indenture further witnesseth and it is hereby expressly agreed, that in case of the death, resignation, incapacity or remove of any or either of the parties of the second part, then it shall and may be lawful and the remaining, acting surviving or competent trustee, and the party of the first part, are hereby jointly empowered to elect and appoint by instrument in writing, duly executed by each of such parties a competent person to fill the vacancy created in manner aforesaid and that each person so appointed trustee on his acceptance of such appointment shall have and passes, and be vested with the same rights and powers as trustee as he would have had and possessed or been trusted with had he been originally made a party of the second part hereto and shall perform the same duties in all respects, and until such appointment withstanding any vacancy or aforesaid said remaining , surviving acting or competent trustee shall have full power and authority to execute each and all the trusts hereby created and his acts in the premises shall be legal valid and effectual in all respects and to all intents and purposes as if the same had been done and performed by both the parties hereto of the second part, and if for any reason the said surviving trustee and the party of the first part hereto should fail to write in the appointment of a trustee as before required, within the space of thirty days after such vacancy occurs, then and in that case, and it shall be the duty of the Secretary of the Company to call a meeting of the bond holders by printed notice, published in tow of the public newspapers of the City of New York, calling such meeting of the bond holders to be held in said City not less than thirty days after the first publication of said notice, for the purpose of filling such vacancy.

At the time and place specified in such notice the holders of said bonds at such meeting, shall proceed to elect a suitable person to act as such trustee to fill said vacancy, and a majority in interest of said bond holders so attending said meeting, or legally represented there at, shall be competent to elect a new trustee, and the person so elected shall immediately on such election, and oh his acceptance in writing of such trust, become vested with all the estate, trust, rights powers and duties of the trustee in whose place he shall have been elected. And in case said appointment shall be made in manor aforesaid or in case of such election as aforesaid, the said party of the first part hereby convents to make execute, and deliver such other of further instruments, deed, indentures or assurances , as may be necessary to enable the person or persons so appointed or elected to execute the trusts hereby created and declared as fully and perfectly in all respects as he or they have executed the same if originally made party or parties of the second part of this indenture.

Notice of the appointment or election of every new trustee shall be given to the Department of Interior.

It is further agreed that it shall be the duty of the said trustees to certify as aforesaid, and deliver immediately to the said party of the first part all such bonds as the said Acts of congress may law fully be issued from time to time as the same shall become issuable, t To be held or used by the said party of the first part. In witness where of the said Union Pacific Railroad company the party of the first part, has caused these presents to be subscribed by its President, and attested by its Secretary and he caused its corporate seal to be hereunto affixed and the said parties of the second part for the purposes of signifying of the trust herein and hereby created, have hereunto subscribed their names and affixed their seal, on the day and year above written subscribed, sealed and   John A Dix (SS) delivered in the presence of   President Union PRRC

By ED Morgan   Attest
Witness Chase Tracy   Chas Tuttle
    John Davenport   Secretary of UPRRC
By Oake Ames   E.D. Morgan (ss)
Witness Chas Tracy
  Amasa Cobb   Oake Ames (ss)
    By J. A. Dix & C Tuttle
Witness: Chas Tracy

                    Charles Nettleton
District of Columbia
Washington. (ss)
     I John R. Callan, a commissioner for the Territory of Nebraska, residing in Washington, and District of Columbia, do certify that on the 13 day of December in the year of 1865, at Washington, in the District aforesaid, before me personally appeared Charles Tracy who being by one duly sworn, did dispose and say that he resides in the City of New York, in the state of New York, that he was one of the subscribers witness to the execution of the foregoing deed, that he knew Edwin D Morgan, and Oake Ames, the persons described in and who executed the said deed, that he saw said Morgan and the said Ames sign, seal and deliver the same, and they acknowledged to him that they executed the same and that he, the said Charles Tracy thereupon become the said subscribing witness to the execution of the said deed which is to me satisfactory evidence of the due execution of said deed.
(ss)   In witness whereof I hereunto set my hand and official seal of Washington in the County of Washington, in the District of Columbia this 13th of December in the year of 1865
          U S Revenue Stamp
          5 cents cancelled
                       John F. Callan
State of New York
     Commissioner for Nebrasla
City and county of New York (ss)

Be it remembered, that on this fifteenth day of December, A. D. One thousand eight hundred and sixty five, before me Charles Nettleton commissioner of the Territory of Nebraska in and for the State of New York, duly appointed and commissioned by the Governor of said territory duly sworn and dwelling in said City of New York, personally appeared John Dix, the president of the Union Pacific Railroad Company and Charles Tuttle the Secretary of the same company to be respectfully known who, being by me severally duly sworn, did depose and say that he the said John A Dix residing in the city , County and State of New York , that he said John a. Dix so as the President, and he, said Charles Tuttle, was the Secretary of said administration Union Pacific Railroad Company; that they each knew the corporate seal of said company, that the seal affixed to the foregoing indenture so as such corporate seal, that the said corporate seal was affixed by the order of the Board of Directors of said Company, and with the assent and authority of the Stock holders thereof, and the said John A Dix as such President as aforesaid, subscribed the said indenture, and the said Charles Tuttle as such Secretary as aforesaid, attested the same by subscribing his name thereto by the like order and authority; and they said John A Dix and Charles Tuttle, acknowledged to me that they executed the same indenture in manner aforesaid, as the act and deed of the said Union Pacific Railroad Company.

(ss) In witness whereof I have hereunto set my hand and affixed my official seal, the day and year above written

US Revenue Stamp

Charles Nettleton

5 cents cancelled

Commissioner for the Territory

Of Nebraska in New York

State of New York

City and county of New York } ss Be it remembered that on this fifteenth day of December A. D. one thousand eight hundred and sixty five before me Charles Nettleton, commissioner of the Territory of Dakota in and for the State of New York, duly appointed and commissioned by the Governor of the said Territory duly sworn and I willing in said City of New York, personally appeared John A. Dix the President of the Union Pacific Railroad

Company   and Charles Tuttle the secretary of the same Company, to me respectively known who, being by me severally duly sworn, did dispose and say that he, said John a. Dix resided in the City, Country and state of New York and that he said Charles Tuttle resided in Rye, in the County Westchester in the state of New York, that he said John A. Dix was the President, and that he, said Charles Tuttle was the Secretary if the Union Pacific Railroad Company, that they each knew the corporate seal of the said Company, that the seal affixed to the foregoing indenture was such corporate seal; that the said corporate seal was so affixed by order of the Board of Directors of said company and with the assent and authority of the stock holders thereof, and that the said John S. dix as such President as aforesaid, subscribed the aid indenture and said Charles Tuttle as the secretary as aforesaid attested the same by subscribing his name thereto, by the like order and authority , and they said John A Dix and Charles Tuttle acknowledged tome that they executed the same indenture in manner aforesaid, as the act and deed of the said Union Pacific Railroad Company.

(ss In witness whereof, I have hereunto set my hand and affixed my official seal, the day and year above written.

Charles Nettleton
Commissioner of the Territory of Dakota in New York

State of New York
City and County of New York]ss Be it remembered that on this fifteenth day of December A. D. one thousand eight hundred and sixty five, before me Charles Nettleton a Commissioner for the Territory of Colorado, in and for the state of New York, duly appointed and commissioned by the governor of the said Territory duly sworn and dwelling in said City of New York personally appeared John A Dix, President of the Union Pacific Railroad Company and Charles Tuttle Secretary of the same Company to me respectively known, who being by me severally duly sworn did dispose and say that he is John A. Dix resident in the City and County and State of New York, and that Charles Tuttle residing in Rye in the County of Westchester in the State of New York, that he said john A. Dix was President and he said Charles Tuttle was the secretary of said Union Pacific Railroad Company, that they each knew the corporate seal of the said company, that the seal affixed to the foregoing indenture was such corporate seal, that the said corporate

seal was so affixed by order of the Board of Directors of said Company, and with the assent and authority of the stock holders thereof, and that the said John A. Dix as such President as foresaid subscribed the said indenture and the said Charles Tuttle as such Secretary as aforesaid attested the same by subscribing his name thereto by the like order and authority and they said John A. Dix and Charles Tuttle acknowledged to me that they executed the same indenture in manner aforesaid as the act and deed of the said Union Pacific Railroad Company.

In witness whereof, I have here unto set my hand and affixed my official seal the day and year above written

(ss)   Charles Nettleton

US Revenue Stamp
Commissioner for the Territory
5 cents cancelled   of Colorado in New York
   State of New York
   City and County of New York]ss Be it remembered, that on this fifteenth day of December A.D. one thousand eight hundred and sixty five, before me Charles Nettleton, a Commissioner for the Territory of Utah in and for the State of New York, duly appointed and commissioned by the Governor of said Territory, duly sworn and dwelling in said City of New York, personally appeared John A. Dix, the President of the Union Pacific Railroad Company, and Charles Tuttle the secretary of the same Company to me respectively known who, being by me severally duly sworn did depose and say that he said John A Dix, resided in the City and County and State of New York, sand that he said Charles Tuttle resided in Rye, in the County of Westchester, in the State of New York, that he said John A. Dix, was the President, and he said Charles Tuttle was the secretary of the said Union Pacific Railroad Company, that the, each knows the Corporate seal of the said Company, that the seal affixed to the foregoing indenture is as such corporate seal, that the said corporate seal was so affixed by the order of the Board of Directors of said company, and with the assent and authority of the stock holders thereof, and that the said John A. Dix as such President as aforesaid subscribed the said indenture and the said Charles Tuttle as such secretary as aforesaid attested the by subscribing his name thereto by the like order and authority and the said John A. Dix and Charles Tuttle acknowledged to that they executed the same indenture in

manner aforesaid as the act and deed of the said Union Pacific Railroad Company.

In witness were of I have here unto set my hand and affixed my official seal the day and year above written

US Revenue Stamp

Charles Nettleton

5 Cents Cancelled

Commissioner for the Territory of Utah

In New York

State of New York

City and county of New York]ss Be it remembered that on this fifteenth day of December A. D. One thousand and eight hundred and sixty five, before one Charles Nettleton, a commissioner of the State of Nevada in and for the State of New York, duly appointed and commissioned under and by virtue of the laws of the said State of Nevada, duly appointed and commissioned under and by virtue of the laws of said State of Nevada, duly sworn and dwelling in the City of New York personally appeared John A. Dix the President of the Union Pacific Railroad company, and Charles Tuttle the Secretary of the same company to me respectively known who being by me severally duly sworn, did depose and say that he said John A. Dix resident in the City County and State of New York, and that the said Charles Tuttle, resided in Rye, in the County of Westchester, in the State of New York. That he said John A. Dix was the President and that he said Charles Tuttle was the Secretary of the Union Pacific Railroad company, that they each knew the corporate seal of the said Company, that the seal affixed to the foregoing indenture was such corporate seal, that the said corporate seal was so affixed by order of the Board of Directors of said company and with the assent and authority of the stock holders thereof, and that the said John A. Dix as such President as aforesaid, subscribed the said Indenture, l and the said Charles Tuttle as said Secretary as aforesaid attested the same by subscribing his name there to, by the like order and authority, and they the said John S. Dix and Charles Tuttle acknowledged to me that they executed the same Indenture in manner aforesaid, as the act and deed of the said Union Pacific Railroad Company.

Ion witness were of, I have hereunto set my hand and affixed my official seal this day and year above written(ss)

Us Rev Stamp   Charles Nettleton
5 cents cancelled   Commissioner for Nevada
                                                 In New York

Received for record January 1ˢᵗ of 69 recorded same
          Date, 10 am
                                     W Thompson Co. Recorder

State of Utah
County of Weber
Mortgage or Trust Deed
Union Pacific Railroad Company
To Edwin D. Morgan and Oakes Ames
Book D of deeds Page 78

Copied 5ᵗʰ day of September 1965

First Mortgage of the Central Pacific Railroad

July 15th 1865

This indenture made and entered into this twenty-fifth day of July 1865, by and between the Central Pacific Rail Road Company of California, a railroad corporation, duly organized under and in pursuance of the laws of the State of Californian, parties of the first part and D. O. Mills and Wm. E. Barron of the City of San Francisco and the said State of California, parties of the second part,

Witnesseth, Whereas, by an act of the congress of the United States of America, entitled, "An Act to aid in the construction of a rail road and telegraph line from the Missouri River to the Pacific Ocean, and to secure to the Government the use of the same for postal, military and other purposes, approved July 1st, 1862, and the Secretary of the Treasury of the United States was authorized to issue to the Central Pacific Rail Road Company of California in accordance with the terms and provisions of the said act, the bonds of the United States for one thousand dollars and payable in Thirty years after date, bearing interest of 6 percent per annum, to the amount of Sixteen of said bonds per mile, for that portion of their line of rail road lying between the foot of K Street in the City of Sacramento, in the State of California, and then western base of the Sierra Nevada Mountains, as fixed by the President of the United States, in accordance with the provisions of said act, the same being distance of eleven and eighteen hundredths miles, and for that portion of their railroad line lying one hundred and fifty miles eastwardly of the said eastern base of the Sierra Nevada Mountains, forty eight of said bonds per mile, for which bonds of the United States retained a line on the said rail road of the said Company, and whereas by the provisions or act of said Congress, amendatory, or said as approved July 2nd, 1864, the said Company was authorized to issue its "first mortgage bonds" on their railroad line to the amount not exceeding the amount of the said bonds of the United States and the said lien of the said United states Bonds, was therein and thereby made subordinate to that of the said bonds of the Company thereby authorized to be issued, and whereas, also by the provisions of an act the said Company further authorized to issue their said six per cent thirty year "first mortgage bonds" payable in any lawful money of the United States, to the extent of one hundred miles in advance of Continuous completed line of construction, and whereas the said Company is about to issue, and intends from time to time, as the same be required for the construction and equipment of their railroad, to said "first mortgage bonds", in form and substance, and to the amount and extend authorized and provided for, in and by the said several acts of Congress, which said bonds have by the provisions of the said acts of Congress, priority or lien on the said railroad line of the said Company, over the said United States Government bonds, and whereas the execution and issue of the said "first mortgage bond' have also been duly authorized and directed by an order and resolution of the Board of Directors of said Company, and whereas the said Board of Directors ordered and directed that the said "first mortgage bonds" should be executed and issued upon that portion of the railroad line of the said Company lying between the City of Sacramento and the Eastern Boundary line of the State of California, to the amount equal to the exceeding the amount of the said United States Government bonds leaving and to be issued thereon. The length of said railroad line from its terminus in the City of Sacramento to the base of the Sierra Nevada Mountains as fixed by the President of the United States in pursuance of said acts of Congress being seven 18/100 miles, and the length of said railroad line from the eastern base of the Eastern boundary line of the State of California and estimated at one hundred and twenty five miles, the said Board of Directors further ordered and directed that the said "first mortgage bonds" should be executed and issued for four several series to be designated by the first four letters of the alphabet, the first of said series to be designated as "Series A" and that said "Series A" should bear date July 1, 1865, and include three thousand of said bonds for $1000, each, "Series B" to include one thousand bonds of $1000 each, "Series C" to include one thousand bonds for $1000 each, "Series D" to be bonds for $1000 each and to include the remainder of said bonds authorized to be issued on said portion of said railroad line under said acts of Congress. The said "Series B, "C and "D" to bear such dated as may hereafter be fixed by the Board of Directors of said Company. Which said bonds are and will be in the following form, to wit; "The Central Pacific Rail Road Company of California, acknowledge them to owe to Eugene Kelly of the City of New York, or to the holder hereof, the sum of one thousand dollars, which sum they promise to pay to the holder hereof, in the City of New York, Thirty years from the date hereof, with interest thereon at the rate of six per cent per annum from the first day of July, 1865, payable semi-annually on the first day of January 1866 and on the first days of July and January of each year thereafter, in the City of New York upon surrender of the annexed coupons, both the principal and interest payable in United States Gold Coin at par, dollar for dollar. This bond being one of the "Series A" of "first mortgage bonds"., which the said Company is authorized to issue upon that portion of their railroad line between the City of Sacramento and the eastern boundary line of the State of California, in accordance with the provisions of an act of the Congress of the United states approved July 2nd., 1864. Entitled,

"An Act to amend an act entitled on act to aid in the construction of a railroad and telegraph line from the Missouri River to the Pacific Ocean, and to secure to the Government the use of the same for postal, military and other purposes. Approved July first eighteen hundred and sixty two, and the act amendatory to the said acts approved March 3, 1865, by the provisions of which acts the said Company ""Series A"" is authorized to issue its first mortgage six ""No.____"" six percent Thirty years Bonds, on its line of railroad, payable in any lawful money of the United States, to an amount not exceeding the amount of the bonds of the United States, provided to be issued to said Company, at and by which also the lien of the United States bonds on the railroad property and equipment's of the said Company is made subordinate to that of the said "First Mortgage Bonds", the holder of any of the said bonds have no preference over any other of said bond holders by reason of priority, in the time of issuing the same or otherwise, the said "Series A" consisting of three thousand bonds for One thousand dollars each. The payments of principal and interest of this and the others of said "First Mortgage Bonds" is secured by a first mortgage, executed by the said Company upon the whole of their railroad from the City of Sacramento to the Eastern boundary line of the State of California and all the rolling stock, fixtures and franchises thereof, to D. O. Mills and William E. Barron of San Francisco and the Counties of Sacramento and Placers, in the State of California, shall not be liable for any of the debts or liabilities of the said Company to nay amount beyond or exceeding the amount of the Capital stock of said company subscribed or which may hereafter be subscribed by them or either of them upon the books   of said Company" in testimony whereof the said Company have caused their corporate seal to be hereunto affixed and the same to be signed by their President and Secretary this first day of July, 1865.

_____   _____

     Leland Stanford

L.S.   I cancelled   I
_____   I U. S.   I
               President
                   I Internal   I
                   I Revenue   I
      E. H. Miller Jr
                   I Stamp   I
                   I $1.   I
         Secretary.
                   I_____I

To each of which said bonds there is attached sixty, interest coupons numbered respectively from one to sixty inclusive of one of which the following is a copy, to wit,

------------------------------------ I
I
                         I
I
                         I
I $30.   Central Pacific Railroad Company of California   60   I
I
                         I
I   for Bond No. __
                         I
I
                         I
I   60
                         I
I   Interest coupons for thirty dollars due July 1, 1896   I
I
                         I
I   Payable   in the City of New York
       E. H. Miller Jr.   I

I

      Secretary.   I

I--
------------------------------------I

And to each of said bonds there is and will be affixed when issued a cancelled U.S. Internal Revenue stamp or Stamps of the value of one dollar, and whereas the Board of Directors of said Company under and in pursuance of said acts of Congress and the laws of the State of California further ordered and directed that to secure the payment of the said "first mortgage bonds" issued or to be issued upon that portion of the railroad line of the said Company hereinbefore described a mortgage of the said Company be executed, sighed by the President and Secretary, and sealed with the Corporate Seal of the Company to the said D. O. Mills and William E. Barron as Trustees for the holders of said bonds upon the railroad of the said Company now constructed or hereafter constructed from Sacramento to the Eastern boundary line of the State of California, and the fixtures, rolling stock and franchises of the Company, as by the said Orders of the said Board of Directors will more fully appear. Now therefore this Indenture witnessed, that the said Central Pacific Rail Road Company of California for better securing the payments of principal and interest of the said "First Mortgage Bonds", issued or to be issued in the several series aforesaid, on the day and at the places therein and herein prescribed for the payment thereof, and also in consideration of the sum of one dollar to it in hand paid by the said parties of the second part, the receipt whereof is hereby acknowledged, have granted, bargained, sold, alienated, conveyed and confirmed, and by these presents doth grant, bargain, sell, alien, convey and confirm unto the said parties of the second part and to their successors duly appointed for the execution of the trusts herein set forth, and to their assigns forever, the following property part of which is now and part of which is hereafter to be constructed, purchased, acquired, held, possessed and owned by the Company, to wit the railroad of the said Company, commencing at the City of Sacramento and running thence in an easterly direction through the Counties of Sacramento, Placer and Nevada, to the eastern boundary line of the State of California, including all of the said line of railroad now completed and in the process of construction as well as that portion of the same which hereafter in whole or in part to be constructed or completed, including therein the roadway and track, together with all the superstructures, depots, depot grounds, station houses, watering places, work-shops, machine shops, machinery, side tacks, turnouts, turntables, weighing scales, fixtures, locomotives, tenders, rolling stock, fuel equipments, and all other property which is necessarily or ordinarily used in operation the said railroad, and all rights and privileges of way or transit which are now or may hereafter constructed, purchased, acquired held, possessed or owned by the said Company and pertaining to said line of railroad and all corporate rights, privileges, and franchises to said Company, together with all and singular the tenements, hereditaments and appurtenances thereunto belonging, or in anywise appertaining, and the reversion and reversions, remainder and remainders, rents, income, issues, profits, thereof with all the right, title, interests, estate, property, possession, claim and demand in law and inequity of the said parties of the first part of, in and to the same, and every part and parcel thereof. To have and to hold the above granted and described premises, property, franchises , with the appurtenances, unto the said parties of the second part and to the survivors of them and to their successors duly appointed upon Trust and for the use and benefit of the person or persons, body or bodies political or corporate, who shall become or be from time to time holders of the said several series of "first mortgage bonds", or any of them, issued or to be issued by the said parties of the first part or their successors as aforesaid, without preference to the holder or any of the said bonds over the others, or any other, by reason of priority in the date or the time of issuing the same or otherwise, provided always and these presents are upon the express condition, that if the said party of the first art or their successors shall well and truly pay or cause or procure to be paid unto the holders from time to time of said bonds, and each and every of them the said sums of money secured to be paid by the said bonds and the interest coupons attached thereto at the places and times and in the manner set forth in the said bonds, according to the true intent and remaining thereof, then these present and all the property, estates, rights, franchises and privileges herein and hereby granted and conveyed, shall cease determine and be void but if default shall be made in the payment of the said sums of money specified in said bonds or in the payment of said interest coupons or either of them, or any part thereof, and if the same shall remain unpaid for the period of six months from and after the time when the same should have been paid, according to the terms of said bonds, then the said parties of the second part, or either of them, upon the refusal of the either, or their successors in said trust, by themselves or their agents or servants in that behalf, may upon request of the holder or holders of not less than fifty of said bonds, on which the interest or principal shall so be and have remained in default as aforesaid, enter into and upon, and take possession of all, or in their or his discursion, any part of the said premise and property hereinbefore described and work and operate the said railroad and receive the income, receipts and profits thereof and out of the same pay first the expenses of running and operating the same, including therein such reasonable compensation as they or he may allow to the several persons employed or engaged in running and superintendence of the same, and a reasonable compensation to the parties of the

second part or their successors or such of them as shall act in the premises for their or his care diligence and responsibility in the premises and second, the expenses of keeping the said road, and the appurtenances and the locomotives and the rolling stock thereof in good and sufficient repair to prevent deterioration in the value thereof and all other reasonable and proper charges and expenses of the cars and management thereof.

And third pay as far as the same will suffice, all interest and principal, if any, which may be due on said bonds, and in the case of deficiency, to apply and receipts after the payment of all said charges and expenses to the payment thereof reasonably, without preference of any kind, or the said parties of the second part may in such case sell and dispose or according to the law, all the rights, property, privileges, franchises, real and personal, with the appurtenances herein and thereby granted, or so much thereof as may be necessary, and out of the money arising from such sale, pay first the costs and charges and expenses of the foreclosure and sale, including therein reasonable council fees for conducting said proceedings and allowed ad fixed upon by the Court but not exceeding thirty thousand dollars and second, any expenses, costs and charges or execution of this trust previously incurred and remaining unpaid, third a reasonable compensation to the trustees, or one of them who may act for their or his care, trouble and service in completing the execution of this trust, and the distribution of the proceeds of sale, to be fixed by the Court, but not exceeding the sum of Fifty thousand dollars, and Fourth to distribute the residue of said proceeds among the holders of said bonds in proportion to their several interests, until all have been paid in full, principal and accrued interest, And the said parties of the first part hereby agree and covenant to and with the said parties of the second part and their successors in the said trust, that they will pay all ordinary and extraordinary taxes, assessments, and other public burdens and charges which shall or may be imposed upon the property herein described and hereby mortgaged and every part thereof, and the said parties of the second part, the survivor of them or their successors in said trust, or any one or more of the holders of said bonds, may in case of default of the said parties of the first part in this behalf, pay and discharge the same and any other lien or encumbrances upon said property which may in any way, either in law or equity become in effect a charge or lien thereon, prior to these presents, or to which this mortgage may be subject or subordinate , and for all payments thus made, the parties so making the same shall be allowed interest thereon at the rate of seven per cent per annum, and such payments with the interest thereon shall be and are hereby secured to them by these presents, and declared to be payable and collectable in the same sort of currency or money, wherein they shall have been paid, and the same shall be payable by said parties of the first part, to said parties of the second part in trust for the party or parties paying the same upon demand, and may be paid out of the proceeds of the sale of said property and franchises as hereinbefore provided, and the said parties of the first part hereby covenant and agree to and with the said parties of the second part and their successors in said trust that they will at any and all times hereafter upon the request of the said parties of the second part, execute a d acknowledge and deliver to the said parties of the second part and their successors in the said trust all and every such further and necessary and reasonable conveyances and assurances of the said premises or any part thereof, as may be by the parties of the second part, or the survivor of them, or his or their successor, in the trust hereby created, be reasonably advised or required for more fully carrying into effect the objects of this convey and the said parties of the second part and their successors in said trust shall be entitled to receive just and proper compensation for all services rendered by them in the discharge of said trust, and the same shall be deemed to be secured hereby. Part and their successors n said trust shall not be responsible for the acts or omissions of any agent or agents employed by him and them in any manner in and about the execution of the trust hereby created, when such agent or agents are selected with reasonable discretion or with the approbation or with the knowledge and without the express disapproval of said parties of the first part, nor shall either of the said parties of the second part be responsible for any act or omission of the other in the execution of said trust. And it is hereby mutually covenanted agreed and declared, that in case either of the parties hereto of the second part shall die or become or be incapacitated from discharging the duties of this trust or shall resign the same by an instrument under his hand and seal duly acknowledged or provided as a conveyance, so as to entitle the same to be recorded, and delivered to the parties of the first part, or the remaining trustee, then the remaining or surviving trustee shall select, and by a like instrument duly acknowledged and proved, nominate to the said parties of the first part, and the said parties of the first part shall and will be by resolution appoint the person so nominated as such new trustee, in place of the trustee so dying , or becoming incompetent or resigning, and so in case of the health, incapacity or resignation of any new or substituted trustee, his place shall be filled in like manner and all the estate, property, rights and interests of the said trustee so dying, becoming incompetent or resigning, shall on the execution, acknowledgement and delivery of such nomination, immediately and by force of this instrument, vest in said new trustee as fully completely in all respects as if he had been herein named as one of the said parties of the second part. And it is hereby further stipulated and agreed, that the City and County of San Francisco and the Counties of Sacramento, and Placer in the State of California shall not be liable for any of the debts or liabilities of the said Company to the amount beyond r exceeding the amount of the Capital Stock of said Company subscribed or which may hereafter be subscribed by them or either of them upon the books of said Company, and the said parties of the second part hereby accept and the trust created and declared by this instrument and agree to discharge the same pursuant to the provisions in the behalf herein contained.

In Witness Whereof the said central Pacific Rail Road Company of California, have caused these presents to be signed by their President and Secretary, and sealed with their corporate seal, and the said parties of the second part have hereunto set their hands and seals the day and year first above written

                                                         Leland Stanford

(_____)   President C. P. R. R.

Co .

    (SEAL)

    (---------)   E. H. Miller Jr.

(L. S.)

                                     Secy. C. P. R. R. Co.

                                     D. O. Mills

(L. S.)

                                     Wm. E. Barron

(L. S.)

State of California   )

) ss

County of Sacramento)

                      On this Twenty sixth day of July 1865, before me Julius Wetzlar, a Notary Public in and for the said county, duly commissioned and sworn, personally appeared E.H. Miller Jr., known to me to be the Secretary of the Central Pacific Rail Road Company of California, which Company is one of the parties described in and who executed the foregoing instrument and the said E. H Miller Jr. duly acknowledged to me that he executed the said instrument as Secretary of said Company as the act and deed of said Central Pacific Rail Road Company of California ,freely and voluntarily and for the uses and purposes herein mentioned, and that the seal affixed to the said instrument is the corporate seal of said company and was affixed there to by its authority. In testimony whereof I hereby set my hand and affixed my official seal the day and year aforesaid.

               (SEAL)

            Julius Wetzlar

State of California)
City and County of)ss
San Francisco)

On this Twenty seventh day of July, 1865, before me H. S. Homans a Notary Public in and for the said City and County, duly commissioned and sworn, personally appeared Leland Stanford, known to me to be the President of the Central Pacific Rail Road Company of California, which Company is one of the parties described in and who executed the foregoing instrument and duly acknowledged to e that he executed the said instrument as an act and deed of the said Central Pacific Rail Road Company of California, freely and voluntarily for the uses and purposes therein mentioned and that the seal affixed to the said instrument is the corporate seal of said Company and was affixed thereto by its authority. And on the same day personally appeared D. O. Mills and William E. Barron known to me to be the persons described in and who executed the said instrument and severally acknowledged to me that they executed the same voluntarily for the uses and purposes therein mentioned in testimony whereof I have hereunto set my hand and affixed my official seal the day and year aforesaid.

(SEAL)
H. S. Homans

Notary Public

Filed July 29 S. D. 1865, at 2 o'clock P. M. and at the request of E. E. Crocker, duly recorded in Book "C" of Mortgages on pages 348, 349, 350, 351, 352, 353, 354, 355, 356, 357, 358, and 359 of the Recorders office of Nevada County in the State of California.

Appendix II

Depositions of Durkee Cases

- Statement of Leonard Blaisdell before the Senate
- Deposition of James McCrocklin Civil Action No 67-c-221
- Deposition of Fredrick T. Frelinghuysen
- Deposition Charles A Nimocks
- Affidavit of Clifton R. Finch
- Deposition William Russell
- Deposition of John T. Dewees

STATEMENT OR LEONARD C. BLAISDELL.

Senate Document Blaisdell

Leonard C. Blaisdell, of Indianapolis, Ind., counselor at law, sworn and examined:

The Chairman. You may proceed and make your statement.

Mr. Blaisdell. The statement which I have to make under oath respecting the subject-matter of claims represented by myself as attorney in fact of claimants against the United States, will be found expressed in case 18003 in the Court of Claims. It is therein set forth that by virtue of the action of the Secretary of the Treasury and of the First Comptroller of the Treasury on April 22, 1884, the rights, privileges, and franchises of these creditors of the Union Pacific, the Central Pacific, and other Pacific Railroad Companies (to which were granted loans by the United States in aid of the construction of these roads and telegraph lines to the amount of $64,623,512), were made subject to the rights of the lawful and just holders of the lien prior and paramount to that of the United States, as expressed in the eighth section of the act of 1864, and as further expressed in the eighth section of what is commonly named the Thurman Act.

That on the said date, a contract or agreement was entered into with myself, by which the United States undertook to issue call bonds on the said Pacific Railroad Companies, payable January 1, 1885, at the sub-treasury in the city of New York. It was further agreed that the amount of interest on the accrued indebtedness, so described as of lien paramount to that of the United States, should be converted into United States sinking fund bonds, bearing the rate of 5 per cent interest, to date from March 3, 1883, and made payable by the United States on August 16, 1894. I further state that the complete statement in relation to all the particulars of this transaction has been hereto before made repeatedly, and finally under the determination of the late President Harrison, and will be found in pamphlet form with the Executive, and also copies with the Secretary of the Treasury, with the Secretary of the Interior Department, and in the Department of Justice. Certified copies under oath will be found in all the Departments.

The Chairman. Have you a copy of that document?

Mr. Blaisdell, Yes; I will furnish full printed copies,

Senator Stewart. I would like to know what this controversy is about.

Mr. Blaisdell. I did not expect to present the matter in full at this time. I expected to get an appointment to do so.

We would have to go to our rooms and bring our papers.

Senator Brice. This is a very important matter, and you should have your documents and an opportunity to present them.

Mr. Blaisdell. I did not expect to be rushed into this subject at all.

Senator Brice. The witness ought to lay before the committee his propositions in proper order.

Senator Stewart. Yes; and submit a statement in writing.

Mr. Blaisdell. I will do that.

Adjourned until Saturday, March 21, at 11 a. m.

Washington, D. C., Saturday, March 21, 1896.

Leonard C. Blaisdell appeared before the committee, and submitted the following statement.

My own personal relation to this matter of Pacific Railroad bonds began about the year 1882. During that year and the succeeding one of 1883 there was a considerable amount of correspondence between myself and the Department of the Treasury. The principal part of such correspondence was between myself on the one part and the late Secretary of the late Secretary of the Treasury, the Hon. Charles J. Folger, and the late First Comptroller of the Treasury, the Hon, William Lawrence, The subject of that correspondence was confined strictly to a single question proposed by me, to wit: "What bonds of indemnity to the United States were signed by Charles

Durkee, the late governor of the Territory of Utah, during his lifetime, and which bonds had been canceled?"

The greater part of this correspondence occurred during the year 1882. During its pendency, however, while there was no satisfactory answer to my question, there was manifested on the part of the officials with whom I corresponded a desire to encourage my further inquiries. At this juncture, or the beginning of the year 1883, it was officially communicated to me "that one of the two or more bonds of indemnity, signed by Charles Durkee, was in behalf of Franklin H. Head and pertained to Indian agency ; that such bonds had been duly canceled." This not being satisfactory (to me) I made further inquiry into what connection, if any, Mr. Durkee appeared to have with either the construction or security for construction of any part of the Pacific Railroad lines.

The reason I had for pressing my inquiries further was that my investigation before this time had fully satisfied me that, no matter in what form consisted the bulk of the estate of Charles Durkee, it had been sequestered from its lawful heirs.

I had informed the Department that the probate records of Kenosha County, Wis., disclosed the fact that a "bargain or assignment" of matters of estate not mentioned in inventory had been made between Caroline Durkee (the widow of Charles Durkee) and one Harry Durkee (an executor of the estate), and that such procedure had been in fraud of the rights of next of kin, claimants as heirs at law, under the ordinance of 1787.

I am satisfied that it was this information alone, unsupported by anything that I personally knew about the assets of said estate, that caused me to receive soon afterwards instructions in official manner, from both the Secretary of the Treasury and the First Comptroller, what course I should pursue, and to report to the Department when I should have complied with instructions and completed the arrangements.

I was directed to make. The directions were to commence a suit in equity procedure in a United States court having jurisdiction over the person of one of the executors of the will of the late Charles Durkee, and that when such suit should have been instituted to report forthwith to the head of the Treasury Department for further advices.

Therefore, having complied literally with these instructions and filed the suit in the supreme court of Cook County, in Chicago, on the 15th day of April, 1884, on the 22d day of that month and year I was presented by the Hon. Joseph Cannon to the Treasury clerk, Amos Webster. Mr. Cannon requested Mr. Webster to look over the papers I had to present him, and, further, to immediately call together such officials as the papers seemed to require to make the required investigations, which all related to Pacific railroad bonds and Charles Durkee's obligations to the United States on bonds of indemnity.

Within a short time there came into the Treasury building Judge Lawrence, First Comptroller; Judge Folger, Secretary of the Treasury; Judge Brewster, Attorney General; Secretary of State Frelinghuysen, and several other officers, each bearing in hand a large bundle of papers. Mr. Webster presented me, and with little delay I, with all these officials, was ushered into a room I understood to be the office of Judge Lawrence, and he further continued the introduction by making the statement that I was the person who had been making all the inquiries of the Department respecting the relations, if any, that the estate of Charles Durkee bore to the affairs and business of such Department.

Immediately Judge Lawrence began to interrogate me as to what knowledge I had acquired relative to the subject matter of the proposed investigation. After ascertaining that I knew practically nothing of Charles Durkee's ownership on Pacific railroad or other bonds (at that time), he proceeded to examine the power of attorney, court papers, and official letters which I had brought with me; and at the conclusion of his examinations he addressed Judge Folger in a formal way, declaring that the powers of attorney presented under the provisions of the ordinance of 1787 constituted me the legal representative of the late governor of the Territory of Utah, and that any business he might have with such estate could be legally transacted with myself. Then Judge Folger arose and stated what the business was that he desired to transact and the purposes to be effected, if found practical, in the joint meeting of officials present and myself.

Judge Folger, then directing his conversation to the Attorney General, Judge Brewster, rapidly recited the enactments of 1862, 1864, and of 1878, respecting Pacific railroads, and concluded by stating that there had been in all some forty or more suits between the Government and these corporations over the question of what constituted "net earnings" and the resultant rights or privileges of the Government to collect moneys from the said corporations for the purposes named in the last enactment mentioned, or the Thurman Act.

At about this stage of the proceedings Judge Folger turned his attention to the vast number of papers, files, and records of various kinds that lay on the tables, picking up different Brewster.

"These," he said, pointing to the first collection, "are the first-mortgage bonds issued by the Union, the Central, and other Pacific railroad corporations, as under the provisions of the act of 1864." Next, he said, "We have here a large amount of bonds, issued by the same corporations, which have been issued to secure payment of interest accrued on the principal bonds. These first-mortgage bonds differ from all others in that they are guaranteed by act of Congress, as lawfully paramount to the right and interests of the United States in respect of its mortgage against the same corporations and each and every one," said he (holding some of them up in his hands, so as to be seen by all present), "are assigned to one, sole, assignee Charles Durkee."

Then, exhibiting some of the interest bonds, Judge Folger explained that these, as well as the first-mortgage bonds, were issued in the form of call bonds, by the terms of which, on any default being made in the payment of the same on the demand of the legal holder or his legal representatives, the right of foreclosure immediately vested in the holder.

"Therefore," said he, "I have contended against the practice heretobefore adopted, of treating these bonds as payments of interest, however good they may be as securities, and have copies in his hand as he continued his remarks to Judge tended that they do not, within the meaning of the law, constitute payment of the interest. To you, Judge Brewster, I present the question for your decision." Judge Brewster promptly replied: "Judge, I fully concur in your conclusion.

That is my judgment also." Then, Judge Folger immediately turned himself about, and, facing me, said: "You have just heard the decision of Judge Brewster, the Attorney General.

What do you want done with these bonds?

"I answered: "I should prefer to leave the whole matter to your discretion, Judge Folger. I cannot determine what disposition shall be made of these bonds; that is for you to say."

"Let me put the question this way: Do you want these mortgages foreclosed?"

Mr. Blaisdell. "That depends upon how much money can be realized out of them without foreclosure."

Judge Folger: "I think that the amount of the Central's bonds, with the interest accrued, might be collected by giving plenty of time."

Mr. Blaisdell: "What is the amount of the Central's bonds?"

Judge Folger: "$25,885,120."

Mr. Blaisdell: "You think that amount could be realized on a call, do you?"

Judge Folger: "Yes, sir."

Mr. Blaisdell: "Let it be called then."

Judge Folger: "At what date?"

Mr. Blaisdell: "At the end of the fiscal year."

Addressing then the accounting officers, Secretary Folger said: "Make an estimate of the value of these bonds with the interest to accrue to date."

It was made, but while being made other conversation was going on between the Secretary and myself, he giving me information and instructions to guide me. Receiving the paper from the accounting officers, on which the estimate had been made, he remarked with apparent surprise

"Why, that amounts to almost as much as the sum total of all the original bonds. I fear that if so much is called at one time there will be a failure. Could you not extend the time on part of the payments?"

"Certainly," I said, "I am not so anxious to get it all at once as I am to at once get good security for the whole. Take as much time as you desire to make the calls in, provided only that we hold the United States securities for our money instead of Pacific railroad bonds."

Judge Folger: "How would the 1st of January next (1885) do?"

"That will do," I said', "I was only solicitous to get the job off my hands and into yours, and the only care that I have is to see that the security shall pass from the Pacific railroads to the United States, so that I shall look to the Government, and not to the Pacific railroads for the payment."

The accounting officers, at this stage of proceedings, picked up their pencils and made a new computation of interest to January 1, 1885.

Judge Folger: "But you must remember that there is a great deal more of this indebtedness to be looked after. What are you going to do with the balance of it; that of the other roads?"

Mr. Blaisdell: "Well, we want to collect it."

Judge Folger: "Should there be an attempt to collect the whole amount due, as under the terms of the forfeiture, the property of these corporations would fail to make anything near the amount required, and the Government would get absolutely nothing. I would like to arrange to save something for the Government."

Mr. Blaisdell: "How will this do. Secure to us the entire principal of the mortgages, and you take just as long time for the Government to pay the accrued interest as you desire?"

Judge Folger. "I will fix the date of the maturity of the accrued interest at that of the maturity of the last bond, or August 16, 1894. At what date shall we begin to compute the interest on the Pacific railroad interest bonds?"

Mr. Blaisdell: "I notice you said that the last payment of interest had been made March 3, 1883. Fix it at that date."

Judge Folger: "Very well. Now, what rate of interest shall this fund bear?"

Mr. Blaisdell: "What rate of interest do sinking fund bonds now bear?"

Judge Folger: "Five per cent per annum."

Mr. Blaisdell: "Will you make it 5 per cent?"

Judge Folger: "I think we can." "Do that, then," said I.

Judge Folger: "Now, what depository do you propose to receive the principal in?"

Mr. Blaisdell: "New York City subtreasury."

Judge Folger: "Why New York City; why not Washington?"

Mr. Blaisdell: "I think it less likely to get mixed up with other funds."

Judge Folger: "Very well, then, that will do. Now, is there any more interest to be paid by the corporations?"

Mr. Blaisdell: "No, sir. From these dates they will all be excused from the payment of any more interest."

Judge Folger: "But I would like in some way to secure to the Government some more net earnings."

Mr. Blaisdell: "Well, I do not know that I have anything to do with that."

Judge Folger: "Not directly; but indirectly it would aid the Government, if you can make a demand upon the Union Pacific for the whole of its net earnings as a matter of default for payment of interest."

Mr. Blaisdell: "Very well; you can fix that to suit the case."

Judge Folger: "On what date did you receive the last interest?"

Judge Folger: "March 3, 1883."

Mr. Blaisdell: "Let it cease on that date, then."

To this proposition Mr. Folger agreed.

This closed the transactions and the conversation with me, excepting that, when he was about to retire, I asked him what I should have to show that these transactions had occurred.

Addressing Judge Lawrence, he said: "You, Judge, will see to it that Mr. Blaisdell is supplied with the proper certificate of ownership of these bonds, and a copy of the proceedings and transactions between himself and the Government, omitting nothing essential to the protection of the interests which he represents."

Mr. Blaisdell (to Judge Lawrence): "When shall I receive these papers and certificates?"

Judge Lawrence: "Oh, you return for them in about a month. I think we will have everything ready about that time."

In about five or six weeks I returned to Washington again, and, being accompanied by Hon. J. G. Cannon, made a personal application for the papers promised. Judge Lawrence manifested a degree of indifference and ignorance on the subject which called forth from Mr. Cannon this remark: "Why, Judge Lawrence, were you not present and knowing to all that transpired in the interview with Mr. Blaisdell?"

Judge Lawrence replied: "Certainly, I was; but, you know, Mr. Cannon, the business was of such a nature that it was not proper to make it a subject of open conversation, and you see this room was filled with promiscuous people. Let Mr. Blaisdell come in this afternoon, and we will have a private talk, and I will tell him all about it."

Then, beckoning with his hand to Joseph A. D. Thompson, Deputy First Comptroller, he said: "Go with these gentlemen and introduce Mr. Blaisdell to Mr. William Armstrong, the Commissioner of Railroads, and tell that officer that hereafter it will be his duty to report Pacific Railroad matters and accounts to Mr. Blaisdell." Mr. Lawrence added, as instructions to Mr. Armstrong, "that he should take particular pains to instruct Mr. Blaisdell as to his rights and prerogatives."

Mr. Armstrong turned to those pages in the last railroad report which referred more especially to the rights and privileges of holders of liens prior and paramount to that of the United States and recited to me the text important to my protection.

Afterwards, handing me the report, he said: "You are entitled to this report, take it along."

From that time to the present, all Commissioners of Railroads have continued to furnish me with railroad reports as they have been published, and have uniformly forwarded them to my address, whether at Champaign, or Chicago, 111.

Although satisfied personally with the treatment received from Mr. Armstrong, I felt disappointed, and returned again to Judge Lawrence, and expressed to him my great dissatisfaction and disappointment in not discovering anything in the reports that identified the late Governor Durkee, of Utah, with any of the matters in which, by reason of the transactions of April 2, 1884, I had become concerned in as legal representative for lawful creditors.

I insisted that Judge Lawrence should so far comply with the known order of Judge Folger (who then had retired on account of sickness) as to deliver to me certificates, or other form of written evidence, that I was the legal representative of the creditors of the Government in these matters. He then promised me that as soon as the terms and agreements made with respect to Pacific railroads in the matter should have been fully carried into effect, and accountings fully completed, that he would supply me with certified copies of every transaction that had occurred in the matter with me.

Accepting this promise as having been made in good faith, I then returned to my home in Champaign, Ill. The time from the second to the third visit to Washington was about six or seven months. During this time a number of letters passed between myself and the Treasury Department. Generally my letters were answered in person by Judge Lawrence. The answers were generally brief, and uniformly evasive on every question of vouchers and certificates.

I came the third time in January, 1885 ; waited on Senator Cullom, who wrote a letter of introduction to the Assistant Secretary of the Treasury, Jonathan Tarbell, requesting such officer to give me special attention for the time I had to spend with him. This he did, and we spent the entire day in the examination of large bundles of papers brought to us by clerks, with the view of selecting the most important, and of finding, if practicable, "how and when Pacific Railroad bonds were assigned to Charles Durkee, deceased, and the papers showing the rights of his heirs."

The result was disappointing to Mr. Tarbell, as well as myself, and he proposed to continue the examination the next day. Owing, however, to my engagements in the suit that had been placed under my management, by an arrangement with the Secretary of the Treasury, that was still pending in Chicago, I felt compelled to return and trust the further investigation to Mr. Tarbell, who promised to do for me the best he could. I returned that night to Chicago.

The Secretary of State, Mr. Frelinghuysen, however, having a personal knowledge of the proceedings of the Secretary of the Treasury, April 22, 1884 (having been present), voluntarily prepared some State papers to be used in the case, to which he attached the great seal of State, and affixed his signature, saying that the purpose of so doing was to enable me to save all the testimony I had received, and to attach thereunto all that I should thereafter receive, in testimony of the transactions had with myself. It was mutually agreed between myself, Secretary Frelinghuysen, and Secretary Tarbell that search for the documents should continue after I should leave, and that as fast as discovered they should be forwarded to me.

There were a few more documents sent me after this, but I never received the certificate of ownership of the bonds.

Mr. Blaisdell dictated to the stenographer the following additional particulars:

THE ENTIRE INDEBTEDNESS EXPRESSED IN UNITED STATES STATUTES.

First. The first-mortgage indebtedness and the subsidy indebtedness being paid, there exists no further liability against the United States.

Second. The United States statutes have provided and the Supreme Court has decided that there is but one class of creditors with higher claim than that of the United States.

(See section 8 of the Thurman Act, and sections 4 and 5 of the act of March 3, 1887.)

Third. No records of the Government show any other claim purporting to be a paramount lien to that of the United States except the claim represented by L. C. Blaisdell.

Fourth. The act of March 3, 1887, is a complete statuary preparation and provision directing the Secretary of the Treasury to clear off such paramount lien.

If the parties claiming to hold paramount lien bonds are correct in their statements, how can the last report of the Secretary of the Interior be correct?

The Secretary of the Interior says that all these bonds are now matured; that the Government holds the second lien and trust protect the property against the first lien. And the statutes declare that the United States has but one lien security the first lien.

See act of May 7, 1878, preamble, pages 318 and 319, section 3743 of the Revised Statutes:

All contracts to be made by virtue of any law and requiring the advance of money, or in any manner connected with the settlement of public accounts, shall be deposited in the offices of the First Comptroller of the Treasury of the United States, the Second Comptroller of the Treasury of the United States, or the Commissioner of Customs, respectively, according to the nature thereof, within ninety days after their respective dates.

Section 306, Revised Statutes of the United States, on liabilities outstanding three years or more, provides : That such sums as shall stand to the credit of any disbursing officer for any purpose, in liquidation of an indebtedness .due to the United States which have for three years or more remained outstanding, unsatisfied, and unpaid shall be deposited by the Treasurer to be covered into the Treasury by warrant, and to be credited to the credit of the parties in whose favor such certificates, drafts, or checks, were respectively issued, or -to the person who are entitled to receive pay there for, and into an appropriation account, to be denominated "outstanding liabilities."

Secretary Foster, in a statement made to one of the Congressional committees, said that it has been the practice of the Treasury Department to treat the interest accrued on the paramount lien obligations of the said Pacific railroad corporations as not maturing until the maturity of the last one of the bonds. A reference to the reply made by the Senate Judiciary Committee, which examined Mr. Foster, will show, as I have been informed, that the committee held to the opposite view and stated that the obligation of the Government in relation to payment of interest accrued on such paramount lien should date from the time when the Government assumed the direct responsibility of payment of the bonds of such lien, to be determined by the date of such assumption.

By reference to the act of March 3, 1887, we shall see that in that act the Secretary of the Treasury is directed to satisfy the claims of the lawful creditors of the paramount lien, as expressed in the act of May 7, 1878. This is the construction which the claimants place on these statutes as applied to their rights. The legal representative of the claimants begs leave to state that, had this been done, as directed in such act, it would have been a saving to the Government of all the interest which has accrued in the period of nine years that has passed since the enactment of that law. And, furthermore, that it would have been to the advantage of the Government, in this respect, that it would have become subrogated to the rights of the paramount lien, by which all the property of the branch lines worth much more than the main lines would have become the security for the payment of the Government interest. This, in the aggregate, would amount to a saving of more than $100,000,000.

The Chairman. Is there anything else that you desire to add to your statement?

Mr. Blaisdell. I have nothing more to offer at present. Our plan is to submit the statute quotations, when we can be questioned by members of your committee. I do not care to offer anything more until the committee begins its interrogations.

The Chairman. Have you citations from the statutes?

Mr. Blaisdell. In abundance. Anything that you want to ask. We have them already printed, and will put them in the record, if the chairman permits us to do so.

The Chairman. You may hand them to the stenographer and have them printed in the proceedings of the committee.

The following papers were handed in by Mr. Blaisdell, and were ordered to be printed:

Case 18003. In Court of Claims. L. C. Blaisdell v. The United States. Application for rule on the Secretary of the Treasury to show cause why judgment should not be entered against the United States, and in favor of the Petitioners and Claimants v. The United States. (Final statement of Case 18003. In Court of Claims. L. C. Blaisdell v. The United States.)

This case was brought before the honorable court through the intervention of the Committee on Claims of the Fifty fourth Congress, from whose files it will appear that the plaintiff had been duly presented by a Member of that Congress, the Hon. Wm. M. Springer of the State of Illinois.

It was filed in the first instance by the present claimant, L. C. Blaisdell, in behalf of not only the heirs at law of the decedent, Charles Durkee, but in behalf of all creditors of the lien prior and paramount to that of the United States, as designated in the several acts of Congress, 1864-1878, and of the act of March 3, 1887.

Thus it appears on the face of the petition that it was a claim filed and founded upon acts of Congress, which acts were in the petition definitely and at length set forth in form and substance, and made exhibits for the purposes of conveying to the mind of the court the foundation upon which all rights claimed by the complainants in the case were to be ascertained. The rights of the complainants, whatever they shall be ascertained by the honorable court to be or to have

heretobefore been, are fully defined in the Pacific railroad laws set up, designated, and pleaded in the preliminary and informal petition; in the more complete petition following on the case or matter of the petition being by the court taken for consideration as in ex-partner; and must finally appear, not necessarily from any or all of the answers of the several Departments, bureaus, and officers of the Government, the information thereby conveyed to the court, but through the information conveyed to the mind of the court through statutes of the United States, and specific acts of Congress defining the particular rights and character of rights set up and appearing in this petition.

It will only be necessary to merely call the attention of this honorable court to the acts of Congress that have been duly presented to it as the authority for bringing this claim herein presented that can be required of the complainants in the case to present.

The information that has been filed with this honorable court by the attorney of record in the case and that particular portion of it which classifies as "official matter" certified by the several Departments, Bureaus, and officers *of the Government disclose a state of facts which precludes the possibility of there being hereafter, at this time, by or through any Department, Bureau, or officer of the Government, a state of facts, to it presented that shall run counter to or in any material form modify the conclusions which the court may draw from that which has been already thus presented.

A summary of these facts thus presented, and that have been on file with this honorable court for the greater part of the two years last preceding the present date, shows to the honorable court all the essential information necessary that it shall have obtained before proceeding to enter final judgment in the cause of the complainants versus the United States.

As they embrace a large part of the history of the Pacific railroad system, their operations, duties, and obligations were as expressed in the United States Statutes ; and so great a portion of the detailed information is to be conveyed to the court through official reports of the Auditor of Railroad Accounts, in the first instance (and Railroad Commissioner's reports in the latter instance) it is deemed in order to present first the annual report of the Auditor of Railroad Accounts to the Secretary of the Interior for the year ending June 30, 1878.

On page 6 of this report occur the words: "The act of Congress approved May 7, 1878 (chap. 96, p.

56, 20 Stat. L., 1877-78), entitled 'An act to alter and amend the act entitled "An act to aid in the construction" of a railroad and telegraph line from the Missouri River to the Pacific

Ocean, * * * approved 1862," * * * and "to alter and amend act of 1864," in amendment of said first-named act, requires:

"That the net earnings mentioned in- said act of 1862, of said railroad companies, respectively, the Central Pacific Railroad Company of California and the Union Pacific Railroad Company, shall be ascertained by deducting from the gross amount of their earnings, respectively, the necessary expenses paid within the year in operating the same and keeping the same in a state of repair, and also the sum paid by them, respectively, within the year in discharge of interest on their first-mortgage bonds."

On the first proposition, to wit, the amount paid by these companies "within any given year in operating their railroad and telegraph lines and in keeping the same in a state of repair," it is not proposed to make any remarks. But the second proposition, namely, "with the amount paid by them, respectively, within the year or at any other time, in discharge of interest on their first-mortgage bonds," with this proposition we do propose to deal.

It is made the basis of the rights set up by the complainants against the United States that the interest accrued upon these first-mortgage bonds, to wit:

Union Pacific	$27,236,512
Central Pacific	25,885,120
Denver Pacific, Railroad and	
Telegraph Company	
(Western Pacific)	1,970,560
Kansas Pacific,	1,600,000
Central Branch Union	
Pacific Railroad Company.	1,600,000
Sioux City and Pacific	
Railroad Company	1,628,320

A total first-mortgage debt and indebtedness lien prior and paramount to that of the United States of $64,623,512, with interest accrued thereon at the rate of 6 per cent per annum, was until the dates, respectively, March, A. D. 1883, and January 1, A. D. 1885, the debt and the expressed indebtedness of these railroad and telegraph companies, jointly and severally, to such parties and persons as were expressed and designated in "certain files and records of the Treasury Department" and which were referred to in these terms by Hon. William Lawrence, under the date of December 3, A. D. 1884, and at such date became, by contract, an indebtedness of the United States.

That the names of "the lawful and just holders of" the said "lien prior and paramount to that of the United States" have not appeared of record within the knowledge of this honorable court, and have never yet been produced (so far as known) before any committee of either House of Congress nor reported in any railroad report required by law to have contained them, constitutes no evidence and no rebuttal of the testimony that first-mortgage creditors answering to that 'description

do not exist, for we cannot consistently believe that when such mortgages of such description and of such character of lien have been so well provided with protection in the expressed provisions of the acts of Congress 1864, 1878, and 1887 that the very "liens" or incumbrance thus openly

recognized by such acts of Congress could exist independently of an expressed ownership of such character of mortgages in the Department of the Treasury and the Department of the Interior, both of which said Departments contain the most conclusive evidence and recorded proofs that such bonds do exist.

The Departments just named above have, it is true, failed to produce the "evidence" called for by the complainants in the first instance and by the honorable court in the second instance, that such mortgage bonds do exist; but these Acts of Congress just referred to, more especially the preamble to the act of May 7, 1878, declare that the Union Pacific Railroad Company named in this and the other said acts of Congress, and the Central Pacific Railroad Company and others therein named, "did and have issued" an amount of "their own bonds" equal to the amount so issued (as therein expressed) to them, and each of them, by the United States.

Furthermore, rights of owners of bonds thus issued are not, in law or equity, to be defeated by the neglect and refusal of said several Departments, or any officer, bureaus, or heads of such Departments to make and preserve proper "files and records" of the various transactions that may have occurred in either one.

In pleading for the protection of the rights of this class of creditors of the United States, I shall submit for the consideration of the honorable court the general proposition that rights thus guaranteed by acts of Congress are not to be defeated by "the neglect and refusal of officers of the Government (more particularly the heads of the two Departments last named) to keep, preserve for the use of this court, and to present the true and perfect record of such transactions occurring therein as have involved the credit of the United States to the total amount named in the said Pacific Railroad bonds." The truth of this last proposition, I believe, (is not questioned by any head of any Department of the Government, so far as I have yet been informed, to wit, the records of the Treasury Department do disclose the "public debt statement; that all interest accrued upon the said bonds are payable by the United States." To whom payable is not disclosed. That the principal of the bonds ($64,623,512) is also "payable by the United States." To whom payable is not disclosed.

Nor is it disclosed (by record or information to Congress given) when, in the history of these bonds, that portion of them became due and payable which represented "interest indebtedness accrued for the period of time which intervened between issue of the principal bonds and the date of April 22,

1884." The Plaintiff in the case has alleged the fact of the transposition of a specific and well-defined and expressed indebtedness of these corporations into an indebtedness of the United States. The Treasury Department corroborates the fact stated, that such indebtedness has become the indebtedness of the United States, but does not show when it so became (debt payable by the United States).

The Interior (Railroad Department thereof) carries the same debt account under the title or name of "Bond indebtedness," and charges the same item against the United States as such, which the Treasury Department terms a cash and "sinking fund indebtedness." The information is thus disclosed to the honorable court that there is a vast discrepancy between the "public debt statement" of the Secretary of the Treasury and that disclosed in the Department of the Interior. The sinking fund as shown by the Commissioner of Railroads, does not show to exceed $27,000,000 (less than $20,000,000 in 1884), while the Treasury Department (unless the Pacific Railroad Committee under Mr. Outwaithe have misstated) shows $64,000,000 of "sinking fund indebtedness of the Government," by reason of these Pacific Railroad obligations, in addition to that shown in the Department of the Interior.

To prove that there is a gigantic discrepancy and erroneous statement of the public liabilities in this respect, as between these two departments the honorable court has but to summons Mr. Outhwaihe as witness, whom, with thirteen other members of that committee (in 1888), declared "that the amount of $64,623,512 in cash" was on the 1st day of January, 1885, an "outstanding liability" of the Government by reason of the amount of cash having been, on that date, deposited with the

Secretary of the Treasury "for the definitely ascertained indebtedness of the several Pacific railroad companies to their lawful creditors" of the lien prior and paramount to that of the United States.

If the liability of the United States, or my statement of its liability in this respect, and as alleged in my petition, both the original and amended, has been disputed by any answer plea, or demurrer filed with this honorable court, I am as yet not made aware of the fact. The statement has gone before the Department of the Treasury, signed and sworn to as set forth in my affidavits, and stands unchallenged so far as I know.

The order of the court for the information that would deny the truth of the statement has gone forth, and does not bring the information that would deny it.

The statement has stood in form and in print before the eyes of every Secretary of the Treasury from the date of January 12, 1889, and not one has attempted to deny it or make any official answer tending to deny the truth, substantially, of my statements, as in petition contained. The President

of the United States (Benjamin Harrison, while Chief Executive) caused all my statements to be placed before himself in official capacity, and in official capacity referred them "for the official action" (note the words) of the Secretary of the Treasury. The Supreme Court in 99 United States Reports supports the statement of my petition, that the United States is in debtor to the "sinking fund" and in favor of the "lawful and just holders of paramount lien," as stated, "to the full amount of the deposits made under the provisions of such sinking fund as contained in the act of May 7, 1878." The committee referred to last has the information that the sum of $64,623,512 is and has been withheld from the "possession of the lawful and just holders of such paramount liens by each and every Secretary of the Treasury, on the plea, or notion, rather, that such officer held discretionary authority to make of such fund a sinking fund."

Congress, by act of March 3, 1887, directed that officer "to clear off such paramount lien incumbrance by payments (by payments, mark the words,) out of the sinking fund and provided that the entire amount be paid, whether the sinking fund was more or less than the amount due to the lawful owners of such bonds, or the "lawful creditors of the paramount lien aforesaid."

For this disobedience of the requirement the direct, positive and special order of Congress the present incumbent in that office is answerable. He cannot and does not answer either Congress or this honorable court that he knows not the lawful creditors of the United States; that he has no legal knowledge of them that he is bound by law to take cognizance of.

He appears .to rest contentedly upon "want of information, such information as would create an official liability on his part to answer" the demands made by me on the United States Treasury. He acts, or rather, neglects to act; and rests upon the assumption that his neglect and refusal to answer me in official manner, either by affirmation or by denial of the claims I have filed, prevents the consummation of my purpose to enforce an accounting from him; and he acts as if he expected that the entire body of Congress and the Supreme Court, including this honorable court, would unitedly be unable to compel him either to affirm or deny my right to an accounting, and thus prevent not only myself and my clients from obtaining the benefits of those acts of Congress upon which we rely for protection, but that all possible creditors of such lien, as Congress provided should be secured to "its lawful holders" (should others than myself and clients proved to be "lawful beneficiaries") would be powerless and the courts named and Congress itself be powerless to enforce against his will the payment of the sums due.

With these statements I have concluded to include the following motion: That the Secretary of the Treasury be, and, with the approval of this honorable court, is hereby ordered to show cause, by his personal appearance before this honorable court, at the next ensuing rule day, why judgment should not be rendered in behalf of the United States for the benefit of the petitioners and claimants in said case and cause, No. 18003 in accordance with the statement of claims against the United States made to this honorable court.

Very respectfully submitted by

Attorney of Record in Case No. 18003.

To the Honorable Chief Justice and Judges thereof.

Washington, D. C., August 19, 1901, at 3 o'clock p. in.

Met pursuant to adjournment to continue taking testimony for complainant. Present same parties as before.

Deposition of James McCrocklin

Civil Action No 67-c-221

James W. McCrocklin being first duly sworn deposes and certifies:

That he has worked assiduously in conducting research of the records of the Library of Congress, the U. S. Archives, and other places in compiling the information contained in this affidavit;

That this affidavit contains factual knowledge of the History of the Financing of the
Pacific Railroads, cheeked for veracity from the records above mentioned, and known to be correct and true as though I were testifying as the witness stand under oath before this Honorable Court; and I respectfully move this Honorable Court to take Judicial Notice of the following History of the Financing of six Pacific Railroads from 1860 to 1968 in Civil Action No. 67-C-221. (Barren and Holtzoff Paras 963 Note 40 and 969 Note 70)

The experience of the Civil War proved the value of rapid transportation of troops, munitions, mail and supplies. Transportation by rail had been proven far superior to wagon trains and other horse drawn vehicles.

Interest in constructing rail lines from the east to the west was first generated in San Francisco at a Pacific Railroad Convention held in September, 1859. The report of this convention recommending the construction of intercontinental railroads was presented to the United States Senate on February 8, 1860. Several members of the Senate recognized the importance of the proposal and introduced investigative type legislation.
At this time, Senators and Congressmen who were friends of the Honorable Charles Durkee, namely Senator Howe, Senator Lane of Kansas, Senator Doolittle of Racine, Wisconsin, Congressman James b. Rollins, Congressman Campbell, and Congressman Edward H. Rollins introduced and backed legislation which resulted in the Act of July 1, 1862 (12 Stat. 489). This Act was introduced in the House by Mr. James S. Rollins on February 3, 1862 and in the Senate by Senator Howe on December 23, 1861. The final Act resulted from consideration by both the House and Senate of several proposed versions of the bill. There was little opposition to the final draft of the bill because it provided stringent controls on the Railroad Companies and gave the United States title to the Railroad Property if the Companies failed. The Bill passed the House on May 6, 1862, the Senate on June 20, 1862, and was enacted into Law on July 1, 1862. The principal provisions of this Act were as follows:

The Act was to aid in the Construction of a Railroad and telegraph line from the Missouri River to the Pacific Ocean, and to secure to the Government the use of the same for postal, military, and other purposes;

The Preamble and Section One appointed 157 members of Congress and promoters of the Railroads plus five Commissioners to be appointed by the Secretary of the Interior to be a body corporate and politic in deed and law and incorporated "The Union Pacific Railroad Company" with authority to construct and operate a railroad and telegraph line along a specified route, and to do all things expected of a corporate body, including sale of 2,000 shares of common stock at $1,000 per share of an authorized 100,000 shares prior to the first meeting of the subscribers, at which meeting, thirteen directors of the Company shall be elected. The President of the United States shall appoint two additional directors to act as Government directors, said government directors not to be stockholders. A majority of the said directors shall constitute a quorum for the transaction of business;

Section Two granted a right of way for construction of the railroad and telegram line, including the taking of public lands along the right of way to the extent of 200 feet in width on each side of the right of way, including additional grounds for buildings, shops, etc., and including the extinguishment of Indian titles to all lands required for the right of way;

Section Three granted additional land consisting of alternate sections to the extent of five alternate sections per mile, within ten miles of the right of way. The Company was not granted mineral rights but was granted timber rights that if the Company had not sold or otherwise disposed of the land within three years after completion of the railroad, the United States could preempt the land for $1.25 per acre;

Section Four prescribed that title to the aforesaid land would pass to the Company after they had completed each consecutive forty miles of first class railroad so accepted by three Commissioners appointed by the President of the United States;

Section Five authorized the Secretary of the Treasury to Issue United States bonds in the amount of $16,000 per mile to the Union Pacific Railroad Company upon acceptance of each forty consecutive miles of completed railroad, said bonds to be payable in thirty years after date and bear six percent interest per year (payable semi-annually), said bonds to "ipso facto" constitute a first mortgage on the whole railroad and telegraph line and equipment; find failure of the Company to redeem the bonds as specified would permit the Secretary of the Treasury to take title to all property covered by the mortgage.

Section Six specified that the grants aforesaid were made on condition the Company pays off its bonds at maturity, keeps the railroads in top condition at all times, authorizes the Government use of the railroad at private rates; and specifies that Government compensation for use of the railroad would apply to payment of the bonds and interest permitting the railroads to pay off the bonds as desired, and further requiring that at least five per centum of the net earnings of said road shall be annually applied to the payment thereof:

Section Seven requires the company to accept the Act within one year, shall complete the railroad by July 1, 1874, shall designate the route within two years and file a map with the Secretary of the Interior whereupon the Secretary shall cause land within 15 miles of the track to be withdrawn from preemption and specifies that the track shall be designed to join up with other railroads.

Section Eight specifies that the Union Pacific track shall start at the 100th meridian at a point approved by the President of the United States and run westerly to the Western boundary of the Territory of Nevada, there to meet and connect with the line of the Central Pacific Railroad Company of California.

Section Nine specifies the routes and authorizes the same land grants and financing for the Leavenworth, Pawnee and the Western Railroad Company of Kansas and the Central Pacific Railroad Company subject to approval of the President of the United States. These Companies had six months to file acceptance of the conditions of the Act with the department of the Interior.

Section Ten specifies the construction schedules for the Leavenworth, Pawnee and Western Railroad company and the Central Pacific and authorizes them to join in construction of the railroads and all conditions applicable to the Union Pacific Railroad Company shall apply, until the railroads shall meet and connect, and the whole line and branches and telegraph are completed;

Section Eleven allows $48,000 of Government Aid for 300 miles of mountainous terrain and $32,000 for other sections as approved by the President of the United States and states that these amounts shall be paid upon completion of twenty miles of consecutive track in lieu of the forty miles specified for the Union Pacific;

Section Twelve specifies routes for the railroads across boundaries of States and Territories, and specifies that ail track shall be of uniform width and construction as approved by the President of the United States so that a single train could traverse from east to west as one continuous line;

Section Thirteen authorizes the Hannibal and St. Joseph Railroad to construct a railroad in accordance with the terms and conditions for the Union Pacific;

Section Fourteen authorized and required the Union Pacific to construct 100 miles of road per year of single line track from the Western boundary of Iowa to the 100th meridian to connect with its lines previously authorized, and failure to do so would cause forfeiture of all rights under this Act, and to construct connecting lines with the Sioux City in accordance with specifications prescribed by the President of the United States;

Section Fifteen authorizes any railroad company now Incorporated to connect with the roads and branches authorized by this Act;

Section Sixteen authorizes the companies named in the act to form themselves into one consolidated company, filing notice thereof with the Secretary of the Interior, and the consolidated companies shall comply with the act;

Section Seventeen prescribes penalties for failure of the Companies to construct the railroads in accordance with this act. Failure to complete the entire track by 1876 would result in Government seizure, and further prescribes that 25% of the bonds specified for construction east of the 100th meridian and the west foot of the Sierra Nevada Mountain shall remain In the U. S. Treasury until such parts wet* completed, and 15% of the bonds specified between the two points aforesaid shall be retained, and if the said road or any part thereof shall fail of completion at the time limited therefor in this act, then and is that ease the said part of said bonds so reserved shall be forfeited to the United States;

Section Eighteen prescribes that Congress can regulate the rates charged by the Companies to belter promote the public interest and welfare, and may alter or amend or repeal this act;

Section Nineteen authorizes the Companies to arrange for existing telegraph companies to install their lines along the rights of way to comply with this act. And in case of disagreement, said telegraph companies were authorized to remove their lines along and upon the lines of railroads herein contemplated without prejudice to the rights of said railroad companies named herein; and

Section Twenty specifies that the Companies named herein shall make annual reports to the Secretary of the Treasury setting forth the following:

First. The names el the stockholders and their places of residence, so far as the same can be ascertained;

Second. The names and residences of the directors, and all other officers of the Company;

Third. The amount of stock subscribed and the amount thereof actually paid in:

Fourth. A description of the lines of road surveyed, of the lines thereof fixed upon for the construction, the road, and the cost of such surveys;

Fifth. The amount received from passengers on the road;

Sixth. The amount received for freight thereon;

Seventh. A statement of the expense of said road and its fixtures;

Eighth. A statement of the indebtedness of said Company, setting forth the various kinds thereof. Which report shall be sworn to by the president of said company, and shall be presented to the Secretary of the Treasury on or before the first day of July in each year.

APPROVED July 1, 1862.

It would appear with the passage of the act of July 1, 1862 that the promoters of the railroad companies would be successful in completing the railroads as planned, but alas this was not possible. They quickly found that they could not sell their common stock of sufficient amount to construct the first sections of the railroads. Coupled with this, they claimed that the cost of materials and labor had doubled. Accordingly, they approached their friends in Congress with a drastic proposal to amend the Act of July 1, 1862.

The Promoters through their agents in Washington and with the influence of the same Senators and Congressmen who pioneered the Act of July 1, 1862, placed their proposals before the House on January 25, 1864 and before the Senate on June 27, 1864.

The principal amendments desired were: -

(1) The common stock authorized would be increased to 1,000,000 shares instead of 100,000 and the price per share would be $190 instead of $1,000.

(2) Change the width of the right of way

(3) Change the construction sections from forty miles to twenty miles so that U. S. aid bonds could be issued as 20 miles of road were completed;

(4) Eliminate Section 17 of the Act of July 1, 1862; and

(5) Authorize the Railroads to issue their own bonds, making them first mortgage bonds and changing the Government Guaranteed Bonds to second mortgage bonds,

These proposals immediately raised the ire of several Senators and Congressmen. They pointed out that the Union Pacific Railroad Company obtains the right of way for a subscription of only $2,000,000 in stock, with a 10% down payment. That nobody knows what the railroads would cost, could be as high as $200,000,000 of which only $200,000 would be put up by the Companies. The Government was financing the railroads and should own or control them. The Companies had done little or nothing since 1862 toward construction of the railroads, and therefore these vast sums should not be handed over to promoters no matter how honest.

The Companies had not submitted a proposed route.

To protect the Government, Construction Contracts should be submitted to the Commissioners and approved by the Government before any bonds were issued.

They also pointed out that many directors appointed by the Act of July 1, 1862 had resigned because of the actions of the promoters who Wall-Street stock-jobbers were building this railroad for personal gain, regardless of the objects of the Congress,

Despite this opposition to the proposed amendment, Congress passed the Act of July 2, 1864 with the following provisions:

Chapter CCXVI - An Act to amend an Act entitled "An Act to aid in the Construction of a railroad and Telegraph Line from the Missouri River to the Pacific Ocean, and to secure to the Government the use of the same for Postal, Military, and other Purposes," approved July first, eighteen hundred and sixty-two.

The Preamble and Section One provided for a change in the capitalization of the Union Pacific Railroad, Increasing the authorized common stock from 100,000 to 1,000,000 shares, and reducing the price per share from $1,000 to $100. This section also specified limits and controls on stock to be held by the Directors of the Railroad Company;

Section Two prescribes controls for the sale of the common stock, including locations of offices, subject to approval of the President of the United States, and authorizes sale of the stock on an Installment plan of $5 down and $5 every six months until fully paid. Assessments will be made on stockholders, and the maximum issued shall not exceed the cost of the road. Transfer agent shall be established in New York;

Section Three prescribes rules for Company acquisition of land grants, including 100 feet each side of the center line but not limited in areas requiring wider right of way. This Section establishes authority and procedure for taking land owned by another party;

Section Four amends sections 3 and 7 of the Act of July 1, 1862, prescribing the sections of land along the right of way which are granted to the Company and the limitations thereon. Lands granted under the Preemptive Land Act and the College Land Grants are not affected by this Act. The Company is not granted mineral rights, including iron and coal, but is granted timber rights within 10 miles of the center line of the track;

Section Five extends the time the Company has to file maps of the route by one year, and reduces the distance the Central Pacific Railroad Company must cover to 25 miles per year and to the state line in four years, and reduces the with-holding of compensation from all to one-half to be applied to the payment of the Government Bonds;

Section Six amended Section Four of the Act of July 1, 1862 by providing three commissioners appointed by the President of the United States for each of the Companies affected by the Act; and authorizes the Central Pacific to file its reports with the office of the U. S. Surveyor General for the State of California Instead of with the President of the United States. Government bonds would be issued on recommendation of the Commissioners after completion of not less than twenty miles of consecutive track;

Section Seven repeals that part of Section 17 which required withholding of bonds to ensure compliance with the Act, and excludes any Company from responsibility of another Company for failure to comply with the Act;

Section Eight authorizes the advance issue of Government Aid Bonds when two thirds of the work on a 20 mile section had been completed and certified, the balance to be paid upon completion of the section. The amount advanced shall not exceed two-thirds of the cost, and in the case of the Union Pacific shall not be advanced more than 300 miles ahead of the completed track west of Salt Lake City;

Section Nine authorizes the Companies to build bridges and ferries, full navigation of navigable waters, in order to connect with each other, but no additional bonds or land grants were authorized;

Section Ten modifies and amends Section 5 and authorizes each Company to issue on the completion of each section to issue their first mortgage bonds on their respective railroad and telegraph lines to an amount not exceeding the amount of the bonds of the United States, and of even tenor and date, time of maturity, rate and character of Interest with the bonds authorized to be issued to said companies respectively. And the lien of the United States bonds shall be subordinate to that of the bonds of any or either of said companies, except as to the rights of the United States relating to the transportation of dispatches and the transportation of mails, troops, munitions of war, supplies and public stores for the Government of the United States;

Section Eleven prescribes that if any Company has already issued bonds which by law take priority over the Government Aid Bonds or the Company First Mortgage Bonds, then the total issued shall be reduced by the amount of the uncancelled bonds so that the total bonds issued shall not exceed the amount authorized per mile; and each Company shall file an affidavit with the Secretary of the Treasury on the over-Issue of any bonds, describing the same in such manner that the Secretary of the Treasury can make the deductions prescribed. These affidavits will be filed by the Secretary of the Interior, and anyone making a false statement shall be guilty of perjury; and also provides that no land grants or bonds issued other than by authority of the Act of July 1, 1868 or this amendment shall be recognized;

241

Section Twelve ensures that the railroad between the mouth of the Kansas River by way of Leavenworth to the City of Lawrence shall be built either by the Leavenworth, Pawnee and Western Railroad Company, now known as the Union Pacific Railroad Company, eastern division or by the Union Pacific Railroad Company by the most feasible route without the issuance of additional bonds; and no bonds shall be issued or land certified by the United States for the main trunk-line west of the 100th meridian and east of the Rocky Mountains, until said road shall be completed from or near Omaha, on the Missouri River to the said one hundredth meridian of longitude;

Section Thirteen provides that the number of directors of the Union Pacific shall be 15 to be appointed by the Company and 5 to be appointed by the President of the United States. That one director shall be appointed to each standing or special committee. That the government directors shall keep the Secretary of the Interior fully informed on progress of construction and answer any inquiries of the Department. That they shall periodically inspect the railroad and report on its management;

Section Fourteen prescribes time and place for meetings and elections of the directors, at New York City on the first Wednesday in October next between the hours of ten a.m. and four p.m. The directors shall serve for one year, and meet annually thereafter;

Section Fifteen prescribes that all railroads will be operated as one continuous line with equal opportunity for use by all, with no discrimination in rates or service, subject to penalty;

Section Sixteen prescribes detailed instructions for the consolidation of any two or more of the railroad companies, and provides that each company is responsible for either the construction of its assigned track or reimbursement therefore to the consolidated company; that consolidation does not relieve any company of Its responsibilities under the Act and authorizes the Central Pacific to construct 150 miles of track east of the stale line of California to join up with the Union Pacific if the Union Pacific fails to do so, and to enjoy the rights, privileges and benefits connected therewith;

Section Seventeen modifies Section 14 of the Act of July 1, 1862 in regard to construction of a railroad from Sioux City to the Union Pacific line. The President of the United States is authorized to designate a Company under the laws of Iowa, Minnesota, Dakota, or Nebraska, to construct the aforesaid railroad, and said Company shall complete the road within 18 months and receive land grants and bonds previously authorized, and if the Company fails to complete the road within 10 years, it shall become the property of the United States;

Section Eighteen provides for the Burlington and Missouri River Railroad Company to construct a railroad through the territory of Nebraska from the Missouri River so as to connect with As main line of the Union

Pacific Railroad at the 100th meridian of longitude, enjoying all land grant rights and financial assistance authorized the other railroad companies, including title to Indian lands consistent with policy;

Section Nineteen grants sections of land to the aforesaid Burlington and Missouri River Railroad Company along the right of way; and provides that the Company shall accept this grant within one year from passage of this act;

Section Twenty provides that the Burlington and Missouri River Railroad Company can obtain title to the land after certification of construction of twenty consecutive miles of track; but no government bonds shall be issued to the said company to aid in the construction; until they had deposited in the Treasury of the Halted States the cost of surveying, selecting,

Section Twenty One provides that no land grants would be transferred to any company until they had deposited in the Treasury of the United States the cost of surveying, selecting and conveying the same, which amount shall, without further appropriation, stand to the credit of the proper account, to be used by the Commissioner of the general land office for the prosecution of the survey of the public lands along the line of said road, and until the whole shall be completed, as provided by this act; and

Section Twenty Two prescribes that Congress may, at any time, alter, amend or repeal this act.

Approved, July 2, 1864.

The first mortgage bonds which this Act authorized the Railroad Companies to issue became known as Paramount Lien Railroad Bonds due to their statutory position as a Paramount Lien on the specified property.

The passage of this most liberal act should have given the promoters of the railroads clear sailing for rapid construction of the railroads. Yet, this was not to be. The promoters have testified under oath before the Congress that they could not sell their common stock or their paramount lien bonds to the public. They could not obtain the assistance of anyone of large means. They contacted such wealthy men as Moses Taylor, William E. Dodge, Commodore Garrison, D O. Mills, Eugene Kelly, John Parroff and many others. All contacted told them that the risk was too great and the profits, if any, too remote.

These promoters also testified under oath that they did not own any of the Paramount Lien Bonds.

Failing to raise the cash needed to construct the advance sections to qualify for issuance of the Government Aid Bonds, the promoters conceived a unique and ingenious scheme to construct the railroads and qualify for the government aid.

The promoters of the Union Pacific, principally Oliver Ames, H.S. McComb, Sidney Dillon, T. C. Durant, James Fisk and others formed a holding company called Credit Mobilier of America, a Pennsylvania Company, to construct the railroad. The directors of both Companies were identical. Credit Mobilier issued contracts to individuals and other companies to construct sections of the road. The Union Pacific transferred common stock and bonds to Credit Mobilier. Credit Mobilier then used the Common Stock and Paramount Lien Railroad Bonds to pay the construction contractors for supplies and work performed. To show cash transactions, instead of credit transactions, Credit Mobilier and the Union Pacific exchanged checks. Credit Mobilier check was used to show on the record that Union Pacific had sold the stocks and bonds for cash. Union Pacific then gave a check of identical amount to Credit Mobilier. On the record it therefore appears that the Union Pacific Railroad Company sold its stocks and bonds for cash and paid cash for the preliminary construction work to qualify for the issuance of Government Subsidy Aid Bonds. However, since there was then no market for a large of stock or any of the Paramount Lien Bonds, the Companies quickly ran into difficulty. They could not pay the contractors in cash with this arrangement. They were forced to make other arrangements to obtain the cash, yet the permanent records show this fabricated procedure between Credit Mobilier and the Union Pacific Railroad Company during the Initial stages of construction.

The Central Pacific Promoters, namely C. P. Huntington and Mark Hopkins stated under oath that they formed a contract company called "The Contract and Finance Company" and seven sub-contracting companies to build the railroad. They too paid for the construction work with their common stock and all Paramount Lien Bonds issued by them.

How did the Honorable Charles Durkee fit into this picture? Mr. Durkee was a prominent and highly respected citizen of his time. He was an intimate friend of President Andrew Johnson, who appointed him as Governor of the Territory of Utah In 1865. He formed a company called John W. Kerr and Company of Salt Lake City, and provided materials for the construction of the railroads. He also was connected with Casemate Brothers of Paynesville, Ohio, who also provided materials to the Railroad Companies.

During this time period, we find that the railroads were constructed on credit, and the promoters were dependent on the Government Aid to pay for the material and workers. As a result, the railroads were not being constructed in accordance with the Acts of July 1, 1862 and July 2, 1864.

The Commissioners appointed by the President, Lt. Col. James W. Simpson, Maj. General Samuel R. Curtis and Hon. William W. White reported to the Secretary of the Interior In early 1866, that the Union Pacific Railroad, Eastern Division, was not complying with the Acts of July 1, 1862 and July 2, 1864 In construction of the railroad. He reported this failure to President Andrew Johnson by letter dated April 20, 1866, and cited Section 17 of the Act of July 1, 1862 as authority for action to be taken against the Company for this failure, due to neglect., He apparently was not aware that this section was eliminated by the Act of July 2, 1864; and that there was no Act of Congress of this character. The Secretary also called attention of the President to the fact that Congress may not be aware of this neglect on the part of the Union Pacific.

By letter dated April 24, 1866, President Johnson informed' the Congress of the report of the Secretary of the Interior and recommended that Congress extend the time for completion of the road, if the Company had otherwise complied with the act.

Congress immediately took notice and members introduced several bills in the House and Senate in regard to correcting this situation. Nothing came of this until 1869.

In the meantime, the Railroad Companies were getting deeper in debt. Their laborers were not being paid and materials were not being delivered. To relieve this situation, the Promoters approached Mr. Durkee for assistance. He had acquired title to a large amount of the Paramount Lien Bonds by purchase, barter and trade. Mr. Durkee then acquired title to all of the Paramount Lien Bonds, then authorized, in principal amount of $64,623,812 and deposited them with the Treasurer of the United States as security for Government Aid to the Railroad Companies. Durkee used his influence with the President, his intimate friend, to accept the bonds as collateral in lieu of the completed construction work on the six Pacific Railroads.

Accordingly, in 1868 and early 1869, Senator James R. Doolittle of Racine, Wisconsin and former Congressman E. H. Rollins of New Hampshire, armed with Powers of Attorney from the Honorable Charles Durkee, deposited all Paramount Lien Bonds with the Government and received Certificates of Deposit which they delivered to Mr. Durkee. Both of these gentlemen had shown great interest in development of the railroads in the passage of the Acts of July 1, 1862 and Ally 2, 1864. Mr. Rollins later became Secretary of the Union Pacific Railroad Company.

In the meantime, Congress was considering passage of an act to protect the interests of the United States.

In testimony on the proposed legislation, there was considerable subterfuge practiced by the promoters of the railroads, the Companies were advertizing that they could provide first class rail service to the West Coast. Passengers had reported to the Committee that this was a fabrication, that the road was not completed that service over the completed part was poor, that they could travel faster and more comfortably by stage lines. It was alleged that the Union Pacific was constructing the road bed to get distance and obtain the Government Aid Bonds, and not trying to complete the road for service.

No Congressman or Senator had any doubt that action had to be taken to control the promoters of the railroads and protect the interest of the United States. They were convinced that the Union Pacific and Credit Mobilier desired to control the road to the California line. They had 1,100 miles of plains to cover, while the Central Pacific had 500 miles of mountains to overcome. The Union Pacific wanted the cream. The Junction point of the two companies thus became a major point of issue. Strong wording was proposed to control them. The promoters heard of this and held an emergency meeting to agree on a Joint terminus. They quickly reached agreement to avoid stringent control and this was reported to the Committee considering the proposed legislation. The Committee then decided to word the legislation so that it confirmed to the agreement. Senator Sherman told the Senate that the only security to the United States was either with-holding further issuance of Government Subsidy Bonds or holding the Paramount Lien Bonds as security. He reported that some of the Paramount Lien Bonds had already been deposited with the Government without any authority of law. He and other Senators further reported that the railroads were being built with the subsidy aid bonds and not with any cash put up by the promoters.

This culminated in the passage of the Joint Resolution of April 10, 1869, which provided the following:

Joint Resolution for the Protection of the Interests of the United States in the Union Pacific Railroad Company, the Central Pacific Railroad Company, sad for other purposes.

The Preamble and the First Section authorized the stockholders of the Union Pacific at a meeting to be held on April 22. 1869, to elect a Board of Directors and establish their office anywhere in the United States. That no other right was conferred nor were say rights of the United States waived to take corrective action for the neglect or act of the Union Pacific heretofore done or omitted which prejudiced the rights the United States and provided that the common terminus of the Union Pacific and the Central Pacific shall be near or at Ogden; and the Union Pacific shall build, and the Central Pacific pay for and own the railroad from the terminus aforesaid to Promontory Summit, at which point the rails shall meet and connect and form one continuous line;

Section Two authorizes the President to appoint a board consisting of five eminent citizens, not interested in any Railroad Company, to examine a* report the condition of the railroads, that they are constructed as a first class railroad in accordance with all of the applicable Acts of Congress;

Section Three authorized the President to with-hold subsidy bonds or receive as security an equal amount of the first mortgage bonds as security to ensure completion as a first-class road of all sections of the roads involved; and authorizes the President, in case of default in the giving of such security, to have the Attorney General file suit In any court of jurisdiction to protect the interests of the United States, and to ensure for all completion thereof as a first-class road as required by law.

Section Four authorized and directed the Attorney General to investigate whether or not the Charter and all the Franchises of the Union Pacific and Central Pacific had not been forfeited, and to investigate whether any of the directors or employees of said companies have or not violated any penal law, or have or have not made any illegal dividends, and if so to take action to have the same reimbursed, and to institute proper criminal proceedings against all persons who have violated such laws.

APPROVED, April 10, 1869

Throughout extensive hearings on the Joint Resolution not one person represented that he owned or knew anybody who owned any of the Paramount Lien Railroad Bonds. Further, it is obvious from study of the Act of July 2, 1864, that the Railroad Companies could not legally issue one such bond, yet the testimony clearly shows that they had issued and used them to pay for construction work in advance of receipt of the Government Subsidy Aid.

With the passage of the Joint Resolution and the deposit of the security by Mr. Durkee, the Subsidy Aid Bonds were released and construction of the railroads proceeded at a rapid pace.

On October 30, 1869, the board of eminent citizens made an ocular report to the Secretary of the Interior that the roads had been completed in accordance with the Acts of Congress. Learning this, Senator Doolittle, representing Mr. Durkee, Collis P. Huntington and E. B. Rollins, called on the President and the Secretary of the Treasury to arrange release of the Paramount Lien Bonds. The Secretary was willing but stated that he had to discuss the matter with the Secretary of the Interior. Mr. Doolittle then arranged for the acceptance of the resignation of Mr. Durkee as Governor of the Territory of Utah so that he could return to Washington to negotiate for recovery of the bonds.

Governor Durkee settled his affairs In Utah, sold his equity in John W. Kerr and Company, and with his wife, Caroline, and brother Harvey[1], departed for his home in Kenosha. Wisconsin, planning to go from there to Washington, D. C. Governor Durkee became very ill with pneumonia and stopped off at Omaha, to rest. While there he informed his wife that he not trust the executors of his estate, and asked her to deliver his personal papers, which were in a black bag, to the Metropolitan National Bank of New York City for safe keeping. These papers included some subsidy bonds which Durkee had purchased and the Certificates of Deposit of the Paramount Lien Bonds which he had deposited in trust with the Secretary of the Treasury. He died at Omaha on January 14, 1870. His widow complied with his dying request and deposited his papers in trust with the Metropolitan Bank in New York City as he had requested. She also complied with his request that she sell some of his assets to Harvey Durkee, but not any of the bonds.

Durkee's bonds were bearer bonds, not registered, and the Treasury Department had prepared ledgers thereon showing date of issue, value, maturity date and accrued interest. The ledgers showed all of these bonds assigned to the Honorable Charles Durkee. The bonds were then wrapped in sealed packages and placed in vaults to the Treasury Department. There they gathered dust until approximately April 22, 1884.

All remained quiet until early in 1873 when it was noticed that the Government was paying out $3,877,410 per year as interest on the Government Guaranteed Subsidy Aid Bonds, while collecting only a little over a million dollars from the compensation authorized by Section 5 of the Act of July 2, 1864. The Secretary of the Treasury reported this accumulative deficit to the Congress in his annual reports. Congress formed standing Pacific Railroad Committees to investigate this, and these committees remained active until World War II.

In 1873, Congress had the Pacific Railroad Committees investigate the financing and management of the Railroad Companies. They conducted an exhaustive investigation of Credit Mobilier and the Central Pacific Railroad Company. At the hearings in 1873, Mr. Durant, Mr. Rollins and Mr. Huntington testified under Oath that they did not own any of the Paramount Lien Railroad Bonds, and admitted that they had not only built the railroads from funds derived from the Government Guaranteed Bonds, but had illegally paid out over $18,000,000 in dividends to stockholders who had paid little or nothing for their stock. They also admitted that the records of all these transactions had been destroyed. They stated that knowledge of the owner of the Paramount Lien Bonds was a matter of record in the U. S. Treasury Department.

In 1873, during the hearings held by Congress, and realizing the once worthless Paramount Lien Bonds were now at a premium due to their position ahead of the Government Guaranteed Bonds, Mr. Rollins, Mr. Durant and Mr. Huntington presented their contracts with Governor Durkee to the Secretary of the Treasury. The Secretary informed them that the records showed all of these bonds were assigned to Charles Durkee, and they would have to get the Probate Court in Kenosha, Wisconsin, to release the bonds since Durkee's will was in probate in that court. Having previously informed the Congress that they did not own any of the bonds, and knowing that Caroline Durkee was under considerable mental pressure, they dropped the matter.

During the Congressional investigation of 1873, the promoters of the railroads became alarmed that the investigation could result in legislation which would divulge their illegal activity and also result in stringent control of the Railroad Companies by the United States Government. They accordingly appealed to the United States Supreme Court for a decision on the necessity of their paying oil their debt to the Government

That time. The Supreme Court ruled, in 1873, that the Railroad Companies were not required to pay their debt until the bonds matured in the 1890s. Section 6 of the Act of July 1. 1862 was not amended by the Act of July 2, 1864, and the United States Supreme Court ruled that the Railroad Companies did not have to pay principal or Interest on the Government Lien until it matured. The provisions of Section 6 of the Act of July 1, 1862 and Section 5 of the Act of July 2, 1864 did not make it mandatory for the Railroad Companies to pay interest as it became due. This was not the Intention of the Congress, for at the time of passage of these acts, the Compensation due the Companies for the transportation of troops, supplies, mail, etc., plus 5% of their net earnings, would have met the annual interest charge.

This ruling by the U. S. Supreme Court slowed but did not deter the Congressional Investigation. To meet the Treasury deficit caused by the excess interest payments on the Government Aid Bonds, Congress passed an Act on the first day of December, 1878 which authorized the Secretary of the Treasury to pay the Interest debt on Bonds issued to Pacific Railways out of any moneys in the Treasury, including customs receipts.

The Congress continued to receive alarming reports of the management and finances of the Pacific Railroad Companies from the Annual Reports of the Secretary of the Treasury, the Secretary of the Interior and the Commissioners of the Railroad,

In 1877, the Judicial Committee of the Senate conducted an investigation which resulted la the Introduction of the famed "Thurman Act" or "The. Railroad Sinking Fund Act." This proposed legislation was introduced in the Senate buy Senator Thurman on March 12, 1877. It was simultaneously considered by the House Pacific Railroad Committee.

In months of argument and discussion, the principal point discussed was whether or not the proposed act was constitutional.

When Senator Thurman was asked way Section 8 of the proposed Act owners of the Paramount Lien Bonds, he replied:

"Section 8 provides that when the fund becomes distributable it shall be distributed according to the priority of lien of the creditors, thereby preserving everyone's right precisely as a chancellor would do in marshalling the assets of an insolvent corporation or firm and distributing them among its creditors. The owners of these bonds have first call on the Sinking Fund without any expense of foreclosure or of any trouble of being compelled to fight the road."

There was no opposition by any Senator or Congressman to this proposal to protect the owners of the Paramount Lien Bonds, Furthermore, despite the many millions of dollars involved, and the importance of this legislation, not one person represented the owners of the Paramount Lien Bonds in over a year of hearings. The record owner of these bonds was the Honorable Charles Durkee who by that time had rested in peace in a Kenosha, Wisconsin cemetery for over eight years.

Several Senators expressed concern over the apparent control of the Railroad Companies over the Departments of the Interior and the Treasury. In fact, it is difficult to understand how these Railroad Companies got away with flaunting the law to the detriment of the United States for a period of 30 years.

It was brought out for the first time in these hearings as to how much those railroads had actually cost. A summary of the Government Subsidy Aid Bonds issued to the six Pacific Railroads was as follows:

Union Pacific	$27,836,512
Central Pacific	$25,888,120
Denver Pacific	1,970,560
Kansas Pacific	6,303,000
Central Branch, UP	1,600,000

Sioux City	I. 628,320
Total	$84,623,512

In addition to the $64,623,512 in Government Guaranteed Subsidy Aid Bonds, the Railroad Companies received the following grants of land:

Union Pacific	12,000,000 acres
Central Pacific	9, 100,000 acres
Denver Pacific	1,100,000 acres
Kansas Pacific	6,000,000 acres
Central Branch, UP	245,166 acres
Sioux City	45.000 acres
Total	**28,490,166 acres**

In the hearings conducted by the Congress from 1866 to 1878, it was repeatedly stated that the Promoters of these railroads received the foregoing bonds and land grants for a personal investment of less than $300,000.

The Thurman Act, after due consideration by the Senate was passed by this Body on April 9, 1878 by a vote of 40-20, and by the House, after one day of hearings, passed the Act of April 24, 1878 by a vote of 40-20 and by the house after one day hearings passed the act on April 24, 1878 by a vote of 243 – 2 and it was enacted into law on May 7, 1878 (20 Stat 56:45 U.S.C. 94, 94) The principal sections of this act which are Germaine to the claim of the Plaintiffs in Civil Action No. 67-C-are as follows:

"See. 3: That there shall be established in the Treasury of the United States a sinking fund, which there shall be invested by the Secretary of the Treasury of the United States Treasury in bonds of the United States; and the semi-annual income thereof shall be in like manner from time to time invested, and the same shall accumulate and be disposed as hereinafter mentioned. And making such investments the Secretary shall prefer the five per centum bonds of the United States, unless, for good reasons appearing to him, and which he shall report to Congress, he shall at any time deem it advisable to invest in other bonds of the United States. All the bonds belonging to said fund shall, as fast as they shall be obtained, be so stamped as to show that they belong to said fund, and that they are not good in the hands of other holders than the Secretary of the Treasury until they shall have been indorsed by him, and publicly deposed of pursuant to this act.

Sec. 7: The said sinking-fund so established and accumulated shall, at the maturity of said bonds so respectively issued by the United States, be applied to the payment and satisfaction thereof, according to the interest and proportion of each of said Companies in said fund, and of all Interest paid by the United States thereon, and not reimbursed, subject to the provisions of the next section.

Sec. 8: That said sinking fund so established and accumulated shall, according to the interest and proportion of said companies respectively herein, be held for the protection, security, and benefit of the lawful and just holders of
Any mortgage or lien debts of such companies respectively lawfully paramount to the rights of the United States, and for the claims of creditors, if any, lawfully chargeable upon the funds so required to be paid into said sinking-fund, according to their respective lawful priorities, as well as for the United States, according to the principles of equity, to the end that all persons having any claim upon said sinking fund may be entitled thereto in due order; but the provisions of this section shall not operate or be held to impair any existing legal right, except in the manner in this act provided, or any mortgage, lien, or other creditor of any of said companies respectively, nor to excuse any of said provisions of this section right, except in the manner in thin act provided, of any mortgage, lien, companies respectively from the duty of discharging, out of other funds, its debts to any creditor except the United States.

Sec. 9: That all sums due to the United States from any of said companies respectively, whether payable presently or not, and all sums required to be paid to the United States or into the Treasury, or into said sinking-fund under this act, or under the acts hereinbefore referred to, or otherwise, are hereby declared to be a lien upon all the property, estate, rights, and franchises of every description granted or conveyed by the United States to any of said companies respectively or jointly and also upon ail the estate and property, real, personal, and mixed, assets, and income of the said several railroad companies respectively, from whatever source derived, subject to any lawfully prior and paramount mortgage, lien, or claim thereon. But this section shall not be construed to prevent said companies respectively from using and disposing of any of their property or assets in the ordinary, proper and lawful course of their current business, in good faith and for valuable consideration."

The promoters of the six Pacific Railroad Companies did little or nothing to oppose passage of the Thurman Act, except to have their lobbyist parade through the halls of Congress while it was being considered. Yet, they appealed again to the United States Supreme Court to find the act unconstitutional. The Supreme Court not only denied their Petition by finding the act constitutional, but also finding that the act the legal rights of the owners of the Paramount Lien Railroad Bonds, No one represented the owners of these bonds at the hearing held by the Supreme Court.

Following the finding of the U. S. Supreme Court, the Secretary of the Treasury by letter dated January 29, 1879, established the Railroad Sinking Fund with the Secretary of that Treasury as Trustee and the Treasurer of the United States as Custodian.

It is interesting to note the following additional provisions of the Act of May 7, 1878, which were the responsibility of the Secretary of the Treasury to administer for the Congress, and which ware the cause of continuous litigation in Congress for the next 15 years. These provisions were:

(1) That the whole amount of compensation which may, from time to time, be due to the railroads, for services rendered for the Government, shall be retained by the United States, one-half to be applied to the liquidation of the interest paid and to be paid by the United States on the Subsidy Aid Bonds and the other half thereof to be turned Into the sinking-fund;

(2) That in addition to the one-half of the compensation for services, rendered by the Central Pacific Railroad Company, the said Company Is to pay into the Treasury for credit to the sinking fund, the sum of $ 1,200, 000, or as much as to make 5% of the net earnings of the Company, the whole sum to the amount of 25% of the net earnings of the Company per year; and the Union Pacific Railroad Company shall pay $850,000 into the Treasury, in addition to the one-half of the compensation for services rendered, so that a total of 25% of the net earnings of this Company is paid into the Treasury for credit to the sinking fund;

(3) That whenever the 75% left to the companies is not adequate to pay the companies legal obligations, the Secretary of the Treasury is authorized to remit as much as may be necessary to pay any Interest due on any lien Paramount to that of the United States;

(4) That the Companies will not vote, make or pay any dividend to any stockholders), in either company as long as they are in default In any payment to the sinking fund as required, or in arrears is payment of interest on any lien paramount to that of the United States; and any dividends so paid shall be recovered and paid into the sinking-fund, and any officer or person who knowingly votes, declares, makes or pays any such dividend, shall be deemed guilty of a misdemeanor, and, on conviction thereof, shall be punished by a fine net exceeding $10,000, and by imprisonment not exceeding one year;

(5) It is the duty of the Attorney-General to enforce this Act in the Courts or otherwise, without regard to matters of form, join of parties, multifariousness, or other matters not affecting the substantial rights and duties arising out of the Acts of July 1, 1862, July 2, 1864 and May 7, 1878;

(6) That if either Company fails to perform all and singular the requirements of this act and of the acts hereinbefore mentioned (July 1, 1862 and July 2, 1864), for the period of six months next after such performance may be due, such failure shall operate as a forfeiture of all the rights, privileges, grants and franchise derived or obtained frost the United States, and it shall be the duty of the Attorney-General to cause such forfeiture to be Judicially enforced; and

(7) That this act shall be deemed, taken and held as in alteration and amendment of the acts of July I, 1862 and July 2, 1864.

This so-called sinking-fund Act should have solved all of the problems of the Government. Unfortunately, the Supreme Court decision in favor of the Union Pacific (91 U. S. 72) which stated that the Railroad Companies did not have to pay principal or interest on the Subsidy Aid Bonds until they matured, was used by the Companies to continue to defy the Government. The ire of Congress was expressed in a proposed amendment to the Sinking-Fund Act as early as March 1, 1880.

This proposed amendment emanated from a letter to Congress by the Secretary of the Treasury on February 21, 1879. By this letter the Secretary of the Treasury concurred in the proposed amendment and recommended that the Trustee of the Sinking Fund be granted permission to purchase the Paramount Lien Railroad Bonds for the account of the Railroad Sinking Fund. He gave as his reason for this desire to purchase these bonds that these bonds earned 6% interest and there was no other long-term investment which paid more than 4%. The Plaintiffs herein presume that the Secretary of the Treasury was not aware that all of the Paramount Lien Bonds were at that time stored in sealed packages in vaults of the U. S. Treasury; or was he possibly confused by the multiple issue of so-called first mortgage bonds issued by these companies.

Although this recommendation of the Secretary of the Treasury and the proposed amendment did not clear Committee, some comments made by Mr. McLane of Maryland who sponsored the amendment ta explanation of why he wanted the Government to purchase the first mortgage bonds were as follows;

"That is the explanation I desire to make to the Gentleman front Texas, that inasmuch as these first-mortgage bonds are a prior lien to the lien of the Government, the Government would have to pay these first mortgage bonds before it could take the road.

But as I have already explained, if the Government owned the entire amount of the first mortgage bonds, no such contingency could occur. If we would take this sinking fund money and invest it from year to year in first mortgage bonds, then it would not be within the power of the railroad companies to foreclose; it would be for the Government of the United States to foreclose.

Did the railroad companies own the Paramount Lien Bonds? Their officers have testified under oath before Congressional Committees that they did not own any of them,
In 1873 and again in 1896.

The principal reason given for the failure of the proposed amendment to pass was that the proposal was too complicated for most of the members to understand, end the matter did not come before the Congress again until 1885.

In the meantime, the will of the Honorable Charles Durkee was under probate in the Kenosha County, Wisconsin, Probate Court. This Court by Judgment dated March 21, 1881 awarded all the residue of the estate of Charles Durkee, which included all Paramount Lien Bonds, to his widow and sole heir, Caroline Durkee. This was confirmed by Probate Court order on January 15, 1968, which also states that no administrator was required for the probate of the estate of Charles Durkee after March 21, 1882, and the act of any Administrator, d,b.n. c.t. a., or otherwise is not binding on the said Caroline Durkee or her heirs.

At the Probate Court bearing on March 21, 1882, it was brought out that the Honorable Charles Durkee had owned some type of railroad indemnity bonds which were held by the Secretary of the Treasury. This caused some of the heirs at law of Charles Durkee to feel that they were legal heirs of his estate. They then hired Leonard C. Blaisdell of Champaign, Illinois, a nephew-in-law of Durkee, to represent them. And Seventeen (17) of them issued Powers of Attorney to Blaisdell to represent them in the matter of the estate of Charles Durkee.

Blaisdell commenced communicating with the Secretary of the Treasury, the Honorable Charles J. Folger and with the First Comptroller, Judge William Lawrence, making many inquiries concerning the estate of Charles Durkee.

About this time, the Secretary of the Treasury, the Attorney General, and the Secretary of the Interior made routine and special reports to Congress on the failure of the Railroad Companies to meet their indebtedness. This flaunting of the laws by the Railroad Companies was beginning to raise the ire of many prominent Congressmen, and it appeared to the Secretary of the Treasury, who was familiar with the problems with the Railroad Companies by virtue of his judicial assignments prior to becoming Secretary of the Treasury, that he must take some type of corrective action.

Part of this trouble with the Railroad Companies stemmed from the fact that they issued many classes of bonds and other indebtedness in violation of Federal Law.

The Promoters of the Union Pacific Railway Company which was formed on January 26, 1880, by the consolidation of the Union Pacific Railroad Company, the Kansas Pacific Railway Company, and the Denver Pacific Railway and Telegraph Company, issued the following bonds:

(1)   Kansas Pacific Railway Corporation
$ 600,000
Denver Extension 7% Mortgage
Leavenworth Branch
Issued 1 January 1866

(2)   Union Pacific Railway Corporation
4,275,350
Eastern Division 7% income
1 July 1866

(3)   Kansas Pacific Railway Corporation
6,500,000
Denver Extension 7% Mortgage
Issued 20 June 1869

(4)   Denver Pacific and Telegraph
2,500,000
Comp. 7% Mortgage
Issued 10 August 1869

(5)   Union Pacific Railroad Corporation
1,086,000
Bridge Mortgages 5%
Issued 1 April 1871

(6)   Omaha Bridge
2,500,000
First Mortgage 5%
Usued 1 April 1871

(7)   Junction City at Fort Kearney
97,000
7% Mortgage
Issued 1 April 1873

(8)   Union Pacific Railroad
16,000,000
Corp. Sinking Fund 8%
Collateral to Union Trust N. Y.
Issued 18 December 1873

(9)   Kansas Pacific Railway
11,724,000

Comp. Consolidated 1st Mortgage 6%
Issued May 1, 1879

(10)   Union Pacific Railway
6,000,000
Comp. 5% Collateral Trust
Issued 2 April 1883

(11)   Union Pacific, Lincoln and
$4,698,000
Colorado Railway Comp.
5% Mortgage
Issued 1 August 1860

(18)   Oregon Shortllne and Utah
13,000,000
Northern Railway Corporation
5% Collateral Trust
Issued 2 September 1889

(13)   Union Pacific Railway Comp.
6,000,000
Bank Collateral 5%
Issued May 1, 1891

(14)   Union Pacific Railway Comp.
74,788
and Kansas Pacific Railway
First Consolidated
Issued 12 October 1893

(15)   Saint Joseph and Grant Island
7,000,000
Guaranteed by U. P.
6% Deed of Trust to Central
Trust Corporation of New York
Issued 1 July 1885

(16)   Kansas City and Omaha
2,713,000
Railroad Comp.
5% Deed of Trust bonds to the
Central Trust Corporation of
New York

Guaranteed by Union Pacific
Issued 1 January 1887

(17)   Leavenworth, Topeka and
          690,000
         South Western Railway
         Guaranteed by Union Pacific
         Date of Issue and int. net known

Total
$84,238,075

It is questionable that the Congress intended to authorize this large amount of bonds in addition to the Common Stock, Government Aid sad Paramount Lien Bonds.

All of the foregoing bonds were foreclosed upon in 1898 as well as the Subsidy Aid Bonds. Payment of interest on these bonds and dividends on common stock caused the Railroad companies to continue to fall to meet the requirements of the Act of May 7, 1878. The clearly violated Section 4 of that Act. Why didn't the Secretary of the Treasury and the Attorney General take action against the defaulting companies as prescribed by Sections 10 and 11 of the Act?

A reasonable explanation is that the Paramount Lien Railroad bonds were a block to the Government taking any positive action to force the Railroad Companies into compliance with the Acts of July 1, 1862, July2, 1864, and May 7, 1878. The Secretary then immediately grasped the opportunity to talk with a presumed representative of the estate of Charles Durkee, namely Leonard C. Blaisdell.

In April, 1884, Blaisdell was invited to come to Washington and meet with the Secretary of the Treasury and the First Comptroller to discuss the matter of the estate of Charles Durkee.

The conference was held in the Treasury Department on April 22, 1884. Present were Leonard C. Blaisdell, Judge Folger, Secretary of the Treasury; Judge Lawrence, First Comptroller; Judge Brewster, Attorney General; Fred. T. Frelinghuysen, Secretary of State; Amos Webster, Treasury Department; Charles V. Parkman, Stenographer who recorded events of the conference; and others.

The Attorney General informed the Secretary of the Treasury that Leonard C. Blaisdell was a proper representative of the estate of Charles Durkee, and that the Secretary could legally do business with him in connection with the bonds assigned to Charles Durkee. They completely disregarded the fact that Caroline Durkee was the sole legal heir to Charles Durkee.

Nonetheless, and despite this error in dealing with an illegal representative, namely Leonard C. Blaisdell, the following agreement was made between Blaisdell and the Secretary of the Treasury, the Trustee of the estate of the Honorable Charles Durkee:

(1) That the Honorable Charles Durkee's Paramount Lien Bonds were different than all others because they were guaranteed by an Act of Congress, as lawfully paramount to the rights and interests of the United States, in respect to its Mortgage against the same corporations;

(2) That the Railroad Corporations owed the Government almost $100,000,000 on its Subsidy Aid Mortgage; had been involved in about forty lawsuits over it, and the Government would lose its investment if Charles Durkee's Estate foreclosed on the Railroad Corporations for the defaulted interest due on the Paramount Lien Bonds;

(3) That the Estate of Charles Durkee, as represented by Leonard C. Blaisdell would cooperate with the Government in order to protect both parties;

(4) That the Government would guarantee the principal amount of $64,623, 512 due on Durkee's bonds, and issue U. S. Sinking Fund Bonds guaranteeing accrued interest provided the estate of Charles Durkee agreed;

(5) That the Government In the name of the Secretary of the Treasury as Trustee of the funds would assume the responsibility of the Pacific Railroad Companies to the estate of Charles Durkee;

(6) That the principal amount would earn 6% per year and the accrued interest of about $70,000,000 would earn 5% per year, both commencing 1 January 1885;

(7) That the principal amount would be deposited in trust in the New York City sub-treasury; and the accrued interest would be invested in sinking fund bonds to mature on August 16, 1894 and which time the total amount of approximately $225,000,000 would be paid to the heirs of Charles Durkee;

(8) Blasidell agreed that Charles Durkee's personal papers on deposit in the Metropolitan National Bank to New York could to acquire by the Secretary of the Treasury;

(9) That Blaisdell would receive a complete record of the meeting, certificates of ownership of the bonds, and a copy of the transaction between himself and the Government; and that he would receive these documents in about 30 days.

This concluded the conference; and in this manner the Government assumed control of the Paramount Lien Railroad Bonds from the Trustee, agreeing that the principal and interest due Charles Durkee's estate would be placed in a statutory trust with the Secretary of the Treasury at Trustee. In addition, this conference executed a voluntary trust which made it an express trust arising out of personal confidence reposing in, and accepted by Leonard C. Blaisdell and Judge Charles J. Folger, Trustee, for the benefit of all parties, in which the scheme or plan was completely declared at the outset, and as further instrument needed to be executed, or no further act done, towards its complete creation of full effect.

About six weeks after the conference, L. C. Blaisdell returned to Washington to pick up his documents. He was given a cold shoulder by Judge William Lawrence who, at the time, refused to cooperate with him. Blaisdell then spent the next few months writing letters to the Secretary of the Treasury and to Judge Lawrence. None of them were answered. Judge Folger had left office shortly after the conference, and died on September 4, 1884, so Blaisdell thus lost his contact with the Trustee.

On January 19, 1885 Secretary of State Fred. T. Frelinghuysen and Doctor T. Robinson, both of whom were present at the conference held on April 22, 1884, realized that somebody in the Treasury Department was not cooperating with Blaisdell, and they issued official documents confirming the meeting of April 22, 1884 and the location of the personnel papers, vouchers, etc. of the estate of the Honorable Charles Durkee.

The Congress was still not satisfied with the conduct of the Railroad and when they received the annual report of the Secretary of the Treasury for 1884, which showed the information listed below, the Senate, OB January 30, 1885, introduced a proposed amendment to the Railroad Sinking Fund Act. The report which caused this action was as follows:

July 1, 1884
States of Railroad Indebtedness
(Government Aid)

Principal Amount Due	$84,623,512
Interest Paid By Government	65.099,504
Interest Paid By Railroads	18,804,122
Annual Interest Due	3,877,410
Average Company Payment	2,266, 625
Applied to Interest	1,253,608
Deposited In Sinking Fund	1,013,017
Net LOSS to Government	2,623,802

The following comment was made in Congress regarding the financing of the railroads.

"It turned out that the bonds which had been given by the Government to aid in the building and endowment of the road, the first-mortgage bonds which the Government permitted to be a lien upon the road and its property prior to its own, the mortgage bonds which were secured by the mortgages made on special properties of the Company, were all divided among the persons concerned in building the read, leaving the road crippled, poor and, embarrassed, and without provision for the security of its indebtedness when it should become due."

The proposed amendment was discussed considerably on the floor of the Senate, and the following is a summary of the information divulged:
      (1) The Companies had sold most of their common stock to the public;

(2) Theft was no record of the public holding the Paramount Lien Bonds;

(3) These was no representative of the owner of the Paramount Lien Bonds

present at any of the hearings on the proposed amendment; and

(4) There would be no trouble in the Government paying off the owner of

the Paramount Lien Bonds.

The following is a summary of the proposed amendment to the Railroad Sinking Fund Act introduced on January 30, 1885:

(1) The Companies would be authorized to issue Redemption Bonds in the amount of the total outstanding indebtedness of both the Government Aid and the Paramount Lien Bonds;

(2) The Redemption Bonds would represent a first mortgage for the United States ahead of all other indebtedness of the Railroad Companies;

(3) The Redemption Bonds would be issued to be repaid over 60 years, with 120th of the principal amount due, plus 3% interest to be paid on semi-annually payments. Commencing six months after passage of the amendment; and

(4) The Government would pay off the Paramount Lien Bonds.

The Proposed Amendment did not pass. The proposal continued to be discussed in the Congress over the next five years.

Judge William Lawrence who was responsible for issuing the documents to Leonard C. Blaisdell in accordance with the agreement of April 22, 1884 retired from his position as Comptroller of the Treasury in March, 1885, and established a law practice in Bellefontaine, Ohio.

From about February 1, 1886 to May 26, 1893. Blaisdell communicated by letter and in person with many Government officials, including the President of the United States, the several incumbent Secretaries of the Treasury, other Treasury Department officials, Congressmen and Senators, delivering certified copies of his knowledge of the meeting of April 22, 1884 to all. None of these officials denied the validity of his claim, and none of them informed him that Charles Durkee left a widow whom he did not represent. Also, during this period he received ten (10) letters and a proposed contract from Judge William Lawrence, in which Judge Lawrence offered to help him, provided his expenses were paid in advance. Be worked with Senator Cullom of Illinois and other Senators in preparing a proposed amendment to the Act of March 8, 1887, which protects the lawful owner of the Paramount Lion Bonds. This was done after the
Treasurer of the United States, Conrad N. Jordan, told Blaisdell that the transactions of the meeting of April 22, 1884 were binding on the Treasury Department; and he would settle if an enabling Act such as the Act of March 8, 1887 were passed. This was seven years before the agreed date of settlement of August 16. 1894.

On January 15, 1887, a Proposed Joint Resolution (H. Res. 170) was introduced in the Senate which would authorize the Secretary of the Interior to investigate the books of the Pacific Railroad Companies.

It was pointed out that the Railroad Companies were due to pay 25% of the net annual earnings of the aided railroads to the Government in accordance with the Act of May 7, 1878. Records of the Secretary of the Interior showed that the Railroad Companies were crediting earnings on the aided roads to the accounts of the unaided roads so that they could avoid paying 25% thereof to the Government. That their books were not being kept properly. Considerable money due the Government had been withheld by the Companies due to mistaken or erroneous reports, settlements, or accounts.
Proceeds of trust funds and land grants had been diverted from their lawful use. To correct these alleged evils and irregularities, the Secretary of the Interior should be granted authority to investigate their books.

There was considerable discussion of the stock issued by the Union Pacific. Several Senators were concerned that Oakes Ames and Jay Gould still controlled this Company. They were informed that they were no longer connected with the reorganized company. That Mr. Charles Francis Adams was now President of the Company, and most of the stock was owned by widows and orphans and they needed the dividends, several Senators took issue with this, stating that they had nothing against widows and orphans, but the dividend payments to them were illegal, and they doubted if the widows and orphans desired to defraud the Government. Most Senators agreed with this.

The implication that Mr. Ames and Mr. Gould were no longer connected with the Union Pacific was not true. They both continued to participate in the affaire of the Company, and Mr. Ames was a Bond Receivership Trustee during the foreclosure proceedings of the Union Pacific in 1895 and he made millions of dollars off of illegally issued bonds.

The Railroad Companies submitted lists of the names of their stockholders to the Senate Judiciary Committee, but despite the threat of the Paramount Lien Bonds to the security of the investment of the Government, no mention was whatsoever as to the owners or alleged owners of these bonds. With discussions spreading over several years in Congress, and the security of an investment of many millions of dollars involved, the owner of these bonds had to be a deceased person or an incompetent person.

During these hearings, several Government Directors wrote letters to Mr. Charles Francis Adams, President of the Union Pacific in support of his position on the proposed joint resolution. One of these Government Directors was the Honorable Franklin McVeigh who later became Secretary of the Treasury, and in 1912 gave Jacob Souder permission to copy the records of the estate of Charles Durkee held by
the Treasury Department, said records showing that the Honorable Charles Durkee owned all of the Paramount Lien Bonds and that the trust fund monies derived there from were held for his estate. Mr. McVeigh wrote a letter dated February 15, 1887 in which he stated that nobody at present threatens the security of the Government but the Government itself.

It is not difficult to agree with Mr. McVeigh, for It is impossible to understand how responsible officials in the Departments of the Interior and Treasury could permit the Railroad Companies to flaunt the several acts of Congress passed to aid them, and in particular the Act of May 7, 1878 which specifically and forcefully gave these Departments all the authority they needed to force these Railroad Companies to comply with the Acts,

As stated previously, Leonard C. Blaisdell was working with Senator Cullom of his home state of Illinois, to amend the proposed House Resolution to protect the owners of the Paramount Lien Bonds.

The proposed Resolution was enacted into law on March 3, 1887. The first three sections authorized the appointment of a Board of Commissioners to investigate the books of the Railroad Companies and report results to the Secretary of the Interior. Sections 4 and 5 concerned protection of the owners of the bonds and the Railroad Sinking Fund. They are quoted as follows:

"94. Liens of United (States; redemption of prior encumbrance.

Whenever, in the opinion of the President, it shall be deemed necessary to the protection on interests and the preservation of the security of the United States in respect of its lien, mortgage, or other interest in any of the property of any or all of the several companies upon which a lien, mortgage, or other encumbrance paramount to the right, title or interest of the United States for the same property , or any part of the same, may exist and be then lawfully liable to be enforced, the Secretary of the Treasury shall under the direction of the President, redeem or otherwise clear off such paramount

I hereby certify that this Affidavit was corrected after it was typed and this apace is blank.

James W. McCrocklin

Deposition of Fredrick T. Frelinghuysen

Office of the Secretary of State
Washington, D. C.
January 19th, 1885

KNOW ALL MEN BY THESE PRESENTS:

On behalf of Leonard C. Blaisdell, Attorney of Record for the Estate of the Honorable Charles Durkee, deceased, Kenosha, Wisconsin, I am herewith setting forth fasts relative to a meeting held in the United States Treasury Department, on April 22, 1884, and causing same to be made of record in this office.

I was present at this meeting, together with the First Comptroller, Judge William Lawrence, Secretary of the Treasury C. J. Folger., Solicitor of the Treasury, Dr. Thomas Robinson, and other Treasury employees, when Judge Folger, Secretary of the Treasury said that Leonard C. Blaisdell had come to the Treasury Department by appointment, with proper credentials to prove that he was the   Attorney-of-Record for the heirs at law for the Estate of the Hon. Charles Durkee.

At this meeting, all of the Treasury and Government Officials heard Judge Folger ask the question of Judge Lawrence: "Have you examined the credentials of Mr. Blaisdell?" and Judge Lawrence replied: "I have examined them and find that he is the proper person for us to do business with." Judge Folger then turned to the Attorney General and said: "We have here all of the First Mortgage Prior Lien Bonds of the Union Pacific and Central Pacific Railroads, in round figures amounting to $64,000, 000, and they are all assigned to one sole assignee: Charles Durkee."

Attorney General Brewster, Judge William Lawrence, Secretary C. J. Folger and myself, all saw the bonds and the assignment of these bonds to Charles Durkee.

After considerable discussion with Mr. Blaisdell, Judge Folger addressed Judge Lawrence with this remark: "You will make a complete record of this transaction of this meeting and deliver to Mr. Blaisdell a perfect record thereof. In addition thereto, you will issue to Mr. Blaisdell an instrument setting forth that the United States Government guarantees, the payment of the principal of these bonds and as much interest as shall be due, up to and including December 31, 1884.

In Witness Whereof I have hereunto affixed my hand and the Seal of the United States this nineteenth day of January, A. D., Eighteen Hundred and eighty-five.

FRED'K   T.
FRELINGHUYSEN,
Secretary of State.

Deposition Charles A Nimocks

Court of Claims Case 18003

Q 16 What, if anything did you find relating to the ownership of bonds by Caroline Durkee Widow of Charles Durkee Deceased?
A. I found that Blaisdell had addressed a letter to the Register of the Treasury asking him if there was any registered bonds in the name of Charles or Caroline Durkee, and he replied that a letter press copy shows that there was $11,500 in registered bonds, in the name of Caroline Durkee.

This may relate to the document that states that Caroline Durkee had bonds with specific serial numbers. The statement does not state if these were government bonds or railroad bonds. The Union Pacific RXR did not sell registered Bonds in 1866-69.

Clark Rush Testimony Treasury Department
Clark Rush Deposition

Answer Sir I saw letters from Folger Sec. of treasury

Question 15 and the following questions by Mr. Plumber; Judge do you remember a meeting in your office on April 22, 1884, between Hon. Charles J Folger Sec. of the treasury yourself and other officials and Leonard C Blaisdell representing Charles Durkee's heirs?"
Answer yes Sir
Question 16 did judge Lawrence make an answer to that as follows: quote there was a meeting. I think laid still went to judge Folgers

Question 18 What kind of bonds?
Answer: Government bonds believe Pacific railroad bonds?
Question 25 know what occurred there is anything?
Answer Mr. Blaisdell showed his power of attorney from the heirs of the estate and wanted him to assist him in looking up the assets of the estate and the sub treasury New York and the wrote to the sub treasurer.

Note Sub-Treasury of New York
Q 27. He wrote at you instance, did he not?
A. Yes, sir; he wrote there to see what he could find of the record.
Q.28 What reply did he get, if any?
A He got a reply that there was $12,000, deposited here in the interest of a Mrs. Durkee---to her order.

Affidavit of Clifton R. Finch

CLIFTON R. FINCH, residing in Denver, Colorado, and Cleveland, Ohio, deposes and states as follows:

"Was born in Philadelphia in 1852, Moved to Cincinnati 1857. Remaining a resident of that city until 1889. "That he attended the Massachusetts Institute of Technology and Harvard University as an engineer in 1880-1886.

"Spent the major portion of my life as a contract engineer for the Cleveland Foundry and Machine Company and Cleveland Machine Tool Company, Cleveland, Ohio, in the capacity of an engineer and sales manager east and. west of the Mississippi river." That I did at different times serve in the capacity of engineer for the companies who were more or less interested in the Pacific railroads, particularly the Union Pacific, Central Pacific and Southern Pacific, A. T. & S. F., Rock Island, Denver, and Rio Grande.

"At certain times discussed with H. M. Hoxie, the man who owned contracts to build a section of Union Pacific Railway from the Missouri River at Omaha, Nebraska; also Robert Lovett, attorney, later President of the First National Bank of Chicago and later Secretary of the United States Treasury; also Secretary of the Interior Department of the United States; Congressman DeWees, attorney, residing at Denver, Colorado; also other officials of the United States government and State officials.

"That it was my duty at various times in connection with large sales of railroad equipment requiring information subject to securities pledged as a guarantee of payment for machinery and rolling stock to check companies which were buying from him for the supplying companies. I also had to check land titles as were required for certain re-organization companies.

"That he made photographic chain of pictures in the United States of railroad Right-of-way for the Harriman group, 1909-1910.

"That I owned my own private car for personal use at various points to contact officials of the Pacific Railroads, at which times he made large sales and arranged financial matters pertaining to the sales and in that manner acquired knowledge which never was made available to the public relative to financial matters of the railroads.

"That I distinctly recall the statement of H. M. Hoxie 'that Governor Durkee, of the Territory of Utah, not only guided the legislation creating the railroad corporations and business destiny of these Pacific Railroads, but, he also furnished the original cash required.

"That I heave knowledge and basis of fact, that Mr. Hoxie procured the original construction contract, and the Governor Charles Durkee also acted as his bondsman to the United States Government. Mr. Hoxie further states that Governor Durkee had acquired many millions of dollars worth of construction bonds of the Union Pacific Railroad in lieu of cash for the supplies which he furnished to the construction companies thru his firm, John W. Keer & Co., Salt Lake City, Utah. "

"That Attorney Robert Lovett, Sr. while traveling with me in my private car between Houston and San Antonio, stated that he was greatly concerned over the fact that banker sin New York had pledged as collateral for the contracts with the Cleveland companies the First Mortgage Bonds of their railroads, or as they were called in those days of construction, the construction bonds, which were issued under the Acts of Congress passed 1862-1864, in aid of the construction of these Pacific railroads. That if they defaulted in payments, as he (Lovitt) knew that these First Mortgage Bonds had been deposited by order of Governor Charles Durkee, who all or most of the, with the Treasury Department of the United States; he also stated that certain bankers had in some a manner acquired these bonds and were using them as collateral for loans; also, since Mr. Durkee's death in 1870, the government, due to their loan to these railroads in the form of subsidy aid bonds in an amount of many million dollars, which constituted a second mortgage on these railroads as called for under the Acts of 1862-1864.

"That Lyman Gauge, Secretary of the United States Treasury, had stated to him (Lovitt) that he should not count on anyone being able to place the First Mortgage Bonds on the Union Pacific Railway Company as collateral for loan or as a collateral against purchase, orders; that these bonds had been redeemed and the funds were held in trust by the United States Treasury Department for the estate of Charles Durkee, former Governor of the Territory of Utah; that he had been obliged to conceal these facts by certain bankers who had pledged to deliver these bonds if they defaulted on purchase contracts; that he believed the railroads under the re-organization plan would be able to meet their loans and purchase commitments, but, that he (Gauge) knew that the cash held in trust would not be surrendered as it belonged to the estate of Charles Durkee and not to the railroad companies or their bankers. "

"That Congressman DeWees in Denver, on or about the year 1893, in the office of Tetter, Vale and Walcott, stated to me that he had at different times tried to purchase all of or any part interested in certain railroad contracts held, owned and controlled by Governor Durkee, but, that the Governor always demanded the certain amounts be taken in bonds of these railroad companies in lieu of cash payments.

"That shortly after Judge Lawrence retired from the office of First Comptroller of the United States Treasury he called on Judge Lawrence on Judge Lawrence at his office in Bellefontaine, Ohio. To the best of my knowledge it was during the year 1890. That Judge Lawrence was asked to state what, if anything, he knew relative to the financial status of the Pacific Railroads as had been given aid by the government in their construction? The Judge replied: "The United States Government is fully protected on its second mortgage for the reason that a call by the Secretary of the Treasury, Judge Charles J. Folger, these railroads deposited with the Government, January, 1886, an amount equal to the total of their first mortgage debt, in lieu of a defaulted interest payment. That this sum could be used at any time to redeem the First Mortgage Bonds of these roads deposited with the Treasury Department of the United States with Charles Durkee as the sole assignee. That he (Lawrence) knew that certain hostile groups were trying to conceal the facts of Durkee's ownership of these bonds from his estate, that they had the support and backing of certain bankers. That he did not know if these would do find a way to get these First Mortgage Bonds into their possession prior to their redemption date. That he believed the Trust Fund into which these bonds had been deposited was now selling these bonds to the Thurman Act Sinking Fund. " Clifton R. Finch _(Seal)

Deposition William R. Russell

Subscribed before Dudley T. Hassan, Examiner in Chancery, this 14th day of November, 1901.

Whereupon, William R. Russell, a witness of lawful age, produced on the part of the complainant, and being first duly sworn according to law, was examined and testified as follows:

Direct Examination by Mr. Wood.

Q. State your name, age, residence, and occupation?

A. William R. Russell; of lawful age; Kensington, Md.; clerk in the U. S. Treasury Department.

Q. How long have you been a clerk in the Treasury Department?

A. Twenty years; I have charge of the vault of the Treasurer's office.

Q. What is the name of that vault?

A. It is called the "Bond Vault."

Q. Do you keep a record of the contents of that vault?

A. I do not; that is kept by the bookkeepers. I merely keep a pencil memorandum.

Q. The United States Treasurer's report of 1869 on page 237, shows that there was deposited in his office the following:

There have been left in the custody of the Treasurer as special deposits, within the fiscal year, as security that certain railroads, hereinafter mentioned, would be completed and equipped according to the requirements of the Government as a condition precedent to the issue of the remaining portion of the Government bonds, subsidies as follows:

First Mortgage Coupon Bonds of the Union Pacific Railroad Company $1,600,000

First Mortgage Coupon Bonds of the Central Pacific Railroad of California 4,000,000

Do you know the location and custody of the first mortgage bonds of the Union Pacific Railway Company mentioned above?

A. I do not; I was not in the Treasury Department at that time.

Q. Is there any record kept of what became of them?

A. If they were in any one of the funds of either of the Pacific Railways, they were probably in the vault when (99) I took charge of it.

Q. Is your vault the only place they would be kept in?

A. I do not know where the bonds were. The probability is they were in the cash room.

Q. Have you ever run across the bonds mentioned in this trust fund?

A. I have not.

Q. Have you any record in your custody of the contents of that Bond Vault, showing who was the owner of the first mortgage lien on the Union, Central, Western and Kansas Pacific Railways?

A. Some of these first mortgage Bonds were in the vault since I have been in charge.

Q. Are they there now?

A. No, sir.

Q. Do you know what became of them?

A. They were sent to the Assistant Treasurer at New York by messengers and by express, for the purpose of redemption by the railway companies, being usually sent in advance of their maturity. I took some of them to New York myself and delivered them to the Assistant Treasurer of the United States at the Sub-Treasury.

Q. Did you make the collection or just delivered them to the Assistant Treasurer?

A. I merely acted as messenger to take them to New York and delivered them to the Assistant Treasurer of the United States for redemption by the said railway companies.

Q. Do you know what amounts you delivered?

A. They varied at the different times the first were dated in 1865 and were 30-year bonds. They began to mature in 1895 from that on to 1899, and were sent out as fast as they became due.

Q. What railroads were they on?

A. Union, Central, Eastern Division of the Union (100) or Kansas Pacific, Sioux City and the Western Pacific Railways.

Q. Do you recollect the total amount of them?

A. I do not.

Q. Then all of these first mortgage bonds have been passed out of your vault and you have none of the first mortgage bonds of the Central, Union, Western or Sioux City or Kansas Pacific Railways, in your vault or under your control?

A. No, sir; they have all been sent or taken to the Assistant Treasurer of the United States at New York.

W. R. RUSSELL.
Subscribed before me this 14th day of November, 1901.

DEPOSITION OF JOHN T. DEWEES

Met pursuant to notice to continue taking testimony for complainant Present D. W. Wood, Esq., for complainant and Mr. Gould, though duly notified, did not appear, and the following testimony was taken subject to his cross examination.

Whereupon, John T. Dewees, a former witness was recalled, examined and testified as follows:

Direct Examination, By Mr. Wood:

Q. Mr. Dewees, to whom did you refer to in your third answer on page 58 of your former testimony in this cause, and what do you mean by saying that he was also furnishing ties for the Union and Central Pacific Railway Companies?

A. Casemate Brothers, of Paynesville, Ohio, had the contract with the Union Pacific Railway Company to lay, construct, back-fill and surfacing of the same, and furnished the ties from Omaha to the junction of the Central Pacific Railway; they also furnished ties for Union and Central Pacific Railway Companies, and that Governor Durkee was also furnishing ties for the Central and Union Pacific Railway Companies and their branches, and to Casemate Brothers and their subcontractors,

and J. W. Kerr & Co., of which firm Durkee was a partner, they were furnishing to the contractors who were building the Central and Union Pacific Railway Companies and their branches, all the ties and material that were required to be furnished, for the construction of the roads .and their branches.

Q. Were they paid in money, or did they receive certificates for their payment?

A. They were paid partly in money and partly in Union Pacific first mortgage bonds; and also in first mortgage bonds on the Central Pacific Railway and its branches, for the supplies which they, Casemate Brothers furnished. (108)

Q. Can you give me an idea of the per cent they received in money?

A. It would depend entirely upon the sub-contract made with Casemate Brothers; the amount of money and the proportion of bonds was a matter entirely within the discretion of the Casemates.

Q. On page 58 of your former testimony, you stated that those bonds were usually $1000 bonds; did you handle all the bonds in Governor Durkee's possession, and are you sure they were all $1000 bonds?-

A. I did not examine all the bonds Governor Durkee had; there were a large amount of bonds in his possession, but a large number of them for $2500 to $5000, were also there. As well as I remember, the bonds were usually of the denominations that were easiest for the contractors and sub-contractors to handle.

Q. In your testimony in regard to the number of times you met Governor Durkee and talked with him, your answers any books or papers of said Pacific Railway Companies that would disclose to whom said certificates or bonds had been issued?

A. I think Mr. Charles Kuntz could give vast information upon the subject and I understand that George Francis Train's private secretary, now living in Denver, Colorado, and who has expressed a perfect willingness to give all the information in his possession to assist in the adjusting of this matter.

Q. Have you any records or memorandums that would determine definitely how long it was after you met Governor Durkee at Cheyenne, Wyoming, where you say you examined these bonds, that you heard of his (Durkee's) death?

A. It took the same length of time for me to go to Salt Lake City that it took Governor Durkee to go to Omaha. I heard the following day that he was dead; the next morning after I reached Salt Lake City, I called at John Kerr & Go's, office and Mr. Kerr showed me a telegram that Durkee had died in Omaha the day before.

Q. Have you any interest in the result of this suit?

A. None whatever.

Q. Are you retained as counsel in this suit?

A. No, sir.

Q. Do you represent any of the heirs-at-law or claimants in this suit?

A. No, sir,- I do not represent any claimant nor have I any interest whatever in the results of this suit.

Q. If Mr. Gould makes a reg/uest for your return for the purpose of cross-examination, will you return upon notice from the Examiner?

A. I will cheerfully present myself for cross-examination.

Q. Do you know or can you set forth any other matter or thing that may be a benefit or advantage to the parties at issue in this case or either of them, or that may be material (111) to the subject of this your examination or the matter in question in this case?

A. No, sir; I do not.

JOHN T. DEWEES.

Subscribed before me this 25th day of November, A.D. 1901.
DUDLEY T. HASSAN,
Examiner in Chancery

Appendix III
Exhibits to Case 67-C-221

Exhibits listing documents found and used in the court case. These list documents where copies have been found.

1. Affidavit by James McCrocklin on certification of evidence,
2. Affidavit on History of Financing Pacific Railroads by James McCrocklin .
3,, Memorandum on Leonard C. Blaisdell.
4. Memorandum on Charles Durkee.
5. Motion for Judicial Notice of Evidence.
6. Act of July 1, 1862 Authorizing Government Guaranteed Financing
7. Act of July 2, 1864 Authorizing Railroad Companies to Issue Own Bonds.
8. Act of May 7, 1878 Establishing Trust in Form of Sinking Fund to Pay Off Paramount Lien Bonds.
9. Act of May 3, 1887 Authorizing Government to Pay Off Paramount Lien Bonds.
10. Act of September 11, 1841 stating That All Trust Funds earn 5% Interest.
11. Act of June 26, 1934 Authorizing Secretary of the Treasury to Pay Off Trust Funds and Report to Congress.
12. Joint Resolution of Congress of April 10, 1869 Requiring Deposit in Trust of Paramount Lien Bonds as Security for completion of Railroads.
13. Administrative Procedure Act, 5 U.S.C. Authorizing Suit against Trustee for an Accounting.
14. Letter dated April 20, 1866 from Secretary of the Interior to the President of the United States.
15. Letter dated November 6, 1869 from Secretary of Treasury to J. C. Bige1ow, Loan Division.
16. Letter dated November 16, 1869 from Secretary of Treasury to C. P. Huntington.

17. Letter dated November 28, 1869 from Treasury to Interior.

18. Letter dated January 7, 1870 from Secretary of Treasury to Treasurer.

19. Letter dated Sept. 7, 1870 from Secretary of Treasury to E. H. Rollins.

20. Letter dated January 29, 1879 from Secretary of Treasury to Treasurer.

21. Official Statement of Fred T. Frelinghuysen, Secretary of State dated January 19, 1885.

22. Letter dated January 19, 1885 from Doctor T. Robinson to the Comptroller.

23. Letter dated January 29, 1886 from House Judiciary Committee to the Attorney General.

24. Justice Dept. memorandum dated April 26, 1934.

25. Attorney General Memorandum dated July 9, 1934.

26. Justice Dept. Memorandum dated August 23, 1934.

27. Memorandum re Racine College dated January 11, 1936.

28. Letter dated October 7, 1965 from Dept. of State to Lawrence Simmons.

29. Extract from Volume 5, Comptroller's Decisions.

30. Forty-First Congress - First Session, Monday, March 15, 1869 Statements by Senators Cassely and Sherman.

31. Forty-First Congress - Senate - First Session - Comment on Railroad Sinking Fund.

32. Fiftieth Congress - First Session - House Report 866 Re. Railroad Sinking Fund.

33. Fiftieth Congress - House - First Session - Resolution of Mr. Anderson.

34. Fifty-Fourth Congress-Senate-First Session-Statement made by Leonard C. Blaisdell under oath.

35. Fifty-Fourth Congress - Senate - First Session – Statement of Collis P. Huntington under oath.

36. Fifty-Fourth Congress-Senate Second Session – Resolutions on Investigation of Treasury Department.

37. Fifty-Fifth Congress - Message of President Grover Cleveland.

38. Supreme Court Decision (99 U.S.700).

39. Leonard C. Blaisdell vs. United States in the Court of Claims Extracts from Case 18003.

40. Power of Attorney signed by Caroline Durkee on June 10, 1895 in attempt to collect Trust Fund.

41. Deposition of Leonard C. Blaisdell dated June 5, 1896.

42. Deposition of C. A. Nimocks dated June 17, 1897.

43. Deposition of M. R. King dated Dec. 12, 1899.

44. Letter dated A p r i l 11, 1883 from Leonard C. Blaisdell to the Solicitor of the Treasury.

45. Letter dated April 19, 1883 from Treasury Department to Leonard C. Blaisdell

46. Letter dated April 21, 1883 from Leonard C. Blaisdell to William Lawrence.

47. Letter dated August 7, 1883 from Leonard C. Blaisdell to the First Comptroller.

48. Letters dated August 16 and August 24, 1883 from Leonard C. Blaisdell to the First Comptroller.

49. Dept. of Interior .Memo dated August 22, 1883.

50. Letter dated August 24, 1883 from the First Comptroller to Leonard C. Blaisdell.

51. Two letters dated A p r i l 3, 1884 from the First Comptroller to Leonard C. Blaisdell and A. B. Baldwin.

52. Letter dated July 21, 1884 from the State Dept. to Leonard C. Blaisdell.

53. Letter dated August 23, 1884 from Leonard C. Blaisdell to William Lawrence.

54. Letter dated Sept. 30, 1884 from Leonard C. Blaisdell to William Lawrence.

55. Letter dated April l 27, 1886 from Crammond Kennedy to Clark Brush.

56. Letter dated Feb. 1, 1887 from William Lawrence to Leonard Blaisdell.

57. Letter dated August 26, 1887 from William Lawrence to Leonard Blaisdell.

58. Letter dated Sept, 1, 1887 from Lawrence to Blaisdell.

59. Letter dated Sept. 25, 1887 from Lawrence to Blaisdell.

60. Letter dated Feb. 2, 1888 from Lawrence to Blaisdell.

61. Letter dated May 4, 1888 from Lawrence to Blaisdell.

62. Letter dated Dec. 18, 1888 from Lawrence to Blaisdell.

63. Affidavit of Leonard C. Blaisdell dated March 2, 1888,

64. Letter dated June 21, 1888 from Blaisdell to First Comptroller.

65. Letter dated July 24, 1888 from Blaisdell to the First Comptroller.

66. Letter dated August 15, 1888 from Blaisdell to the First Comptroller.

67. Letter dated August 17, 1888 from Blaisdell to the First Comptroller.

68. Letter dated August 23, 1888 from Blaisdell to the First Comptroller.

69. Letter dated January 5, 1894 from Lawrence to A. Bryan.

70. Petition of Jacob Souder dated November 25, 1913.

71. Four Affidavits of Lillie Souder Walker.

72. History of Pacific Rail Road Paramount Lien Bonds by Jacob Souder.

73. Affidavit of Christian S. Pearce made on Oct. 12, 1933.

74. Affidavit of Robert W. Walters made on Aug. 2, 1921.

75. Affidavit of Charm. Thompson made on Feb. 14, 1936.

76. Affidavit of Charles Dick made on Jan. 23, 1936.

77. Affidavit of Clifton R. Finch undated.

7.8. Affidavit of Joshua T. Butler made on Jan. 14, 1947.

79. Affidavit of J. Forrest Johnston executed in 1965.

80. Affidavit of Homer R. Foulkes made on Oct. 4, 1965.

81. Affidavit of Mengard Miller made on March 3, 1967.

82. Affidavit of James W. McCrocklin Re. Sinking Fund made Aug.3, 1963

83. Affidavit of James W. McCrocklin Re. Secretary of Treasury Reports to Congress made on Aug. 3, 1963.

84. Affidavit of James W. McCrocklin made on July 20, 1967.
85. Report of Foreclosure of Union Pacific Railroad Company.
86. Senate Document Number 161 - 55th Congress Re. Sinking Fund.
87. Senate Rep ort 293 Page 60 Re Pacific Railroads.
88. Last Will and Testament of Charles Durkee.
89. Probate Court order on estate of Charles Durkee dated March 21, 1882.
90. Last Will and Testament of Caroline Durkee.
91. Probate Court order on estate of Caroline Durkee dated Nov. 6, 1912.
92. Acceptance of Bequest by Board of Trustees of Racine College
93. U. S. Archives Letter dated March 31, 1967.
94. Probate Court order dated January 15, 1968 re the estate of Char 1es Durkee.
95. Probate Court order dated January 15, 1968 re the estate of Caroline Durkee.
96. Letter of Stanton Minter and Bruner, Certified Public Accountants, dated July 26, 1966.
97. Affidavit of Rt. Rev. Donald H. V. Hallock, D. D. Bishop of Milwaukee.
98. Brief on Laches, etc.
99. U. S. Archives Letter dated Nov. 30, 1966.
100. Will of Durkee: Haire, Appellant 164 Wis. 41.
101. Articles of Incorporation of Board of Trustees of Racine College.
102. President Andrew Johnson's Letter to Senate and House dated April 24, 1866.
103. Affidavit of James W. McCrocklin re: John A. Kuykendall.
104. Affidavit of James W. McCrocklin re. Howard T. Foulkes.
105. Affidavit re. Press Release.
106. Motion and demurrer on L. C. Blaisdell Case 18003.

Appendix IV

- Will of Charles Durkee
- Will of Caroline Durkee
- Contract Between Caroline Durkee and Harvey Durkee
- List of Heirs in Court case 18003

Durkee Will

I, CHARLES DURKEE, a resident of the City and County of Kenosha, in the State of Wisconsin, (for two years past and upwards at Salt Lake, Utah), of sound, disposing mind and memory and mindful of the uncertainty of this life, do make this my last will and testament hereby revoking all others heretofore made:

I do hereby devise, bequeath and convey by this, my will, unto my executors, Harvey Durkee, of Kenosha, aforesaid, and Franklin H. Head, late of Kenosha, now of Utah and to which of them may act as executor and to the survivor of said executors all my real and personal estate rights and credits
with the right to sell, dispose and con vey the same without order of any court or officer, in such amounts, and on such terms, as they may deem for- the best intentions of this, my will always taking adequate security where credit may be given. This is upon the following trusts, to-wit :

First. To pay all my debts, funeral expenses, and for a suitable monument for my grave.

Second. Whereas my beloved wife, Caroline Durkee, has now settled upon her an annuity during her life of six hundred dollars annually, and she has a life lease of my homestead in Kenosha City I do herefore, in addition thereto and in lieu of all dower and right of dower (which she will relinquish
to my executors in due form), direct my said executors to invest in interest-paying securities so much of my assets that the annual interest thereon will amount to one thousand dollars annually; which sum of one thousand dollars annually accrued my acting executor will pay one in semi-annual portions, during her natural life, to my said wife, Caroline.

Third. If my said wife, Caroline, shall have any child or children of mine born to her either before or after my decease at any time, then my acting executor will pay out of the residue of such assets, whenever such child or children arrives at the age of twenty-one years, the sum of five thousand dollars to each; and if there be a lack of funds, then so much as there may be, share and share alike, after deducting expenses of administration.

Fourth. Out of said assets my acting executor will pay to the board of officers of the free schools of Kenosha City, Wisconsin, five thousand dollars, to be, by said board, expended in and towards procuring a telescope for the use of the free schools of said City of Kenosha; which board or corporate power of said free schools will make such rules and regulations as to the care and use of said telescope as shall make it useful to the teachers and scholars in said schools for all time to come.

Fifth. All the balance and residue of my assets and property, of whatever name and kind, my executors, or the acting one, will expend for the cause of education of the youth of both sexes, in such way and manner as my executor or executors shall deem best for the good of the youth as citizens of our common country; and when on the decease of my wife, Caroline, the said securities invested to make the annuity to her, shall be freed from that charge; then whatever may remain, after providing for the matters stated above under the third and fourth subdivisions, to be appropriated under the fifth subdivision. .

Sixth. If for any cause there shall be no executor, then I will and declare that the administrator duly appointed with this, my will annexed, shall have all the powers and duties and obligations of my said executors, such powers, duties and obligations of administrator to be supervised by the proper court in probate that may make the appointment and executors and administrators to make due report to the proper court annually. My desire is that my body be buried in the cemetery, near the South Ward, in the City of Kenosha.

Seventh. My will also is, that my gold watch, chain and appendages, be the property of my nephew, Charles, named after me, the son of said Harvey Durkee, and that my executors deliver the same to him as, and for, his property the gift of his uncle. Note In the third item above the words "of mine" duly interlined.

Signed and sealed at Kenosha, Wisconsin, this 12th day of February, A. D. 1869.

(SEAL) CHARLES DURKEE.
This instrument executed this twelfth day of February, 1869, by Charles Durkee in our presence, who then & there declared it to be his last Will & testament, & he requested us to sign the same as witnesses, which we now do, in his presence & in the presence of each other.

Will and Testament of Caroline Durkee

Know all men by THESE Presents: That I Caroline
Durkee, do hereby make my LAST WILL AND
TESTAMENT, hereby revoking all others,
First. . 1st. I direct that all my just debts and funeral
expenses be paid, to include a reasonable sum for a stone or
monument at my grave, but' I do not desire an expensive
one, preferring rather that my memory may be preserved in
the permanent and living charities hereinafter provided for.
Second. 2nd. If before my decease I shall not have done so,
I direct my executors place proper memorial stones at the
graves In a lot of my father in the cemetery at Kenosha,
Wis. of the following personal vis. Anna Lake, my mother,
Jared Lake, Jr., my brother, Albert Lake, my brother, & an
infant son of my sister Angelina, (their remains having been
removed from Ft. Wayne, Indiana, by reason of some
encroachment upon the cemetery there, for railway
purposes, by «y direction some years since.)
Third. 3rd. I do hereby give and bequeath to the "St. Luke's
Free Hospital of Chicago, " to endow a Hospital Bed to be
called the "CAROLINE DURKEE BED, " Five Thousand
dollars:- said principal sum to bo invested and re-invested
forever so as to keep the principal undiminished,- the
income only to be expanded for the support of said charity
forever,- no part of the principal sun to be expended in
buildings nor for any other purpose whatever, but to be kept
invested upon good security so as to produce a certain and
assured income forever to support said charity.

Fourth 4h. All the rest and residue of my estate real & personal and whatever situate, I direct to be converted into money or good personal interest bearing securities, and to be paid over to the Board of Trustees of Racine Collage to be held by them in Trust forever upon the following trusts and conditions:- (said College situate at Racine, Wis)

First. no part of said principal sum shall be expended In Buildings.

Second. The whole thereof shall be invested and kept invested forever upon Bond and mortgage upon good improved real estate, but no loan shall be made except upon a first mortgage, and for no amount to exceed the one half of the fair cash value of the estate over and above all improvements thereon.

Third. That the annual Income to be derived therefrom and the whole thereof shall be forever devoted to the support of the chair of the "Professor of Chemistry" to which chair may be added, if not already all other natural sciences.

FOURTH. Said Fund is to be known in perpetuity as the "Caroline Durkee endowment of the Chair of Chemistry or Applied Natural Sciences."

Fifth. With full poser to carry out these provisions, I nominate and
appoint *it*. K. Fairbank, a Trustee of St. Luke's Hospital and James R.
Doolittle, Jr., a Trustee of Racine College of Chicago, executors and of 3rd day of December, 1887, set my hand and seal, and do herby publish and declare sa such in the presence of Witnesses.

CAROLINE DURKEE   (SEAL)

Signed, Sealed, Acknowledged, published and declared by the above named Caroline Durkee as and for her Last Will and Testament, in the presence of us who at her request, and in her presence, and in the presence of each other, have subscribed our names thereto the day and year above written.

James R. Doolittle
Racine, Wisconsin

Hetta M. Elkins Ave., Chicago — 1706 Indiana

Jane S. James Chicago — 71 - 23rd 3rd St.

Sarah L. Anger Chicago — 71 - 23rd 3rd St.

Harriet P. Hurlbut Place, Chicago — 39 Winthrop

Contract between Caroline Durkee and Harvey Durkee

For, and in consideration of the sum of Sixteen Thousand Dollars, ($16,000), in hand paid "by Harvey Durkee of Kenosha, Wisconsin, the receipt whereof I hereby acknowledge, and for the further consideration of the agreements and covenants of said Harvey Durkee hereinafter appearing, I, Caroline Durkee do hereby sell, assign, transfer and set over to said Harvey Durkee all ray right, title and interest in and to the property rights, credits and estate of my late husband, Charles Durkee, deceased, and the proceeds thereof save as hereinafter excepted – said estate being now in process of settlement by F. H. Head, Executor of. the last will and testament of said Charles Durkee - and the said

Harvey Durkee by reason of this sale and transfer shall have the same - rights end authority which I myself should have in the premises to receive from the executor any and all the property and assets hereby

sold and transferred or the -proceeds thereof and to execute receipts therefor. But the following property and assets are not included in the foregoing sale and transfer and are excepted therefrom, to-wit:-

FIRST)- The Homestead now occupied by the said Caroline Durkee in Kenosha, Wisconsin,

SECOND- All the household furniture of said deceased and all- the other personal -property now-in said homestead.

THIRD - One half of the mining claims mentioned in the inventory of the executor now on file.

FOURTH - One half of the proceeds of the twenty acres of land near San Diego, California mentioned in said inventory on file.

FIFTH - All other the property, rights and credits and assets belonging or appertaining to said estate which is not included in the inventory aforesaid made by the executors and filed June 16th, 1870, in the County Court of Kenosha County - and to render certain as between the said Caroline Durkee and Harvey Durkee what is not so included in said inventory it is hereby stipulated and agreed that the following articles and non others are so included in said inventory, to-wit.

Dec. 30, 1869 for the aggregate sum of .Forty Three thousand Dollars in principal besides interest, One Note against Pardon Dodds for one Thousand Dollars, - One note against F. Heath for Four Hundred and Seven Dollars and Fifty-three cents, - One note against Mr. Miffin for one Hundred Dollars, - One note against J. S Rich for about Fifty Dollars, - One note against Mr. Goforth for .Sixty Three Dollars,

One account against Wm. Rydalch for One Hundred Dollars, - One against Harvey Durkee for Twelve Hundred and Forty Four Dollars and Fifty-nine cents, - One gray mare at Salt Lake City. - five and. one-half cords of wood and small lot of household furniture at Salt Lake City, and a claim against Z. G. Simmons for Three Hundred Dollars, - about Eleven Thousand feet of mining claims at Pahranagat, Nevada, - Cash in hands of F. H, Head to the amount of Four Hundred Thirty Three Dollars and Sixty-four cents.

The homestead in the City of Kenosha and all the personal. Proper therein, -.all of the property in said inventory mentioned and the proceeds thereof - Excepting the said homestead and the personal property therein and , one-half of said mining claims and one half of the proceeds of said twenty acres of land near San Diego - and the amount heretofore paid to said Caroline Durkee by the executors - comprises the sale hereby made to said Harvey Durkee and it is understood and agreed that all the property rights, credits and assets and the proceeds thereof so as aforesaid excepted from this sale and transfer shall be exempt from any and all costs and expenses of , the settlement of said estate and from all debts and liabilities of said estate and from all the valid charges and legacies named in said Will, and I, the said Harvey Durkee, covenant and agree that the said rights credits, property and assets of said estate not included in this transfer and sale shall be and remain to said Caroline Durkee undiminished and unencumbered by or on account of any said costs, expenses, debts, liabilities or charges and legacies, sold and transferred to him, subject to the costs and expenses of the settlement of said estate of said Charles Durkee deceased and to the debts and liabilities of said estate and the said valid trusts, charges, and legacies mentioned in said will of said Charles-Durkee – and the Harvey Durkee is hereby authorized- to receive from the executor any annuity hereafter to be paid or provided for said Caroline Durkee if any under the provisions of said will to his own use.

In witness whereof the parties hereto have hereunto set their hands and seals this twenty third day of May 1871,

Caroline Durkee (Seal)

(Rev. stamp)

Harvey Durkee (Seal)

All the money heretofore paid, to said Caroline Durkee by the executor is to be deducted by the executors from the property and proceeds hereby sold and transferred to said Harvey Durkee;-and no part of it from that part of the estate not so sold and transferred.

Caroline Durkee (Seal)

Harvey Durkee (Seal)

List of Heirs of the Durkee Estate
Filed in Court of Claims Case 18003

Leonard Blaisdell
Harriet Durkee Blaisdell of Champaign Illinois
Harvey Durkee of Charles City Iowa
Caroline C. Johnson of Mapleton Indiana
Charles C. Durkee of Roseville California
George Durkee of Deforest Wisconsin
John Durkee of Hot Springs Arkansas
Joseph E Durkee of Sioux Rapids Iowa
Mary Louise Durkee Hendrix of Rochester New York
Mary Durkee of Malone New York
Martha Kate Durkee Smith of Malone New York
Bessie Durkee of Malone New York
William Durkee of Cincinnati Ohio
Hattie Flueut of Alexandria South Dakota
Mary Furness of Charles City Iowa
Louisa Hoag of Charles City Iowa
Ellen Church of Charles City Iowa
Laura Huntington of Charles City Iowa
Joseph Durkee of Sioux Rapids Iowa
Charles Boardman of Fredonia New York
George Boardman of Washington DC
George W. Boardman
Mary Fargo Stewart of Ward Island New York
Jessie H. Moneghan of Grand Forks Dakota Territory
May A. Fargo of San Francisco California
Ellen Church of Washington DC

www.ingramcontent.com/pod-product-compliance
Lightning Source LLC
Chambersburg PA
CBHW021759190326
41518CB00007B/366